MW01196122

TIDES OF FORTUNE

TIDES
OF FORTUNE

The Rise and Decline of Great Militaries

ZACK COOPER

Yale

UNIVERSITY PRESS

New Haven and London

Published with assistance from the Louis Stern Memorial Fund.

Yale University Press books may be purchased in quantity for educational, business, or promotional use. For information, please e-mail sales.press@yale.edu (U.S. office) or sales@yaleup.co.uk (U.K. office).

Set in Janson type by IDS Infotech Ltd.
Printed in the United States of America.

Library of Congress Control Number: 2024937405
ISBN 978-0-300-26867-6 (hardcover : alk. paper)

A catalogue record for this book is available from the British Library.

This paper meets the requirements of ANSI/NISO Z39.48-1992 (Permanence of Paper).

10 9 8 7 6 5 4 3 2 1

Contents

Preface

By nurturing the nation's strength we should ride the tide
of fortune.

—PRINCE HIROHITO (1920)

How WILL THE UNITED STATES and China compete militarily in the
years ahead? Many experts believe the answer to this question is largely
unknowable. But this book argues that the U.S. and Chinese militaries
are following a well-trod path. For centuries, the world's most powerful
militaries have adhered to a remarkably consistent pattern of behavior,
determined largely by their leaders' perceptions of relative power shifts.
This book traces the rise and decline of the twentieth century's leading
militaries and finds that the U.S., German, British, French, Japanese,
and Russian militaries each adhered to a common logic—here termed
perceived relative power theory—as they struggled to manage their rise and
decline. In short, these militaries altered their defense objectives, strategies, and investments in predictable ways as their power shifted. The
U.S. and Chinese militaries are once again following these paths today.

The Puzzle: China's Pursuit of Power Projection

The puzzle that initially inspired this book is a simple one: Why is
China building a power-projection military just when its decades-long
pursuit of anti-access capabilities is calling into question U.S. military

dominance in Asia? Many experts believe that China's anti-access capabilities—including conventionally armed ballistic missiles, anti-ship cruise missiles, and diesel submarines—have leveled the playing field between China and the United States. If these systems work as designed, Beijing's comparatively cheap anti-access weaponry could neutralize Washington's more advanced and expensive power-projection systems, such as aircraft carriers and forward military bases.

Recently, however, China's leaders have shifted their focus and begun to invest more in traditional means of power projection, including aircraft carriers and forward bases. In short, China is abandoning an approach that seemed to be working. To explain China's transition from an asymmetric anti-access approach to a more symmetric strategy, scholars have referenced structural, domestic, and cultural factors.[1] But these explanations leave open major questions about the nature and timing of Beijing's transition toward power projection. Why is China adopting more power-projection capabilities? Why is it doing so now? And will these trends accelerate if China continues to grow stronger, or could they reverse if China's power peaks in the years ahead?

The Theory: Changes in Perceived Relative Power

How do militaries change as nations rise and decline? International relations scholars tend to attribute changes in defense policies to structural explanations concerning the distribution of capabilities, geography, technology, or resources; domestic explanations concerning the interaction of individuals or groups pursuing parochial interests; or cultural explanations determined by national or organizational cultures. These factors all play important roles in determining defense policies. But these theories leave out a critical piece of the puzzle: perceptions of relative power changes.

This book argues that the world's most powerful militaries have adhered to a remarkably consistent pattern of behavior, determined largely by their leaders' perceptions of relative power shifts. Leaders evaluate both relative power levels and relative power trends as they choose how to adjust national defense policies. The pages that follow explain this theory and trace the rise and decline of the twentieth century's leading militaries. This research suggests that leaders in each country adhered to a common logic—perceived relative power theory—as they struggled to manage their rise and decline. In short, leaders altered their defense objectives, strategies, and investments in predictable ways as their national power shifted.

This book puts forward a novel theory, which begins with the simple premise that national leaders adopt defense policies consistent with their perceived relative power. Leaders focus on two separate but related factors: (1) perceived *levels* of relative power and (2) perceived *trends* in relative power. Levels of relative power range from weak to strong, while trends in relative power vary from rising to declining. Based on these two variables, states can be assigned to one of four categories: (1) weak but rising, (2) strong and rising, (3) strong but declining, or (4) weak and declining. These categories reflect the four phases of rise and decline.

In each phase of relative power, leaders adopt distinct defense objectives, strategies, and investments. All else equal, strong states seek more extensive objectives than weak states. These extensive objectives require strategies that enable the control of territory. Control strategies in turn necessitate investments in sustainable systems. Conversely, weak states seek more limited objectives requiring only denying control to one's adversary. Denial strategies can be accomplished with cheaper, expendable systems. Thus, strong and weak states pursue different objectives, strategies, and investments.

National leaders care not only about perceived levels of relative power but also about perceived trends in relative power. All else equal, rising states seek more expansionist objectives than declining states. Expansion requires an offensive strategy, which in turn necessitates investments in mobile systems. On the other hand, declining states aim to consolidate their position. This can be accomplished with a defensive strategy using less mobile systems. Therefore, just as strong and weak states pursue different objectives, strategies, and investments, so should rising and declining states.

As explained in detail in chapter 1, this theory hypothesizes that states pursue different defense policies across four phases of relative power. In phase 1, weak but rising states adopt expendable mobile systems—here termed an *anti-access defense policy*. In phase 2, strong and rising states pursue sustainable mobile systems—classic power projection. In phase 3, strong but declining states favor sustainable immobile systems—a garrison fortification approach. And in phase 4, weak and declining states seek expendable immobile systems—an area-denial scheme.

By combining elements of the literature on power transitions, offense-defense balance, and asymmetric conflict, this theory helps to resuscitate compelling but often overlooked theories. Foremost among these is the distinction between offensive and defensive strategies and how they interact with the concepts of control and denial. This book defines these concepts, molding them into a coherent theory of defense policy, and making a variety of specific and testable predictions about defense policy changes.

The cases examined in this book concern states transitioning from one phase of perceived relative power to another. Chapters 2 and 3 discuss the rise of the United States and Germany around the turn of the twentieth century. Chapters 4 and 5 review the peaking of Great Britain and France before World Wars I and II, respectively. Chapters 6 and 7 address the decline of Japan during World War II and that of the Soviet Union at the Cold War's end. Chapter 8 then concludes by drawing lessons from these cases and discussing the implications for the evolving military competition in Asia.

The Implications: The Sino-American Inversion

If perceived relative power theory is correct, then it helps to explain why China is turning toward power-projection capabilities just as some leaders in the United States are advocating turning away from them. Leaders in Beijing now see China as relatively strong, leading them to adopt different defense objectives, strategies, and investments. When its leaders viewed China as relatively weak, they sought anti-access capabilities to deny foreign powers the ability to intervene in regional disputes. But as China's leaders have come to believe they can challenge the United States symmetrically, they have embraced power projection, shifting Beijing's objectives, strategies, and investments. This argument has the potential to explain both the nature and timing of China's shifting defense policies, as well as those of other rising and declining powers. It can also help to predict how China's military modernization will evolve in the years ahead.[2]

Across the Pacific, this book should spur action on the part of U.S. leaders. Officials in Washington have been far too complacent about both the shifting balance of power in Asia and the emergence of smaller, cheaper, and more expendable military systems. Today, improvised explosive devices menace ground forces, smart mines and anti-ship missiles threaten naval forces, advanced air defenses increase the risks to aircraft, and space and cyber networks are under near-constant attack. Heretofore, the U.S. military has stuck with a set of increasingly untenable defense policies as power projection has become more costly. But the price of projecting power is increasing, which incentivizes militaries to invest more in denial strategies and expendable systems.[3]

This book, however, provides reason for continued U.S. optimism. Relative power trends may be working against the United States at the moment, but technological trends are shifting in the United States' favor. U.S. leaders have a fleeting opportunity to embrace new technologies and strategies that can stabilize the military balance in Asia. This burgeoning debate is exemplified by the U.S. Marine Corps considering a shift toward expeditionary advanced base operations, the U.S. Navy examining distributed maritime operations, the U.S. Air Force considering agile combat employment, and the U.S. Army proffering a concept of multidomain operations. Each is an acknowledgment that projecting power is becoming harder, so new strategic concepts are needed. These recent reforms are notable, but the cases presented here demonstrate that defense policies change slowly, depend greatly on individual leadership, and are most difficult when states are experiencing relative decline during peacetime. By acknowledging these challenges, this book provides the theoretical and historical foundation for embracing new defense policies, which could have far-reaching consequences for both the sustainability of U.S. power and the postwar order more generally.[4]

Acknowledgments

THIS BOOK IS THE product of a decade of research and writing made possible by the support of numerous institutions as well as advice and feedback from dozens of friends and mentors. This project emerged from the doctoral program in security studies at Princeton University. Professors Aaron Friedberg, Tom Christensen, and John Ikenberry supervised my dissertation—their wisdom and insights have been critical throughout this project. Harvard University's Steve Rosen kindly served as an outside reader and has provided thoughtful guidance and feedback over many years. In addition, I am thankful to Karen McGuinness, Ann Lengyel, Cindy Ernst, and numerous other staff, faculty, and students at Princeton for making my experiences as a student and lecturer at Princeton so rewarding.

Over the past decade, I have also been lucky to have had the support of some fantastic people and institutions in Washington, D.C. I began writing this book while working at the Center for Strategic and Budgetary Assessments, where Andrew Krepinevich, Jim Thomas, Evan Montgomery, Eric Edelman, and others introduced me to the concepts of control and denial. I later shifted to the Center for Strategic and International Studies, where John Hamre, Mike Green, and Kath Hicks supported a book project that melded my policy and academic interests. Finally, the American Enterprise Institute has been my most recent intellectual home, where I owe a debt of gratitude to Arthur Brooks, Robert Doar, Dany Pletka, Kori Schake, and many others.

In addition to these institutions, I could not have completed this book without research support from Princeton's Center for International Security Studies, the National Institute for Social Science, the Bradley Family Fellowship, and the Smith-Richardson Foundation. Several other institutions also permitted me to research or present elements of this book in the United States, Europe, and Asia, for which I am deeply grateful. Additionally, I have benefited from teaching at Princeton and Georgetown University, both of which have allowed me to use their libraries and other resources to conduct much of this research.

Throughout the past decade, I have also incurred debts to numerous individuals who provided encouragement and helped to shape this project. In addition to a number of anonymous reviewers, I am grateful for the advice of Dima Adamsky, Rich Armitage, Omar Bashir, Hal Brands, Kara Bue, Jeff Cooper, David Edelstein, Stacie Goddard, Sheena Greitens, Marina Henke, Mike Horowitz, Mike Hunzeker, Richard Jordan, Mara Karlin, Robert Keohane, Pattie Kim, Dan Kliman, Alex Lanoszka, Darren Lim, Jennifer Lind, Julia Morse, Rohan Mukherjee, Vipin Narang, Mira Rapp-Hooper, Laura Rosenberger, Robert Ross, Elizabeth Saunders, Jake Shapiro, Travis Sharp, Mike Sulmeyer, Caitlin Talmadge, Tom Wright, and Keren Yarhi-Milo. Emily Carr, Ally Schwartz, Thomas Causey, Noah Burke, and Connor Fiddler provided valuable editing and assisted with revisions. Yale University Press's team was patient and thoughtful, including Jaya Chatterjee, Amanda Gerstenfeld, Jeff Schier, and Andrew Katz. Of course, all errors remain my own.

Most importantly, I would like to thank my wife, Laurie Ball Cooper, and our children, Alexis and Austin, for enduring what has turned out to be quite a long process. They have shared much of the burden and could not have been more supportive. This book is dedicated to them. I look forward to watching their continued rise as I experience my eventual (perhaps even ongoing) decline.

CHAPTER ONE

Determinants of Defense Policies

> The fundamental cause of wars among states and changes in international systems is the uneven growth of power among states.
>
> —ROBERT GILPIN, *War and Change in World Politics* (1981)

THIS BOOK SEEKS TO explain why states change defense policies. To that end, this chapter begins by briefly reviewing the literature on defense policies and identifying some of its limitations. The chapter then outlines a new theory connecting perceptions of relative power to shifts in defense objectives, strategies, and investments. The chapter concludes by proposing six hypotheses on defense policies and describing the research design for assessing their validity.[1]

Literature on Defense Policies

Scholarship on the roots of defense policies includes structural explanations related to the distribution of capabilities, geography, technology, or resources; domestic explanations concerning the interaction of individuals or groups pursuing parochial interests; and cultural explanations determined by national or organizational cultures. Each is outlined in the following sections.

Structural Explanations

Realist scholars typically argue that defense policies result from features of the international system. The most basic realist proposition on defense policy is that states imitate each other. The founder of neorealism, Kenneth Waltz, wrote that "competition in the arts and the instruments of force . . . produces a tendency toward the sameness of the competitors." Therefore, Barry Posen asserts, "successful practices will be imitated. Those who fail to imitate are unlikely to survive." As a result, many realists suggest that states will imitate leading powers, as long as they have similar material capabilities, geographic positions, and technological access.[2]

Capability: Other scholars believe international pressures drive states to differentiate themselves. John Mearsheimer argues that states "look for new ways to gain advantage over opponents, by developing new weapons, innovative military doctrines, or clever strategies." What might cause states to innovate in this way? One factor is differences in capabilities. Robert Gilpin observes that "dominant states have sought to exert control over the system in order to advance their self-interests." Conversely, weaker states are forced to pursue more limited aims. Stephen Walt notes, "great powers have both global interests and global capabilities, weak states will be concerned primarily with events in their immediate vicinity." If these scholars are correct, then weaker states should differentiate their defense policies from those of stronger states.[3]

Geography: Another factor that determines defense policies is geography. Jack Levy and William Thomson argue that "sea powers differ from dominant continental powers in their goals, strategies, and behavior." This fundamental difference is reflected in the views of Halford J. Mackinder and Alfred Thayer Mahan. Mackinder wrote, "who rules eastern Europe commands the Heartland; who rules the Heartland commands the World Islands; and who rules the World Island commands the World." Conversely, Mahan advised that control of the seas "is the chief among the merely material elements in the power and prosperity of nations." As Mackinder and Mahan suggest, geographic differences lead states to adopt distinctive defense policies.[4]

Technology: Capability and geography are critical factors, but so too is technology. Thomas Schelling suggested that an "inherent propensity toward peace or war" is "embodied in weaponry, the geography, and the military organization of the time." If this is correct, then technological differences should lead to distinct defense policies. The leading theory that describes this relationship is the offense-defense balance. First proposed by Robert Jervis and George Quester, the offense-defense balance refers to the ease of distinguishing between offensive and defensive forces and the relative strength and cost of each. Extending this concept, Gilpin noted that offensive innovations "stimulate territorial expansion and the political consolidation of international systems by empires or great powers." Defining and measuring the offense-defense balance has proven problematic, but even if scholars differ on how to quantify its impact, technology certainly plays a role in determining defense policies.[5]

Resources: Some scholars argue that resource scarcity or abundance drives foreign policies, thereby determining whether and how states seek to obtain new territorial control. Michael Klare suggests that the pursuit of limited natural resources, particularly energy sources, forces states to compete for access to the resources and sometimes gain access to new territory. Michael Barnhart explains how this logic drove "Japan's drive for self-sufficiency" and altered its defense policies. Similarly, Melvyn Leffler asserts that U.S. defense policies were driven by a complex mix of commercial considerations and interests, which ultimately transformed U.S. national objectives. Taking a different angle, Jonathan Markowitz asserts that "the more resource-dependent a state is, the stronger its preference for projecting power to seek control over resource rents."[6] What these different approaches have in common is that they see defense policies as driven by diverging resource endowments or economic interests.

Domestic Explanations

Although structural factors are often given preference, domestic politics clearly affect defense policies. Richard Rosecrance and Arthur Stein note that "the narrow constituents of realism—material power, changes in the distribution, and external threat—are radically incomplete. . . . Domestic forces may actually be increasing in scope and importance." Even Waltz admitted, "The causes of war lie not simply in states or in the state system; they are found in both." Thus, the roots of defense policies lie in both as well. Critics of domestic explanations argue that it is impossible "to formulate in a systematic and exhaustive fashion the domestic determinants of the foreign policies of states." Yet, three domestic factors appear critical: domestic structures, bureaucratic politics, and individual leadership.[7]

Domestic Structures: If domestic preferences matter, then adjudication mechanisms are critical. Deborah Avant suggests, "Domestic institutions might vary in several ways: on a continuum of capability and legitimacy (from strong to weak states), mode of authority (from democratic or autarchic), or constitutional arrangement (parliamentary to presidential)." Connecting domestic politics to defense policies, Jack Snyder roots expansionary impulses in domestic coalitions favoring "imperial expansion, military preparations, or economic autarky." Elizabeth Kier examines how "the interaction between constraints set in the domestic political arena and a military's organizational culture determines choices between offensive and defensive doctrines." In short, "the social structures of the political unit can affect its ability to generate military power, offensively and defensively," as Steve Rosen has written.[8]

Bureaucratic Politics: James Q. Wilson concluded in his pioneering work on organizations, "The key difference between the German army in 1940 and its French opponents was not in grand strategy, but in tactics and organizational arrangements." Similarly, Michael Horowitz finds, "domestic political and military organizational factors are vital in shaping the way military organizations behave." Fareed Zakaria notes that the United States in the late 1800s was a strong nation with a weak state due to the lack of a capable central government. Militaries, like all organizations, harbor many biases. Militaries are surprisingly resistant to change and often oppose innovations that threaten traditional roles and missions. Barry Posen finds that militaries "generally prefer offensive doctrines because they reduce uncertainty in important ways." And

Dan Markey explains that military organizations often prefer symbols of prestige "to demonstrate their power." Thus, defense policies are shaped by militaries' resistance to change, offensive biases, and desire for prestige.[9]

Individual Leadership: Ultimately, all policies are determined by individuals. Henry Kissinger once noted, "As a professor, I tended to think of history as run by impersonal forces. But when you see it in practice, you see the difference the personalities make." Although scholars admit that "individuals set the ultimate and secondary intentions of a state," the study of individuals has proven difficult to systematize. Nevertheless, recent work explores how individuals are influenced by references to historical events and analogies. For example, Keren Yarhi-Milo explains how "decision makers tend to rely on kinds of information that are particularly vivid." One implication is that individuals are often slow to change their views, meaning that it can take "the replacement of one generation by another to let the impact of external changes take its full effect." Human perceptions and biases therefore shape defense policies in multiple ways.[10]

Cultural Explanations

A final driver of defense policies is culture. Jeffrey Legro describes military organizational cultures as "patterns of assumptions, ideas, and beliefs that prescribe how a group should adapt to its external environment and manage its internal structure." Colin Dueck suggests that culture shapes strategic choice in three ways: "First, culture influences the manner in which international events, pressures, and conditions are perceived. Second, it provides a set of causal beliefs regarding the efficient pursuit of national interests. Third, it helps determine the actual definition of those interests, by providing prescriptive foreign policy goals." Thus, Tom Mahnken argues that a state's "way of war ... represents an approach that a given state has found successful in the past. Although not immutable, it tends to evolve slowly." In this way, culture provides an explanation for Paul Kennedy's observation of a time lag "between the trajectory of a state's relative economic strength and the trajectory of its military/territorial influence."[11]

Limitations of Existing Theories

Structural, domestic, and cultural factors all play a role in determining defense policies, but existing theories suffer from three major limitations. First, few theories delineate when or why defense policies change. Structural and cultural explanations are particularly weak in this regard because they often rely on static variables. Although domestic theories can better explain rapid policy shifts, they often struggle to identify the root causes of changes in domestic preferences. Therefore, scholars lack a leading theory of what triggers shifts in defense policies.[12]

Second, few theories address the full spectrum of defense policies, from objectives to strategies to investments. Most scholarship focuses on only one link in the ends-ways-means chain. Many structural explanations address either objectives or strategies, without commenting on the investment decisions. Similarly, many domestic explanations focus on objectives but bypass the strategies or investments needed to attain them. And cultural explanations often touch on security strategies but ignore both interests and investments. As a result, scholars lack a leading theory that connects defense objectives, strategies, and investments.[13]

Third, most existing theories are either parsimonious, with limited predictive power, or predictive, with limited cross-case applicability. Unfortunately, structural explanations often overvalue parsimony, while domestic and cultural explanations are often difficult to apply across cases. None of these factors is fatal for existing explanations, but they indicate the need for a theory that parsimoniously explains changes in defense objectives, strategies, and investments.[14]

A Theory of Perceived Relative Power

The theory of perceived relative power suggests that national leaders alter defense policies as states undergo cycles of rise and decline. After all, "The most basic realist proposition," according to Randall Schweller, is that "states must recognize and respond to shifts in their relative power." The core of perceived relative power theory is the recognition that leaders shift defense policies as their perceptions of levels and trends in relative power change. Leaders typically perceive states to be in one of four phases of relative power: (1) weak but rising, (2) strong and rising, (3) strong but declining, or (4) weak and declining. In each phase, leaders adopt different defense policies based on their assessments of current and future relative power.[15]

Independent Variables: Perceptions of Relative Power

This theory begins with two aspects of perceived relative power: one static and the other dynamic. The static element is the current perceived levels of relative power, measured on a spectrum from strong to weak. The dynamic aspect is perceived trends in relative power, measured on a spectrum from rising to declining. Each of these variables focuses on relative power, rather than absolute power, because defense policy is inherently competitive. When one state's capabilities increase, its competitors worry that their relative capabilities have decreased. These calculations will differ depending on the leader but typically compare a state's power with that of the country its leaders perceive as their greatest threat. Therefore, this theory relies not on abstract calculations of relative power but instead on the views of national leaders. After all, as William Wohlforth writes, "If power influences the course of international politics, it must do so largely through the perceptions of the people who make decisions on behalf of states."[16] Which leaders' views matter therefore depends on who influences defense policy making in individual countries.

Perceived Relative Power Levels: Scholars have long studied how different static levels of relative power affect defense policies. For example, Mike Mastanduno, David Lake, and John Ikenberry argue, "powerful states will emphasize international strategies more than will weak states." Strong states can adopt more extensive objectives, strategies, and investments than can weak states. This is not to suggest that strong states win all wars or attain all their objectives. In fact, research by Ivan Arreguín-Toft shows that weaker actors have won an increasing percentage of asymmetric conflicts. Yet, strong states still have defense policy options that weak states do not enjoy. Of course, it is not the actual levels of power that matter but perceptions of them. And as Zakaria notes, "statesmen's perceptions of national power shift suddenly, rather than incrementally, and are shaped more by crises and galvanizing events like wars than by statistical measures."[17]

Perceived Relative Power Trends: Theorists have long acknowledged the importance of power trends. George Modelski suggested that in "the ascending phase and the descending phase ... the nation-state plays distinct, and contrasting, roles." And Gilpin noted how "a change in a state's power and wealth usually causes a corresponding change in the foreign policy of the state." Power changes incentivize states to expand when windows of opportunity open or to consolidate before those windows close. As A. F. K. Organski argued, rising states "are most likely to have goals that involve changing the status quo, whereas declining nations and nations near the peak of their power are most concerned to preserve the existing order." Synthesizing this literature, Dale Copeland describes how "states in decline fear the future" and roots much state behavior in "the simultaneous interaction of the differentials of relative military power between great powers and the expected trend of those differentials."[18] Leaders' views of current power levels and expectations about future power trends are central drivers of defense policies, each affecting them differently. This book examines how these perceptions shape defense policies, but it treats the causes of changes in leadership views as exogenous.

Dependent Variable: Defense Policies

This theory focuses on three specific defense policies: objectives, strategies, and investments. Defense objectives are the national security ends that leaders seek. Defense strategies are the ways they intend to accomplish these objectives. Defense investments are the means leaders provide to pursue these strategies. States may not always proceed in an orderly fashion from one to the other, but together these policies form links in the chain from ends to ways to means. In choosing their policies, states adopt a mix of objectives, strategies, and investments. Even the most offensively oriented states fortify command and control facilities, and the most defensively oriented states retain mobility for reserve forces. France's defensively focused Maginot Line, for example, still required some degree of rapid transportation to move troops and supplies to the front. All states are likely to pursue a combination of forces. As Mearsheimer notes, states are "both offensively-oriented and defensively-oriented. They think about conquest themselves, and they balance against aggressors." The key question is therefore not whether a country adopts a specific defense system but what mix of capabilities national leaders pursue. This book asserts that it is usually possible to identify states' primary defense priorities, as demonstrated in the case studies.[19]

Objectives: Defense objectives can generally be categorized along two dimensions: the degree and scope of territorial aims. First, states can adopt either extensive or limited objectives. Extensive objectives aim to exert substantial authority over a given area, while limited objectives require only the partial exercise of power. For example, militaries can seek to conduct either extensive nation-building or more limited counterterrorism missions. Second, states can seek either geographic expansion or consolidation. After all, as Robert Pape notes, "the principal issue in serious international disputes is usually control over territory." Expansionist objectives increase the scope of geographic authority, whereas consolidation aims only to maintain authority over existing holdings. Accordingly, defense objectives can be categorized as either extensive or limited and either expansive or consolidative.[20]

Strategies: Defense leaders must next identify the best strategy to achieve these objectives. Strategies vary along two axes. First, states can adopt either control or denial strategies. Control strategies exert influence over an area through sustained physical presence, whereas denial strategies exert influence without sustained presence. Experts often differentiate between two types of denial—anti-access and area denial—which differ primarily by the distance at which they are practiced. Second, states can pursue offensive or defensive strategies. Keir Lieber defines offense as "the use of military force to attack, seize, and hold a portion or all of a defender's territory" and defense as "using military force to prevent an attacker from seizing territory." Thus, strategies can pursue either control or denial and either offense or defense.[21]

Table 1. Perceived Relative Power Theory's Causal Claims

			Defense policies		
			Objectives	Strategies	Investments
Perceived relative power	Level	*strong*	extensive objectives	control strategies	sustainable investments
		weak	limited objectives	denial strategies	expendable investments
	Trend	*rising*	expansive objectives	offensive strategies	mobile investments
		declining	consolidative objectives	defensive strategies	immobile investments

Investments: The final decision is the defense investment mix needed for a given strategy. Investments vary along two dimensions. First, states can invest in either sustainable or expendable systems. Sustainable systems, such as most ships and aircraft, are designed to be used in combat through multiple engagements. Expendable systems, such as missiles and mines, are consumed or destroyed when used in an engagement. This often amounts to a trade-off between more complex and expensive sustainable systems, on the one hand, and cheaper and more numerous expandable ones, on the other. Second, states can invest in either mobile or immobile systems. The degree of mobility is determined by the speed at which a system can move toward and engage an adversary over a variety of distances. Some systems are perfectly immobile, such as land mines and fortifications. Others, including most tanks, ships, and aircraft, can move rapidly to engage an adversary. Therefore, investments can be categorized as either sustainable or expandable and either mobile or immobile.[22]

The theory of perceived relative power is rooted in two independent variables—perceived relative power levels and trends—but it makes numerous predictions about defense policies. This book focuses on six specific hypotheses about defense objectives, strategies, and investments, each of which consists of two mirror-image propositions.

Defense Objective Hypotheses

H1: PERCEIVED STRONG (WEAK) STATES ADOPT EXTENSIVE (LIMITED) OBJECTIVES

Existing literature suggests that strong states pursue extensive objectives, while weak states pursue more limited objectives. As Andrew Krepinevich notes, asymmetries "exist in terms of competitor goals and objectives." To this end, Organski notes, "As the power of a state increases, the relative cost of changing the system and of thereby achieving the state's goals decreases (and, conversely, increases when a state is declining)." By virtue of strong states' relative power advantage, they are capable of exerting significant authority over distant areas. Authority here refers to the degree to which the "right to rule" is exercised. Weak states are seldom capable of exercising similar authority abroad and must therefore settle for more limited objectives. As discussed later, this basic asymmetry has substantial implications not just for objectives but also for strategies and investments.[23]

H2: PERCEIVED RISING (DECLINING) STATES ADOPT EXPANSIVE (CONSOLIDATIVE) OBJECTIVES

Rising and declining powers experience a parallel set of incentives and constraints, but they tend to focus on the geographical scope of their authority rather than the functional extent. Rising powers typically have an incentive to expand their authority geographically. After all, the distribution of territory in the international system seldom reflects the rising power's improving position. Conversely, Schweller advises that declining powers are "the principal beneficiaries of the status quo" and "they more than anyone else have a vested interest in preserving it." Declining states are therefore largely satisfied with the current distribution of territory. Thus, this theory follows Organski's lead in identifying four categories of states, "1. The powerful and satisfied, 2. The powerful and dissatisfied, 3. The weak and satisfied, 4. The weak and dissatisfied." Table 2 depicts the predicted objectives for each of these four phases.[24]

Table 2. Relative Power Perceptions and Defense Objectives

	Rising powers	Declining powers
Strong powers	Extensive expansion	Extensive consolidation
Weak powers	Limited expansion	Limited consolidation

Defense Strategy Hypotheses

H3: PERCEIVED STRONG (WEAK) STATES ADOPT CONTROL (DENIAL) STRATEGIES

Leaders typically align their strategies to accomplish their objectives. As Emily Goldman notes, "The strategy a state pursues is a product of its relative power." Strong states pursue control strategies because they have extensive objectives abroad. Gilpin explains that "as the power of a group or state increases, that group or state will be tempted to try to increase its control over its environment. In order to increase its own security, it will try to expand its political, economic, and territorial control." Weak states, on the other hand, adopt denial strategies because they have limited objectives and less need to exercise substantial authority abroad. Barry Posen describes these as deterrent doctrines, implicitly differentiating denial strategies from offensive and defensive approaches. Archer Jones found that asymmetric strategies provided the "means for a weaker adversary to use against a stronger," because they "functioned for the weaker adversary as a substitute for the more effective and less costly persisting strategies that were beyond their strength." Similarly, Kissinger notes, "The guerrilla wins if he does not lose. The conventional army loses if it does not win." In this way, asymmetric objectives lead to asymmetric strategies.[25]

H4: PERCEIVED RISING (DECLINING) STATES ADOPT OFFENSIVE (DEFENSIVE) STRATEGIES

Leaders also shift strategies as states rise and decline. Jack Snyder writes that "choice of an offensive or a defensive strategy should depend on national aims. . . . A state particularly needs an offensive

Table 3. Relative Power Perceptions and Defense Strategies

	Rising powers	Declining powers
Strong powers	Offensive control	Defensive control
Weak powers	Offensive denial	Defensive denial

strategy when it seeks to conquer or coerce others." As previously hypothesized, rising states should adopt expansionist objectives, so they should pursue offensive strategies. Posen finds a similar pattern, noting that "expansionist powers will prefer offensive doctrines," whereas "status quo states will generally prefer defensive doctrines." Declining powers have a more complex calculus because they have an incentive to engage in preventive war. Kier contends that while "revisionist states can require offensive doctrines, both offensive and defensive doctrines can defend the status quo." Furthermore, Scott Sagan points out that "offensive military doctrines are needed not only by states with expansionist war aims, but also by states that have a strong interest in protecting an exposed ally." Nevertheless, the empirical evidence for these claims is mixed. Declining powers may have reason to consider offensive strategies, but they have far more incentive to adopt defensive strategies than their rising peers do.[26]

Defense Investment Hypotheses

H5: PERCEIVED STRONG (WEAK) STATES ADOPT SUSTAINABLE (EXPENDABLE) INVESTMENTS

Leaders should ideally choose their objectives and strategies before making investments. If they do so, Goldman writes that strong powers should "invest in sustaining capabilities." After all, control strategies require continued physical presence, so strong states need systems that are sustainable. Sustainability provides the ability to project power, but this endurance increases complexity, vulnerability, and cost. Conversely, weak states are more likely to invest in expendable systems since they can accomplish denial strategies more cheaply. Moreover, recent advancements in missiles and mines have enhanced the effectiveness of expendable systems and denial strategies. On land, improvised explosive devices have made it more difficult for ground forces to occupy territory. At sea, high-speed missiles threaten aircraft carriers and other surface ships. In the air, missiles menace planes, and cruise missiles threaten their airstrips. And in space and cyberspace, critical infrastructure is increasingly under attack. In short, technology has made control more difficult. As a result, weak states have substantial incentives to adopt expendable systems to accomplish denial strategies.[27]

H6: PERCEIVED RISING (DECLINING) STATES ADOPT MOBILE (IMMOBILE) INVESTMENTS

Leaders must also decide on their systems' degree of mobility. Most scholars believe mobility—the speed of travel across a border with an adversary—aids offense, whereas firepower and protection aid defense. According to Charles Glaser and Chaim Kaufmann, "Nearly all advances in military mobility—chariots, horses, cavalry, tanks, motor trucks, aircraft, mobile bridging equipment—are generally considered to have favored the offense, while major counter-mobility innovations—moats, barbed wire, tank traps, land mines—have favored defense." Because rising powers typically embrace offensive strategies, they have incentives to invest in mobile systems. On the other hand, declining powers have less need for mobility because they rely more on defensive strategies. Mobility, after all, is costly and typically comes at the expense of firepower and protection. One need only recall the famous phrase, "A single shot can sink a ship, while a hundred salvos cannot silence a fort." Thus, pursuing mobility when immobility would suffice is inefficient, particularly for declining powers.[28]

Synthesis: Four Phases of Relative Power

It is now possible to trace how defense policies change as states rise and decline. States undergo four phases of relative power. In the first phase, states are weak but rising. In the second phase, states are still rising and now strong. In the third phase, states are still strong but have peaked and are now in relative decline. In the

Table 4. Relative Power Perceptions and Defense Investments

	Rising powers	Declining powers
Strong powers	Sustainable mobility	Sustainable immobility
Weak powers	Expendable mobility	Expendable immobility

fourth phase, states continue their decline into a relatively weak position. These four phases are depicted in figure 1.[29]

How do defense policies change through these four phases? In the first phase, leaders view their states as relatively weak but rising, leading them to adopt limited expansion objectives. They want to "change the rules governing the system," but "weak states are more constrained in their ability to achieve their goals through international action." As hypothesized earlier, limited expansion should necessitate strategies of offensive denial and investments in expendable mobile systems. Such defense policies are best summarized as anti-access approaches.[30]

In the second phase, leaders in rising powers see their states as strong. They experience "the urge to control and to dominate, to imprint a pattern on events," according to Modelski. The desire for a rising power to "extend its territorial control" leads to extensive expansion objectives. Achieving extensive expansion requires strategies

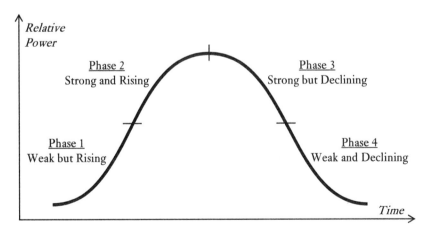

Figure 1. Four phases of relative power. (Source: Zack Cooper, 2024)

Table 5. Summarizing the Theory of Perceived Relative Power

	Rising powers	Declining powers
Strong powers	Phase 2: Power Projection *Objectives:* Extensive expansion *Strategies:* Offensive control *Investments:* Sustainable mobility	Phase 3: Garrison fortification *Objectives:* Extensive consolidation *Strategies:* Defensive control *Investments:* Sustainable immobility
Weak powers	Phase 1: Anti-Access *Objectives:* Limited expansion *Strategies:* Offensive denial *Investments:* Expendable mobility	Phase 4: Area Denial *Objectives:* Limited consolidation *Strategies:* Defensive denial *Investments:* Expendable immobility

of offensive control and investments in sustainable mobile systems. These defense policies are classic power projection.[31]

In the third phase, states have reached the pinnacle of their power and enter a period of relative decline. Such states are still relatively strong, but as Dale Copeland warns, "states in decline fear the future." Declining states have incentive to lock in the status quo, so Paul K. MacDonald and Joseph M. Parent argue that declining powers should retrench because "the rigors of great power politics compel them to do so." Strong but declining states should therefore adopt extensive consolidative objectives, which necessitate strategies of defensive control and investments in sustainable immobile systems. These defense policy call for garrison fortification.[32]

In the fourth phase, states continue to decline and become relatively weak. Some states experience drastic declines due to domestic upheavals or failed wars. Although leaders in these states seek to maintain the status quo, their weakness limits their objectives. Thus, weak and declining states should adopt limited consolidation objectives. Accomplishing limited consolidation requires strategies of defensive denial and investments in expendable immobile systems. These defense policies are best termed *area denial.*[33]

Perceived relative power theory makes predictions for how leaders in rising, peaking, and declining states will change their defense policies. However, actual relative power balances often differ substantially from perceptions of those balances. Perceptions of power levels and power trends are driven by a number of factors, which are often separate from changes in power and capabilities. Yarhi-Milo finds that leaders pay selective attention to certain factors, including the vividness of information and subjective views of the credibility of different types of signals. David Edelstein shows that leaders—especially of declining powers—are slow to acknowledge change and even slower to adapt to it. The case studies in this book build on these observations by demonstrating how misperceptions of power levels and trends can lead to unsound defense policies, often with disastrous results.[34]

Research Design

To evaluate this theory, this book examines defense policy changes in six great powers. Each chapter traces how defense policies shifted as leaders altered their relative power perceptions, generating multiple causal-process observations. The hypotheses presented earlier are tested against other explanations rooted in structural, domestic, and cultural factors, such as a desire for prestige and the influence of strategic culture. Two caveats are in order. First, the cases focus on the past 150 years. History is replete with denial strategies, but for technological reasons, these strategies relied less on expendable systems until the late 1800s. After all, as Giulio Douhet noted in 1927, "It was impossible to invade the enemy's territory without first breaking through his defensives lines. But that situation is a thing of the past for now it is possible to go far behind the fortified lines of defense without first breaking through them." Second, although this theory applies to all states, the cases focus on great powers. Great powers are more likely to experience all four phases of relative power. In addition, their leaders' relative power calculations are simpler because they are more likely to focus on other great powers. The conclusion discusses how these scope conditions could be relaxed to apply the theory beyond recent great powers.[35]

The cases examined here include six of the twentieth century's great powers. Each case examines a great power as it shifts from one quadrant to another. And each case is paired with another, to ensure that both a maritime and a continental power are evaluated during each transition. Cases begin with an assessment of national leaders' perceptions of relative power and then trace whether and how changes in perceptions led to changes in objectives, strategies, and investments. These cases include substantial variation in structural, domestic, and cultural conditions, which can help to establish the conditions under which the theory holds.[36]

Chapters 2 and 3 review rising powers transitioning from weakness to strength, namely, the United States (1890–1910) and Germany (1890–1910). The first case study examines the rise of the United States and explains why U.S. leaders embraced power projection in the late 1890s after having explicitly rejected it in the 1880s. The chapter concludes that the U.S. embrace of power projection was caused by a change in U.S. leaders' relative power perceptions. The chapter on Germany describes why a continental power surrounded by formidable armies built a large navy in the 1890s, despite the hazards of doing so. After 1897, Kaiser Wilhelm became confident in Germany's relative strength and radically altered Germany's defense policies by devoting more resources to its power-projection capabilities. Thus, although the United States and Germany had different geographic positions, domestic influences, and strategic cultures, they followed surprisingly similar paths. Readers will note many similarities between these decisions and recent changes in China's military modernization efforts.

Chapters 4 and 5 analyze peaking powers transitioning from rise to decline, focusing on Great Britain (1890–1910) and France (1918–1938). Perceived relative power theory suggests that states passing their apex should shift their defense objectives from expansion to consolidation, necessitating more defensive strategies and less mobile systems. In short, states starting to decline should transition away from power projection. Around 1904, a series of shocks convinced British leaders that they were in decline relative to Germany. As a result, Britain shifted toward consolidation, defense, and immobility. But many British leaders remained resistant to change, resulting in slower and smaller defense reforms than expected. Understanding why is critical to setting the conditions under which this theory holds, which has many implications for the United States today. The paired chapter on France analyzes its defense policies from 1918 to 1938, explaining why France embraced garrison fortifications in 1927 but not earlier. As leaders in Paris came to terms with the Republic's relative decline, André Maginot and his adherents won support for what became the Maginot Line. These cases help to explain when a clear threat can convince leaders to rapidly alter their defense policies, even in declining powers.

Chapters 6 and 7 assess declining powers transitioning from strength to weakness, looking at Japan (1935–1945) and the Soviet Union (1980–2000). The former chapter explains why Japanese leaders embraced defensive approaches in 1942 but refused to authorize kamikaze attacks until 1944. Two shifts in Japan's relative power occurred during World War II. Initially, many leaders in Tokyo believed that Japan was a strong and rising power. But after the battles at Midway and Guadalcanal in 1942, it became clear that Japan was declining. And by 1944, it was apparent that the empire was relatively weak. As expected, Japan jettisoned its power-projection strategy around 1942 and adopted an area-denial strategy by 1944. The final case study examines Moscow's defense policies from 1980 to 2000. It explains why Russian defense reforms relied so heavily on nuclear weapons. During this time, Soviet (and later Russian) leaders came to appreciate that they were experiencing relative decline. Yet, Russian leaders saw few serious threats in the early 1990s. It was not until the late 1990s that leaders in Moscow perceived a serious external threat that prompted them to thoroughly reconfigure their strategy and investments, eventually resulting in greater reliance on nuclear weapons.

Chapter 8 concludes by evaluating the theory, discussing implications for scholars, and highlighting policy implications for the competition between China and the United States. It begins by describing five key lessons from the historical case studies as well as five areas for further study. The chapter then turns to the consequences for the emerging Sino-American strategic competition. Returning to the initial puzzle, this chapter explains China's recent defense reforms and then applies perceived relative power theory to predict its future defense policies. The book concludes by discussing how the United States should respond. It makes the case for urgent defense reforms that take into account both the United States' relative power position and changes in technology that advantage denial. The chapter argues that the time has come for the United States to stabilize the military balance in Asia by taking urgent action to respond to the shifting tides of fortune.

CHAPTER TWO

America's Rise

A new consciousness seems to have come upon us—the consciousness of strength—and with it a new appetite, the yearning to show our strength. It might be compared with the effect upon the animal creation of the taste of blood. Ambition, interest, land hunger, pride, the mere joy of fighting, whatever it may be we are animated by a new sensation. We are face to face with a strange destiny. The taste of empire is in the mouth of the people even as the taste of blood in the jungle. It means an imperial policy, the Republic, renascent, taking her place with the armed nations.

—EDITORIAL, *The Washington Post* (1898)

THE UNITED STATES EMERGED from the Civil War a united but exhausted nation. Across the Atlantic, Britain was industrializing and acquiring colonies, France was thriving, Germany was unifying, and Russia was expanding. Across the Pacific, the Meiji Restoration would soon bring about Japan's own development and modernization. Meanwhile, two decades after the Civil War, the United States remained largely inward focused. The emphasis was on rebuilding the South, not the army or the navy. In 1890, the U.S. Navy totaled 122,000 tons, while the British Navy displaced 802,000 tons, the French 515,000 tons, the Russians 246,000 tons, the Italians 203,000 tons, and the Germans 188,000 tons. The United States had fallen woefully behind in the naval competition. Despite the country's booming population and economy, the Civil War appeared to have shattered the United States' ambitions abroad.[1]

Yet, within a few short decades, the United States reemerged onto the world stage. A new set of U.S. leaders sought an enhanced international role. The United States not only built a great navy but openly competed with European powers for influence. This transformation took place largely from 1890 to 1910. It was made possible, and indeed was personified, by two individuals. The first, Alfred Thayer Mahan, became famous worldwide for his treatises on naval history and served as the world's most prominent proponent of naval power. The second individual, Theodore Roosevelt, put in place much of Mahan's vision as a young official in the Department of the Navy and then as president of the United States. Together, Mahan, Roosevelt, and their supporters transformed the United States into a global power in just two decades.

This chapter evaluates perceived relative power theory against the rise of the United States from 1890 to 1910. This chapter focuses in particular on how and why the U.S. Navy changed before and after William McKinley's election in 1896. This election brought to power a set of leaders more confident in the United States' strengthened relative power position. Perceived relative power theory makes three predictions about states shifting from perceived weakness (Phase 1) to perceived strength (Phase 2). Hypothesis 1 asserts that these states should change from limited objectives to extensive objectives. Hypothesis 3 asserts that these states should shift from denial strategies to control strategies. And Hypothesis 5 asserts that these states should move from expendable investments to sustainable investments. In short, perceived relative power theory suggests a transition from anti-access defense policies toward power-projection defense policies. These hypotheses are evaluated against the historical record in the pages that follow.

U.S. Defense Policies Pre-1896

Late nineteenth-century U.S. defense policies were in many ways an outgrowth of the Civil War. The United States had largely completed its expansion across the North American continent, and there were indications that U.S. leaders might look farther afield. Secretary of State William Seward acquired Alaska in 1867, but public condemnation of "Seward's folly" made clear a preference for more limited objectives. Potential threats from European powers, North American neighbors, and American Indian tribes did not require projection of power at great distances. In 1869, Secretary of State Hamilton Fish proclaimed that "the acquisition of outlying territory has not been regarded as desirable by us." The U.S. appetite for adventurism seemed to have dimmed. As a result, U.S. defense objectives remained limited, U.S. strategy mostly denial focused, and U.S. investments weighted toward systems that could not be sustained in a conflict.[2]

Defense Objectives: Limited

Throughout the 1880s, leaders in Washington echoed the public's skepticism of overseas commitments. In 1885, President Grover Cleveland explained, "I do not favor a policy of acquisition of new and distant territory or the incorporation of remote interests with our own." Cleveland reflected the prevailing view that U.S. interests were largely limited to the defense of existing territory. Even Theodore Roosevelt, who would later promote extensive U.S. goals abroad, expressed concern about foreign entanglements. In 1886, Roosevelt criticized supporters of manifest destiny as "statesmen of easy international morality."[3]

Nevertheless, the United States' growing international ties forced its leaders to consider new missions, such as protecting trade routes. With business booming from 1880 to 1890, total wealth increased 50 percent in nominal terms. Trade expanded in line with economic growth. By 1890, the United States accounted for roughly one-tenth of world trade, roughly equal to that of France and Germany. Although high tariffs took a toll on trade, particularly after the economic scare of 1893, manufacturing trade continued to grow. From 1890 to 1900, manufacturing exports jumped from 20 to 35 percent of U.S. exports. By 1900, the United States was importing $885 million in goods but exporting $1.4 billion, with over one-third of this total going to Europe.[4]

The United States' growing trade was the result, in part, of its booming population and economy. Between 1860 and 1890, the number of Americans doubled to over sixty million. This amounted to twice the population of England and Wales, easily surpassing Germany, France, Russia, and Japan. Furthermore, the steady addition of new immigrants from Europe and Asia rapidly added to the U.S. population and slowed population growth abroad. By 1892, U.S. gross domestic product per capita was nearly equal to that of England, 50 percent higher than that in Germany or France, double that of Spain and Italy, and three to four times that of Japan and Russia. By the early 1890s, the United States was the world's top economy as measured by gross domestic product.[5]

Yet it was not until the mid-1890s that the United States' newfound strength became apparent to its political leaders. William McKinley's election brought into office a president who recognized U.S. strength and believed that the United States could assert itself on the international stage. McKinley initially remained focused on digging the United States out of the economic depression that followed the panic of 1893. Nonetheless, McKinley and other Republicans also supported calls for "the acquisition of such territory, far and near, as may be useful in enlarging our commercial advantages, and in securing to our navy facilities desirable for the operations of a great naval power." McKinley was encouraged in these efforts by a group of young leaders with increasingly extensive objectives abroad.[6]

Theodore Roosevelt would serve as McKinley's assistant secretary of the navy and later as his vice president. By 1896, Roosevelt had repudiated his earlier comments about the manifest destiny concept. He announced, "[I] feel very strong about . . . Hawaii. . . . I am a bit of a believer in the manifest destiny doctrine. . . . I don't want to see our flag hauled down where it has been hauled up." The historian Howard Beale explained, "Roosevelt had been preoccupied with theories of the spread of civilization through the expansion of control by 'superior races' over 'backward' areas."

Meanwhile, Roosevelt's good friend Henry Cabot Lodge warned against seeing "South America parceled out as Africa has been": "We should then find ourselves with great powers to the South of us and we should be forced to become at once a nation with a powerful army and navy with difficulties and dangers surrounding us."[7]

These sentiments demonstrated a renewed interest not only in operating abroad but also in challenging European powers. This was a clear break from past U.S. objectives. One advocate was the naval strategist Alfred Thayer Mahan, who had a substantial impact not only on Roosevelt but also on other American politicians. Mahan and Roosevelt shared a vision of a renewed United States with a strengthened navy. Roosevelt—who had himself written a popular study of U.S. naval policy in the War of 1812—heralded Mahan's work and embraced the more extensive objectives he proposed. As McKinley, Roosevelt, and Mahan gained a newfound appreciation of U.S. power, they transformed U.S. defense policies.[8]

Defense Strategy: Denial

The shift in U.S. defense strategy is most visible in the navy's transformation. In the late 1800s, the U.S. Navy primarily practiced sea denial. Rather than attempting to meet foreign navies head-to-head, U.S. strategy called for commerce raiding and coastal defense. Those vessels equipped to operate offshore were lightly armed and armored, so they could act only against merchant ships, not foreign warships. Meanwhile, coastal defenses were intended to deny opponents the ability to carry out raids from the sea. U.S. naval strategy remained rooted in the country's first naval operations, using privateers to carry out raids against enemy shipping. As the historian J. H. Patton noted, "The American privateers maintained the honor of the nation as much as the regular navy." This sea-denial strategy remained dominant for most of the 1800s.[9]

Throughout the 1880s, leaders in Washington insisted that sea denial should be the navy's primary goal. This view was rooted not in the United States' expanding interests but in its perceived weakness as a naval power. A House committee reported that the United States remained "infinitely smaller in real fighting power" than the European powers. As one observer noted, "A strong mobile navy in the age of steam necessitated overseas bases and coaling stations, and the seaborne commerce needed to sustain a country's wealth and strength required overseas markets and sources of raw material." Such activities overseas appeared dangerous to many Americans. Thus, in 1881, the Naval Advisory Board recommended "construction of cruisers and gunboats rather than battleships, because it decided that the purpose of the navy was protection of commerce, 'showing the flag' in foreign ports, and coastal defense, not major fleet actions against other naval powers." Navy Secretary William Whitney called these unarmored cruisers "commerce destroyers" and noted, "we shall soon be in condition to launch a fleet of large and fast cruisers against the commerce of an enemy."[10]

Meanwhile, the 1880s witnessed a renewed push for coastal defenses. Congressman George Robeson commented in 1883, "It is ridiculous to build an offensive navy to go out and strike at the commerce of foreign nations if you have nothing to defend your harbors and seaports; if you have the accumulated capital and property in the maritime cities at the mercy of any ironclad that may come in." This concern resulted in a study recommending improved coastal defenses rather than seagoing ships. In 1890, Congressman William McAdoo argued, "Mr. Jefferson, as is well known, advocated strenuously that the first step to be taken was the defense of our coasts; he held that the main line of action for us, being not an offensive, but a defensive naval power, was to protect our 12,000 miles of seacoast. This is good sense now as then." Most U.S. coastal defenses took the form of small ships designed not to control the coasts but to deny adversaries the ability to linger near the coasts themselves.[11]

Nevertheless, a strategic transformation took hold as U.S. trade expanded. In 1890, Mahan warned that the United States was "weak in a confessed unpreparedness for war, . . . [lacking] warships of the first class, without which ships no country can pretend to control any part of the sea." Mahan's growing influence turned the tide against both coastal defenses and commerce raiding. Rejecting coastal defenses, Mahan wrote, "the enemy must be kept not only out of our ports, but far away from our coasts." Discarding commerce raiding, Mahan insisted, "It is not the taking of individual ships or convoys, be they few or many, that strikes down the money power of a nation; it is the possession of that over-bearing power on the sea which drives the enemy's flag from it. . . . This overbearing power can only be exercised by great navies." To Mahan, coastal defense and commerce raiding were losing strategies because they were incapable of winning victory.[12]

Instead of sea denial, Mahan advocated sea control. He explained, "Military control depends chiefly upon two things, position and active military strength." Position would require that the United States "take possession, when it can be done righteously, of such maritime positions as contribute to secure command." Meanwhile, military strength meant building a blue-water navy capable of concentrating against an enemy's fleet. As the naval officer Harris Lanning wrote in 1895, the United States "was attempting to become a great Naval power": "Our people had to compete with other nations and a larger Navy was necessary to ensure us free use of the trade routes across the sea." Although Mahan realized that total sea control was outside the navy's grasp, he made clear that even partial sea control was preferable to sea denial. This would signify quite a shift for the U.S. Navy.[13]

The navy's transformation proceeded slowly at first. Roosevelt warned, "The American people must either build and maintain an adequate Navy or else make up their minds definitely to accept a secondary position in international affairs." In 1896, he admitted, "It is very difficult for me not to wish a war with Spain, for such a war would result at once in getting a proper Navy." The next year, Roosevelt told a friend in confidence, "I should welcome almost any war, for I think this country needs one." The seeds of a sea-control strategy—and war with Spain—had been planted, but they would not fully spring to life for several years.[14]

Defense Investments: Expendable

Through the 1880s, many naval officers viewed a seagoing navy as unnecessary because limited U.S. objectives did not require sea control. The naval officer Bradley Fiske noted, "our Navy was maintained simply as a measure of precaution against the wholly improbable danger of our coast being attacked." Thus, the U.S.

Navy remained far smaller than its rivals. By 1883, Britain possessed 61 armored ships, 186 unarmored ships, and 100 smaller
torpedo boats. France had 58 armored ships, 159 unarmored ships,
and 70 torpedo boats. Against these, the United States had only 91
ships total, with a small proportion of armored ships and only a
single torpedo boat. The maritime revolution was already under
way abroad, with new construction shifting from wood and sail to
iron and steam. Yet, Washington was slow to adopt these modern
elements. Navy Secretary William Whitney assessed in 1885, "The
United States had no vessel of war which could have kept the seas
for one week as against any first-rate naval power."[15]

The Naval Affairs Committee of 1880 admitted, "We cannot
expect at once to build up a Navy powerful enough to meet in
mid-ocean and successfully contend with the monster iron-clads of
England, France, and Italy, nor do we desire that the attempt
should be made." In 1882, Lieutenant Commander Henry Gor-
ringe warned, "It would be folly for us to build a fighting fleet to
match that of England, and it would be still greater folly for us to
build a fighting fleet inferior to those of England, France or Italy."
Instead of a real fighting fleet, the United States focused on *Monitor*-class ships designed for coastal protection over seaworthiness
and a small number of fast but underarmed cruisers. The *Monitor*
class was unable to travel substantial distances. Admiral David Por-
ter commented that they were "simply useless . . . [and could] not
go to sea without being towed." Although naval leaders did not
want to expend these ships in a conflict, they were not designed to
be sustained through an engagement with a capable adversary.[16]

The first push toward a seagoing fleet was the Navy Act of
1883. This act represented the beginning of a new age of U.S.
shipbuilding. It resulted in the so-called ABCD ships—the USS
Atlanta, USS *Boston*, USS *Chicago*, and USS *Dolphin*. These ships
had steel hulls and both sail and steam power. Although they took
years to come into service, the ABCD ships eventually formed the
basis for the "squadron of evolution" that would help launch the
"New Navy." Yet, these new seagoing ships were not intended for
sea control. Rather, the ABCD ships were built for commerce raiding, fulfilling the wishes of Navy Secretary William Chandler. In
1883, Chandler explained that the ships were needed "to assert at

all times our natural, justifiable, and necessary ascendancy in the affairs of the American hemisphere." These ships still would not permit the navy to project power against a serious opponent. In 1886, House Naval Affairs Committee chairman Hilary Herbert lamented, "we have not a single vessel of war that could keep the seas against a first-class vessel of any important power."[17]

The first move toward sustainable ships came in 1886, but it would take years to gain traction. The Naval Affairs Committee suggested construction of two armored vessels "capable of keeping the sea for long periods." Many experts continued to believe that capital ships of this sort were unnecessary. Lieutenant Commander W. W. Reisinger argued that the navy "shall never need, the large fleets of heavy ironclads. . . . [Rather] a fleet of powerful vessels with the latest and best torpedo outfits . . . and high-powered guns, will prove the best coast defense, supplemented by the fast sea-going torpedo boats." Without a significant threat, arming for war with a major power seemed unnecessary to some leaders. Meanwhile, Congress would only permit a modest seagoing fleet. Between 1886 and 1889, a limited number of battleships were developed. These ships, although capable of deploying at greater distances, remained far slower than other modern fleets. While acquiring this fleet of battleships, the United States continued to invest in new coastal defenses. Mahan objected to such expenditures but also admitted that "guns, lines of stationary torpedoes, and torpedo-boats," could complement "a navy able to keep the sea."[18]

Efforts to establish a sustainable fleet meandered through the early 1890s. Admiral Stephen Luce warned, "The battleship is the very foundation of the Navy. The United States has no battleships, therefore she has no Navy." President Benjamin Harrison entered office determined to rectify this weakness. Harrison announced at his inauguration, "the construction of a sufficient number of modern warships should progress as rapidly as is consistent with care and perfection in plans and workmanship." Navy Secretary Benjamin Tracy testified, "The best ship in the world is the cheapest at any money—I don't care what it costs. The people of this country, in my judgment, will never approve and take pride in any second-class ship." Tracy commissioned a Policy Board, which recommended what one historian calls "coast-defense battleships of 'limited coal endurance,' since the nation was not yet prepared to take the full leap to an ocean-going fleet." Nevertheless, the ships were not funded.[19]

In time, Mahan's growing popularity brought additional political support to the quest for seagoing battleships. Mahan argued, "The backbone and real power of any navy are the vessels which, by due proportion of defensive and offensive powers, are capable of taking and giving hard knocks. All others are but subservient to these, and exist only for them." In 1892, Navy Secretary Tracy won support for what one observer calls "his first ocean-going capital ship, although it was still described as a 'sea-going coast-line battle ship' in the authorizing legislation." These coastal defense battleships displaced nearly 10,000 tons and could carry up to 1,600 tons of coal (although they were usually given only 400 tons). The ability to deploy and sustain these ships, however, improved only gradually. Although an 1893 test experimented with coaling at sea, no further efforts were attempted until after the Spanish-American War.[20]

Meanwhile, the United States continued to invest in smaller coastal-defense vessels, even as it sought advanced seagoing battleships. At the time, the navy included just four "first rate" armored cruisers of 6,000 to 8,100 tons; six protected cruisers of 3,700 to 4,500 tons, four "second rate" cruisers between 3,000 and 3,200 tons; three "third rate" cruisers of 2,000 tons, five *Monitor*-class vessels between 3,800 and 4,000 tons, six gunboats of 1,000 to 1,700 tons, several smaller gunboats and torpedo boats below 1,000 tons, and a harbor defense ram. To simplify the fleet, Secretary Tracy proposed just three major ship types: "First, the armored battleship of 10,000 or more tons; second, the armored cruiser of from 8,000 to 9,000 tons; and third, the commerce protecting and destroying cruiser, of extreme speed, of 7,500 tons." Tracy's plan called for larger, faster, and more sustainable ships of all classes. Nonetheless, a bifurcated force continued to gain support in Washington. President Grover Cleveland noted, "If we are to have a Navy for war-like operations, offensive and defensive, we certainly ought to increase both the number of battleships and torpedo boats." His navy secretary, Hilary Herbert, decided to do just that.[21]

This struggle between an oceangoing fleet and commerce raiding or coastal defenses would continue until William McKinley was elected in 1896. McKinley inaugurated a revolution in U.S. shipbuilding. Soon the United States became one of the leading builders of large battleships that could be sustained at a distance for long periods. The United States' limited objectives, sea-denial strategy, and unsustainable ships would soon be remnants of history.

U.S. Defense Policies Post-1896

By the latter half of the 1890s, some leading figures were embracing the United States' newfound strength and openly advocating an extensive U.S. agenda abroad. As Mahan stated in 1897, "Americans must now begin to look outward." A decade later, Roosevelt predicted, "There will be an awakening, but it will be gradual." This awakening was jump-started by the Spanish-American War, which presented a prime opportunity for increasingly confident U.S. leaders to push through a new set of defense policies. The result was a rapid shift toward extensive objectives, a control strategy, and sustainable systems. By the time William Howard Taft came to power in 1909, the United States no longer saw itself as a weak nation. Rather, the United States had transformed into a strong world power, with the power-projection military to prove it.[22]

Defense Objectives: Extensive

Nothing put the United States' newfound strength on display more than the Spanish-American War. In 1898, the U.S. Navy was in no way prepared to take on a strong colonial power such as Britain or France. But Spain was much weaker. Spanish warships were old, and Spanish decision-making was hampered by the long distances involved. U.S. ships had superior firepower and implemented a blockade of Cuba that permitted them to remain relatively close to the U.S. coastline. In this way, the U.S. fleet offset its limited sustainability. Thus, the Spanish-American War both exaggerated U.S. strength and motivated leaders in Washington to capitalize on the United States' newfound glory.

The United States' wartime successes owed much to Theodore Roosevelt. As assistant secretary of the navy, Roosevelt had used the prospect of war to prepare the navy. On assuming the job in 1897, Roosevelt said the United States should "take the position to which it is entitled among the nations of the earth." When Navy Secretary John D. Long took a day off shortly after the sinking of the USS *Maine*, Roosevelt became acting secretary for the day. He took advantage. Roosevelt ordered coaling ships to prepare for action and arranged for the purchase of auxiliary cruisers. He also ordered the U.S. Asiatic Squadron to prepare for operations against Spanish forces in the Philippines. When Secretary Long was informed of Roosevelt's actions, he was disturbed. But he chose not to rescind the orders. Two months later, the war with Spain was under way, and the U.S. Navy was well prepared.[23]

Roosevelt's motivation for these reforms derived from his increasing confidence in U.S. power. In 1895, Roosevelt declared, "No amount of material prosperity can atone for lack of national self-respect." The next year, Roosevelt insisted, "the United States . . . should be dominant in the Western Hemisphere." And the year after, Roosevelt looked beyond the Americas, telling Mahan, "As regards Hawaii, . . . if I had my way, we would annex those islands tomorrow." In response to concerns that annexation of Hawaii might provoke a foreign response, Roosevelt declared, "The United States is not in a position which requires her to ask Japan, or any other foreign Power, what territory it shall or shall not acquire." But Roosevelt worried that the American people were too slow to realize the dangers around them, commenting, "It is very difficult to make this nation wake up. . . . I sometimes question whether anything but a great military disaster will ever make us feel our responsibilities and our possible dangers." The USS *Maine*'s sinking proved the perfect wake-up call.[24]

War with Spain reinforced the desire for overseas territories. The first target was Hawaii, a vital coaling station for travel to Asia. President McKinley noted, "We need Hawaii just as much and a great deal more than we did California. It is manifest destiny." Roosevelt declared, "We did not create the Hawaiian Islands, they already exist. We merely have to face the alternative of taking them ourselves and making them the outpost for the protection of the Pacific Coast or else of seeing them . . . transformed into the most dangerous possible base of operations against our Pacific cities." This description of offensive U.S. actions as inherently defensive would pervade Roosevelt's speeches for years. He noted, "We cannot help Hawaii's being either a strong defense to us or a perpetual menace. We can only decide whether we will now take the islands when offered to us as a gift, or by force try to conquer them from the first powerful nation with which we may become embroiled."[25]

James Bryce, later British ambassador to the United States, observed that Roosevelt was now motivated by "the notion that it is a fine thing for a great country to have vast territories, and to see marked as her own, on the map of the world, dominions beyond her natural borders." This drive would not stop with Hawaii. Farther to the west, the United States landed troops to gain control of the Philippines after Admiral George Dewey soundly beat the Spanish at Manila Bay. Many Americans criticized this seizure of Spanish territory. Roosevelt's former supervisor, Navy Secretary Long, argued, "If I could have my personal preference, . . . I would . . . be rid of the Philippines and of everything else except our own country." Nevertheless, when the Treaty of Paris was concluded, Washington controlled Hawaii, the Philippines, Guam, and Puerto Rico.[26]

Proponents justified these extensive commitments abroad in several ways. Mahan plainly stated, "if a plea of the world's welfare seems suspiciously like a cloak for national self-interest, let the latter be accepted frankly as the adequate motive which it assuredly is." Roosevelt now found himself advocating the colonialism he had rejected as immoral just a decade earlier. Roosevelt insisted, "Peace must be brought about in the world's waste spaces. . . . Peace cannot be had until the civilized nations have expanded in some shape over the barbarous nations." He admitted, "I am an expansionist," and insisted, "our whole national history has been one of expansion." In 1900, Roosevelt's popularity drove him from the New York governorship to the ticket of sitting president McKinley. During the race, Roosevelt continued to advocate a broader conception of U.S. objectives. He insisted, "We must work out our own destiny by our own strength. A vigorous young nation like ours does not always stand still. Now and then there comes a time when it is sure either to shrink or to expand. Grant saw to it that we did not shrink, and therefore we had to expand when the inevitable moment came." After winning the vice presidency, he noted, "Our people are neither cravens nor weaklings and we face the future high of heart and confident of soul eager to do the great work of a great world power."[27]

The United States' triumphant rise had been announced. And this vision of strength and extensive engagement abroad attracted adherents. Senator Henry Cabot Lodge commented, "A great nation must have great responsibilities. It is one of the penalties of greatness." Senator Albert Beveridge suggested that God had "marked the American people as His chosen nation to finally lead in the regeneration of the world." Woodrow Wilson assessed, "This great pressure of a people moving always to new frontiers, in search of new lands, new power, the full freedom of a virgin world, has ruled our course and formed our policies like a Fate." Similarly, the British naval attaché C. L. Ottley observed, "The successful issue of the war with Spain in 1898 has given an added impetus to the policy of naval expansion in the United States, of which the earliest indications were apparent in 1883. . . . The country in general is in favor of a fleet commensurate with the wealth of the nation and strong enough for all purposes."[28]

Roosevelt assumed the presidency in September 1901. The next year, Roosevelt publicly endorsed the Monroe Doctrine, commenting that "if the Monroe Doctrine did not already exist, it would be necessary forthwith to create it." He pushed for an even larger global role as the United States was "becoming, owing to our strength and geography, more and more the balance of power of the whole globe." U.S. control of the Philippines resulted in an insurgency that raged for years, but Roosevelt was unwilling to give up the new territory. He explained, "The question now is not whether we shall expand for we have already expanded—but whether we shall contract. The Philippines are now part of American territory. To surrender them would be to surrender American territory." Roosevelt rejected the idea that this amounted to imperialism, noting, "The simple truth is there is nothing even remotely resembling 'imperialism.' . . . The words mean absolutely nothing as applied to our present policy in the Philippines."[29]

During his time in office, Roosevelt fundamentally reshaped U.S. defense policies. Roosevelt declared, "We have definitely taken our place among the great world powers, and it would be a sign of ignoble weakness, having taken such a place, to shirk its responsibilities. Therefore, unless we are willing to . . . acknowledge ourselves a weak and timid nation, we must steadily build up and maintain a great fighting navy." Senator Beveridge concurred, "Our rapidly-increasing power determined [the need for colonial administration]; our commercial needs determined it; more than either, geography determined it; and, most of all, our duty to the world as one of its civilizing powers determined it." Roosevelt himself explained that the United States now "came in as a strong man and not as a weakling." Roosevelt would claim that it was Admiral "Dewey's canon, that waked the world, that bid the older nations know that the young giant of the West had come to his glorious prime." But Roosevelt himself had ushered in much of this transformation. Thus, by the time Roosevelt stepped down from the presidency in 1909, the United States had transitioned from limited to extensive goals abroad.[30]

Defense Strategy: Control

New defense objectives mandated a new defense strategy. Just as Mahan has suggested, the navy shifted from commerce raiding and coastal defense to long-distance sea control. As the historians Harold and Margaret Sprout note, "Mahan's philosophy of sea power entered the White House in the person of Theodore Roosevelt." Even before he took office, Roosevelt had become a chief proponent of a control strategy, noting, "If we have a great fighting fleet . . . to equality with the greatness of our people; if we have such a fleet, capable, of offensive no less than of defensive work, there will be small chance that our people will be forced to fight." As assistant secretary, he increased dry-dock capacity, refit older vessels with modern equipment, and ensured the availability of coal for the Asiatic Squadron. Moreover, he ordered the Asiatic Squadron to be prepared to conduct "offensive operations" against Spanish forces in the Philippines. As one naval historian observes, Roosevelt "initiated a series of actions that had the potential to shift the basic mission of the U.S. Navy from coastal defense to power projection."[31]

The shift in U.S. strategy proceeded with remarkable speed after the Spanish-American War. By 1899, the British director of Naval Intelligence L. A. Beaumont warned, "the United States mean to be the strongest Naval power [along their eastern coast] and it will be difficult to prevent it." Navy Secretary Hilary Herbert was somewhat more circumspect: "It is not contended that we should attempt to compete in numbers with the great navies of England and France, but we ought surely to move up steadily into a higher rank than we now occupy, and into the pace of nations whose necessities are far less than ours." Politicians such as Chester A. Arthur argued, "I cannot too strongly urge upon you my conviction that every consideration of national safety, economy, and honor imperatively demands a thorough rehabilitation of our navy."[32]

The navy's sea-control transformation accelerated after the turn of the century. The U.S. Navy still trailed the British in overall tonnage, but by 1900, it had surpassed Italy and nearly equaled Russia and France. The United States' warship tonnage jumped from 240,000 to 333,000 in the decade before 1900 and, in the next decade, added nearly 500,000 tons of modern warships. The president of Bethlehem Steel would later note, "In 1902, the United States Government launched us on a larger and modern naval program." Only Germany was able to keep up with this percentage increase in warship tonnage. The historian Craig Symonds writes that early nineteenth-century navalists "yearned for empire" and that "a naval fleet was physical evidence of national adulthood."[33]

With a growing navy, sea control now seemed attainable. Yet, the United States remained constrained by geography. Mahan's vision of sea control required a unified fleet, but the United States had to operate in both the Atlantic and the Pacific. Indeed, when Roosevelt considered shifting vessels to the Atlantic in 1902, Mahan warned, "To remove our fleet—battle fleet—from the Pacific would be . . . a confession of weakness. . . . It would mean a reversion to a policy narrowly American, and essentially defensive." Protecting both coasts became an even more difficult task after 1905, when Japan's alliance with Great Britain and its defeat of Russia permitted Japan a freer hand in the Pacific. Roosevelt's answer was the Panama Canal. But he was not content simply to build the canal. Instead, Roosevelt desired that it be "wholly under the control of the United States, alike in peace and war." Other experts suggested that "fortified naval bases could be established in Cuba and Puerto Rico": "our Navy can control the Caribbean."[34]

This new focus on sea control extended far beyond the coasts of the United States. Congressman Richmond Hobson wrote in 1902, "The finger of fate is pointing forward. America will be the controlling World power, holding the scepter of the seas, reigning in mighty beneficence with the guiding principle of a maximum of world service. She will help all the nations of the earth. Europe will be saved by her young off-spring grown to manhood." To accomplish this mandate, the 1903 General Board suggested "a) a forty-eight-battleship fleet, . . . b) an American policy to be automatically conditioned by naval development abroad, . . . c) a fleet always stronger than likely enemies, and d) a commensurate increase of personnel as well as materiel." No longer would the United States accept a role as a weak state at the mercy of stronger powers. Instead, one naval historian observes, "Commerce raiding and coastal defense strategy were discarded and a forward strategy was adopted in which a fleet powerful enough to defeat any potential enemy fleet would do so far out at sea." The United States had fashioned a sea-control strategy; the challenge now was to construct the requisite fleet.[35]

Defense Investments: Sustainable

Extensive defense objectives and a sea-control strategy required sustainable naval systems. Existing U.S. warships were not up to the task. One historian writes, "Prior to 1898, battleships had been needed only for coastal continental defense. The government now realized that it needed battleships with greater range to protect its newly acquired territories and foreign interests, . . . ships with higher speeds and greater cruising radius." In 1899, Congress required that new capital ships have "great radius of action," although they still designated the new batch of vessels as "coast line" battleships. Larger and more expensive ships came at a cost, namely, the smaller cruisers and other ships that were not sustainable at sea. Roosevelt insisted to the chairman of the House Naval Committee, "Heavy cruisers were very well in their way, but heavy battleships are what we need. We do not need light cruisers at all." Mahan argued, "the recourse of the weaker maritime belligerent is commerce-destruction by cruisers on the high sea." As a result, Mahan advised, "Seaworthiness, and reasonable speed under all weather conditions, are qualities necessary to every constituent of a fleet."[36]

Politicians in Washington sought ships that could be sustained at sea and symmetrically confront potential adversaries. Seaworthy battleships were the goal. Larger, more sustainable ships were enabled by the transition from coal to oil. Half a ton of fuel oil was equivalent to one ton of coal, so this nearly doubled the range of oil-fueled ships. Thus empowered, Navy Secretary William Moody announced in 1904, "we have under construction and authorized by the Congress a greater tonnage than has any other nation in the world except Great Britain." Battleships crowded out funding for smaller ships that "did not have the endurance or stability to be useful away from American shores." As Commander William Sims acknowledged, "A fleet of small vessels would have considerably less coal endurance than a fleet of large ones. . . . The fleet of large vessels, while avoiding decisive action and preventing its enemy from proceeding in any given direction, can ultimately attack when the latter is obliged to abandon the open sea." American navalists soon become envious of the British dreadnought. The dreadnought was not only heavily armored and gunned but also capable of high speed. The United States quickly followed suit, but sustainability remained a priority. Captain C. W. Dyson noted, "The areas to be covered are great and the distances to bases and from base to base in some cases are magnificent. Fuel economy is of the highest value, even predominates over speed."[37]

By 1907, the Great White Fleet was cruising around the world. Roosevelt justified this as "absolutely necessary for us to try in time of peace to see just what we can do in the way of putting a big battle fleet in the Pacific." The navy learned a great deal about sustaining a force at sea and the importance of colliers and distant outposts. This lesson was vital because earlier observers had noted, "The United States have never deemed it needful to their national

Table 6. Estimated Warship Tonnage (1890–1910)

	1890	1900	1910
Britain	679,000	1,065,000	2,174,000
France	319,000	499,000	725,000
Italy	242,000	245,000	327,000
United States	240,000	333,000	824,000
Germany	190,000	285,000	964,000
Russia	180,000	383,000	401,000
Japan	41,000	187,000	496,000

Source: Table reproduced and adapted from Paul M. Kennedy, *The Rise and Fall of the Great Powers: Economic Change and Military Conflict from 1500 to 2000* (New York: Vintage Books, 1989), 203.

life to maintain impregnable fortresses along the world's highways of commerce." At the time, the United States was building two colliers but had no more. In 1909, *Scientific American* wrote, "Undoubtedly, the greatest need of the navy to-day is a fleet of large and fairly fast colliers, built expressly for naval purposes." The next year, five colliers were added to the budget. This development supplied the final missing piece in the shift from a coastal-defense force to a navy with global power-projection capabilities. Finally, U.S. ships were not only seaworthy but also sustainable. At last, the United States was able to compete symmetrically with all but the British Navy.[38]

In many senses, Roosevelt's departure from office marked the completion of the navy's transformation from an unsustainable coastal-defense and commerce-raiding force into a sustainable oceangoing navy. The nation had acquired overseas territories, distant coaling stations, and colliers. The navy had built first-class battleships and demonstrated the ability to deploy and sustain them anywhere on Earth. These trends continued after Roosevelt departed. William Howard Taft, for example, created "a still more 'top-heavy' navy," even choosing to sacrifice "cruisers, destroyers, and the other essential components of a fighting fleet." Thus, by the beginning of World War I, the United States had one of the world's largest and most sustainable battlefleets. And it was oriented almost entirely toward control of distant seas.[39]

Assessment

U.S. defense policies were transformed from 1890 to 1910. When the country's leaders viewed the United States as relatively weak, they favored limited objectives, adopted denial strategies, and avoided expensive investments in sustainable systems. Yet, expansive objectives abroad soon ruled the day, due in part to U.S. leaders' recognition of their newfound power. As Roosevelt proclaimed in 1899, "Nations that expand and nations that do not expand may both ultimately go down, but the one leaves heirs and a glorious memory, and the other leaves neither." Roosevelt and his adherents were determined to extend their control across the seas.[40]

There is no doubt that other forces were also at work. Yet, most structural and cultural explanations struggle to explain the timing of this shift toward power projection. From the mid-1890s onward, U.S. leaders largely emulated stronger powers rather than developing new innovations. But the imitation hypothesis suggests that this should have been a constant tendency. Although changing geographic boundaries provide a possible explanation, U.S. expansion from coast to coast had been largely completed years earlier. Similarly, technological explanations fail to explain why U.S. leaders did not pursue new naval systems before the mid-1890s. And cultural arguments struggle to explain why U.S. objectives, strategies, and investments changed so rapidly in the 1890s despite the fact that manifest destiny had been a theme in U.S. strategic thinking since the 1820s.

Another group of possible explanations relates to domestic politics and individual leadership. Although the United States entered the 1890s as a rapidly growing economy, it remained largely focused on the North American continent, and its navy was ill prepared even for coastal defense and commerce raiding. Yet, domestic support for the navy expanded around this time. In particular, Mahan's writings won political support for activities abroad. These set "the American ship of state upon the much bolder and more comprehensive program of politico-naval imperialism which was envisaged and justified in Mahan's larger philosophy of sea power." Mahan's personal influence, along with that of Roosevelt and others, shifted funding toward the navy and power projection.

Nevertheless, it is important to remember that Roosevelt was initially opposed to entanglements abroad. It was not until Mahan wrote in 1893, "we have come upon the sea . . . in our natural, necessary, irrepressible expansion," that Roosevelt became more supportive of extending U.S. objectives. Moreover, Roosevelt rose to the presidency after the United States had already seized Hawaii, Puerto Rico, Guam, Palmyra Island, the Philippines, Wake Island, and American Samoa. Thus, individual leadership was critical, but it was not the only factor.[41]

No single factor is wholly responsible for the United States' defense policy reforms. Geography, domestic politics, and individual leadership played a role. But the fact that U.S. defense objectives, strategy, and investments shifted so rapidly after U.S. leaders recognized their newfound strength aligns with the predictions of perceived relative power theory. Some underlying force appeared to trigger U.S. leaders to espouse similar views around the same time. Many Americans followed Roosevelt's path from opposing manifest destiny in the 1880s to embracing extensive objectives abroad. The 1890 Policy Board foreshadowed these changes. That group noted, "our Navy is insignificant and totally disproportionate to the greatness of the country." This would change in just two decades, as U.S. leaders came to believe that "the determining factor would be the control of the sea." And this sea-control strategy required not only a larger fleet but also ships capable of being sustained at sea. These shifts are perhaps best summarized by a contemporary historian, who wrote, "The growth of the U.S. Navy's power and size merely paralleled the concurrent increase in American political and economic influence." Thus, this case provides confirming evidence for Hypotheses 1, 3, and 5.[42]

CHAPTER THREE

Germany's Rise

We realize that without power, without a strong army and a strong navy, there can be no welfare for us. The means of fighting the battle for existence in this world without strong armaments on land and water . . . have not yet been found. In the coming century the German nation will be either the hammer or the anvil.

—CHANCELLOR BERNHARD VON BÜLOW, REICHSTAG SPEECH (1899)

BY THE END OF the nineteenth century, the German economy was booming. Wilhelm II succeeded his father on the Prussian throne in 1888, and over the next twenty-five years, German imports and exports tripled. German trade expanded as its merchant fleet grew from under one hundred thousand tons to over five million tons. This expanding merchant fleet raised Germany's share of world shipbuilding from 7.3 to 13.8 percent in only fifteen years. Wilhelm basked in the glory of Germany's newfound might and proclaimed, "The German Empire has become a world empire."[1]

German leaders now attempted to transform the Reich into a global power. Although Prussia had traditionally focused on its army, Germany chose to build one of the world's great navies. In 1899, the navy budget was 133 million German marks, but it would grow to 467 million marks within fifteen years. Wilhelm explained, "Germany is a young and growing empire. . . . Germany must have a powerful fleet to protect that commerce and her manifold interests in even the most distant seas." To accomplish that goal, Wilhelm appointed Alfred Tirpitz to lead the Imperial Navy Department in 1897.[2]

In many ways, Germany's rise paralleled the United States' ascent. While Alfred Thayer Mahan was inspiring navalism in the United States, Alfred Tirpitz was doing the same in Germany. The historian Gary Weir explains, "The Americans and Germans were similar both in strategic theory and in their stage of naval growth." Tirpitz noted the parallels in German and U.S. strategy development, commenting, "Whilst we were discovering these things quite empirically on the 'small practice-ground' by Kiel Bay, the American Admiral Mahan was simultaneously evolving them theoretically from history." The historian Dirk Bönker notes, "In each country navalists fused these shared ideas to particular concepts of national destiny, empire, and the world, which permeated the expansionist discourses among the national intelligentsia in each country." The result was that both Germany and the United States rapidly developed power-projection navies.[3]

This chapter examines German defense policies from 1890 to 1910. Germany's army sought supremacy on the continent and became an even more potent power-projection force, but only the navy could secure foreign trade routes and challenge Great Britain. This chapter therefore focuses on how the German Navy transformed during this period. Perceived relative power theory makes three predictions about states shifting from perceived weakness to perceived strength. Hypothesis 1 predicts a change from limited objectives to extensive objectives. Hypothesis 3 predicts a shift from denial strategies to control strategies. And Hypothesis 5 predicts a move from expendable investments to sustainable investments. As expected, when German leaders became more confident in their relative strength in the late 1890s, they extended their objectives, adopted a sea-control strategy, and developed a sustainable battlefleet.

German Defense Policies Pre-1897

Wilhelm II was only twenty-nine years old when he ascended to the German throne after his father and grandfather died over the course of three months. Young Wilhelm was eager to put his stamp on German history, but he was not enthusiastic about foreign entanglements. In his first speech to the Reichstag, Wilhelm announced, "Germany needs neither glory in war nor any form of conquest now that it has finally won the fight to be entitled to stand as an independent nation." This vision of Germany as a pacific nation aligned with the views of Wilhelm's closest advisers. Yet, Germany's limited objectives, denial strategy, and unsustainable naval forces were living on borrowed time. Within a decade, Wilhelm would jettison this worldview and its supporters.[4]

Defense Objectives: Limited

In 1888, Wilhelm inherited not only the throne but also his grandfather's powerful chancellor, Otto von Bismarck. Bismarck had masterminded German unification. Wars with Denmark in 1863, Austria in 1866, and France in 1870 allowed "the Prussian eagle to spread his wings." Once Prussia reigned supreme over Germany, Bismarck focused on consolidating the Reich. He avoided overseas commitments, commenting in 1870, "I do not want colonies. They are only suitable as supply bases. . . . This colonial business for us would be similar to the silken pelts of Polish noble families who do not possess even shirts." Going further, Bismarck remarked, "As long as I am chancellor we will carry on no colonial policies." Nevertheless, under pressure from nationalist groups in the mid-1880s, Bismarck supported limited colonization. Germany acquired South-West Africa, Togoland, Cameroon, German East Africa, New Guinea, and the Marshalls. The Reich would later add Nauru, Palau, the Marianas, Kiaochow, and Samoa.[5]

Wilhelm's first speech to the Reichstag presented a modest vision of Germany's overseas ambitions. Wilhelm appeared concerned about overexpansion. One solution lay in an alliance with Great Britain. Germany and Britain both feared France and Russia. Germany dreaded a two-front land war, while Britain worried about dual naval engagements. The stage was thus set for Wilhelm's suggestion to British leaders, "We ought to form an Anglo-German alliance, you to keep the seas while we would be responsible for the land; with such an alliance, not a mouse would stir in Europe without our permission." During a visit to Britain, Wilhelm insisted, "we should reinforce the peace together; you with your strong fleet and us with our great army."[6]

Wilhelm was no stranger to the British. His own mother was the eldest daughter of Queen Victoria and retained strong ties to her homeland. But Wilhelm's difficult relationship with Britain began at birth. His arm was injured during delivery, and Wilhelm later blamed his mother and her British doctors for this as well as for his father's premature death. When the time came to marry, Wilhelm's mother objected to his choice of wife. And on his accession, Wilhelm's own grandmother Queen Victoria complained, "It is too dreadful for us all to think of Willy [Wilhelm] and Bismarck and Dona [Wilhelm's wife] being the supreme head of all now! Two so unfit and one so wicked." Despite these tensions, Wilhelm was made an admiral of the British Navy in 1889. At the time, Wilhelm commented, "Germany possesses an army which answers to her needs, and if the British nation possesses a fleet sufficient for the needs of England, this in itself will be considered by Europe in general as a weighty factor in the maintenance of peace." An Anglo-German alliance appeared logical, despite the family infighting.[7]

If Bismarck had remained chancellor, such an alliance might have been accomplished. Although the British did not trust Bismarck, they knew he was a pragmatist. Bismarck was well aware that the British fleet remained supreme on the seas. Despite his pursuit of colonies in the 1880s, Bismarck was largely focused on continental aims. An alliance with a continentally focused Germany might have been appealing to British leaders. Yet, Queen Victoria was unwilling to delegate continental policy to Germany. Years earlier, she had commented that England "must not stand aloof; England must show the world that she is not prepared to abdicate her position as a great Power." Bismarck, for his part, had no intention of negotiating an alliance out of weakness. He insisted, "We have a desire for peace but we will also not shrink from a decision to take up arms if that is forced upon us. We Germans fear God, but nothing else in the world." Thus, despite the logic of an alliance, London and Berlin were unable to conclude one.[8]

In 1890, Bismarck's reign as chancellor came to a surprising end. Wilhelm, seeking to exercise his prerogative as Kaiser, argued with Bismarck over control of the government. The resulting disagreement ended in a scathing resignation letter from Bismarck and Wilhelm's "dropping the pilot." The end of Bismarck's time as chancellor ushered in a new era of "personal rule." Bismarck had foreseen this when he commented of Wilhelm in 1886, "Some day that man will be his own chancellor." After dismissing Bismarck, Wilhelm shocked Berlin by selecting the former chief of the imperial navy Leo von Caprivi to take his place.[9]

Wilhelm was growing increasingly concerned about Germany's place in the world. Bolstered by the confidence that German leaders had "succeeded in the difficult task of welding the German race into a strong union," Wilhelm now began to reconsider German ambitions abroad. At the time, Wilhelm continued to insist that his aims were pacific, suggesting, "Far be it for me to use this strength for aggressive purposes. Germany needs neither warlike glory nor acquisitions in any part of the globe." Yet, Wilhelm increasingly saw the British as a threat. He commented, "my attention was called to our dependence upon England, owing to the fact that we had no navy and that Heligoland was in English hands." This concern was due in part to Wilhelm's desire for expansion. As he explained that effort to "extend [Germany's] colonial possessions ... could happen only with England's permission" and that this was "an unworthy position for Germany."[10]

Chancellor Caprivi, despite having led the German Navy, was a Prussian army officer, and he remained determined to strengthen the Reich's continental defenses. As one naval historian writes, "Caprivi's concern [was] for using the navy as an instrument of national defense (in an imminent Continental war)." But Caprivi was already losing influence. In 1892, Caprivi's role as prime minister passed to Botho Eulenburg. By 1893, Wilhelm lamented that the

German military "compares still more unfavorably with that of [its] neighbors than it did last year." Wilhelm panicked, saying, "Our prestige is at an end, if we can take no leading part. World-power—without that, a nation cuts a deplorable figure! What are we to do?" The next year, Wilhelm replaced Caprivi as chancellor, and the Prince of Hohenlohe took over. Unlike Caprivi, Hohenlohe connected Germany's newfound power to its interests abroad. He presaged a change in German policy, noting, "Unless we are prepared always to give way and to abandon our status as a World Power, we must be respected. ... And to impress the seafaring Powers we need a fleet."[11]

Defense Strategy: Denial

As German leaders came to recognize their nation's newfound strength, they not only extended their aims but also debated their strategy. The German Navy became a major focus, but it had traditionally been assembled for coastal defense and commerce raiding. The navy that Alfred Tirpitz joined in 1865 was capable only of sea denial. The historian Rolf Hobson notes that in the early 1870s, "the navy's tasks were to defend the coast, prevent an invasion from the sea, and protect trade." Yet as German power grew, leaders in Berlin contemplated a new posture. Officials noted the need for Germany's "own offensive potential, not only to destroy enemy sea trade, but also to attack enemy coasts and harbors": "To carry out the defensive part of our mission we need to be able, under certain circumstances, to seize the offensive." A naval historian observes of the growing German fleet, "The first conundrum was the 'mission' of the navy. Was it coastal protection, defense of trade, or naval supremacy, at least in the Baltic?"[12]

The initial steps toward a new strategy had been initiated decades earlier under Albrecht von Stosch, a general who would serve as the first head of the Imperial German Navy. In 1871, he commented, "We need ships that are also suitable for the offensive protection of the merchant fleet, and the squadrons that we station in distant lands must also contain such ships." This emphasis on operating at a distance presented the fleet with a major new mission. Yet only two years later, Stosch wrote, "The mission of the battlefleet is the defense of the coasts of the nation. . . . Against larger sea powers the fleet has only the significance of a 'sortie fleet.' Any other objective is ruled out by the limited naval strength that the law provides." Thus, despite the navy's ambitions, it was only sufficient for sea denial rather than sea control.[13]

Sea denial was ingrained in the early German Navy. Many German naval theorists were influenced more by the French than the British. French and German leaders shared a similar dilemma with regard to the British fleet. How could a weak continental navy deter a larger British force? The French provided an answer, which a prominent naval historian characterizes as "two distinct strategies, depending on who the enemy was: *La grande guerre* against an inferior naval power; coastal defense and commerce warfare by cruisers against a superior opponent." This equated to a strategy of control against weak states and denial against strong ones.[14]

But as technology advanced, some German naval leaders hoped to challenge Great Britain "by adopting a guerre de course strategy which mainly relied on fast cruisers and highly sophisticated torpedo boats." Caprivi embraced this strategy when he took over for Stosch in 1884. Caprivi wanted Germany to face France and Russia with the strongest army possible, so he favored cheap coastal defenses and commerce raiding. Caprivi advised, "the only naval question is how small our Fleet can be—not how big." In 1887, more commerce-raiding cruisers were built. German naval experts hoped that a "cruiser war, even if slow in its effects, can none the less become decisive." Caprivi did, however, start to build a more robust coastal-defense fleet. He noted that "one cannot dispense with armored ships and heavy artillery." Thus, Tirpitz would later credit Caprivi with helping "to prepare a strong coastal defense for the next war against Russia and France."[15]

When Wilhelm II took the throne, he immediately made his displeasure with Caprivi's naval policy known. Wilhelm claimed that sea denial was insufficient and that the French "had not read their Mahan." A month after Wilhelm came to power, Caprivi was replaced by Admiral Alexander von Monts. He lasted only a year, dying in 1889, after which time the Admiralty was split into two sections. The High Command would handle strategy and fleet command, while the Imperial Naval Office would manage warship construction and political support. Both would report directly to the Kaiser. The result was a strengthened role in naval affairs for Wilhelm but constant bureaucratic infighting between navy leaders. Admiral Eduard von Knorr led the High Command, and Admiral Friedrich von Hollmann led the Imperial Naval Office. Soon a third position was added, chief of the Naval Cabinet, led by Admiral Gustav von Senden-Bibran, who also reported directly to the Kaiser.[16]

During this period, a debate emerged on German defense strategy. Increasingly, the emphasis both on land and at sea was on offensive action. Some war planners suggested that protection of the coast "will always and best be solved through the defeat of hostile naval forces on the high seas." In 1893, Count Alfred von Schlieffen argued, "the fundamental laws of combat remain the same, and one of those laws is that one cannot defeat the enemy without attacking." Similarly, leading naval officers such as Captain Alfred Stenzel asserted, "At all times it is necessary to press for the offensive; without the offensive a fleet has no function." The naval strategist Curt von Maltzahn suggested that offensive ideas were "designed to spring us loose from our coasts." This shift in strategy brought Tirpitz to the forefront.[17]

Early in his career, Tirpitz had endorsed theories of fleet warfare. He noted that in naval battles, the "sole goal is the annihilation of the enemy. Land battle offers other tactical possibilities, such as taking terrain, which do not exist in war at sea. Only annihilation can be accounted a success at sea." Tirpitz later reflected, "the strongest power at sea has a greater advantage than the strongest power on land, owing to the unlimited area that it controls." Therefore, Tirpitz fought for sea control and a power-projection navy. Tirpitz credited Stosch with being "way ahead of his time in the energy with which he drove [Germany's] sea power forward after centuries of neglect." In 1892, Tirpitz wrote a memo suggesting that control of the sea would only end when "one or the other of the hostile fleets has been definitely defeated." Tirpitz's preference for sea control over sea denial was his hallmark. He later reflected, "Throughout my whole career I have always had to oppose two ideas, especially beloved of the lay mind—the idea of a special coastal defense, and that of a cruiser fleet."[18]

Nevertheless, opponents of sea control remained powerful in the early 1890s. By 1893, Caprivi was chancellor, and he continued to insist that a small coastal navy could accomplish German objectives. He commented, "We do not need the armored ships to seek adventure abroad but to ensure our existence in a land war; for if we cannot count on imports during a war, our existence can be dangerously threatened." Yet, a consensus was forming that the navy required large armored ships. Coastal defense and commerce raiding would no longer suffice. As Captain Stenzel commented, "Our harbors and our coast can only be protected by a fleet which seeks out the enemy at sea and fights." In 1894, Tirpitz hailed this shift "from the coastal-defense idea to the High Sea Fleet." Admiral Alexander von Müller said in 1896 that this shift toward sea control was due to the fact that Germany had "risen to a completely different understanding of its ability and duty to expand." The shift from sea denial to sea control was under way.[19]

Defense Investments: Expendable

German fleet design initially focused on small ships for coastal defense and commerce raiding. Throughout the 1860s, the Prussian Navy included armored batteries and gunboats for coastal defense and a small commerce-raiding fleet. The only ships designed for fleet action were lightly armored frigates. As Germany rose, its leaders sought vessels better equipped for commerce raiding. This offensive sea-denial strategy would best be accomplished by cruisers. As Stosch explained, "I consider large battleships still to be erroneous and superfluous for our conditions, since we cannot for a long time be called to fight a naval battle." The resulting plan aimed for eight armored frigates, six armored corvettes, seven armored monitors, two floating batteries, twenty corvettes, eighteen gunboats, and twenty-eight torpedo boats.[20]

Throughout the 1880s, the German Navy debated its core mission, resulting in a muddled acquisition program. Stosch wanted commerce-raiding cruisers. Caprivi favored coastal-defense ships, gunboats, and torpedo boats. Caprivi explained, "The torpedo-boats are a weapon that is of particular value for a power that is weaker on the high seas." A third faction, led by Tirpitz and other young officers, proposed battleships for fleet action. By 1888, Wilhelm was frustrated, noting, "Whereas, at my accession to the throne, I had found the army in a condition which merely required development upon the foundations already laid, the navy, on the other hand, was only in the first stage of development."[21]

Wilhelm's first task was to devote additional resources to the navy. In 1888, the German army included over 485,000 men, while the navy had only a peacetime strength of 15,480. Indeed, the German Navy was still headed by an army officer. Wilhelm sought new resources for the navy, but then-Chancellor Caprivi insisted that the navy "depend first on protecting [Germany's] coast through armored ships and torpedo-boats in order to keep the entrance into harbors open for [its] ships": "We do not need the armored ships to conduct adventures, but to secure our existence during a land war." To that end, Germany constructed four *Brandenburg*-class battleships and eight smaller coastal-defense battleships, each of limited endurance. The navy's High Command reported that this construction was necessary to remedy "the relative and absolute strength of the fleet from declining significantly since the mid-1880s."[22]

Tirpitz initially believed that torpedo boats were an important asset. He had, after all, gained fame for his role as a leading developer and advocate of the torpedo. Tirpitz called torpedo boats "our only true asset" and said they might "repel a badly executed English offensive." Yet, Tirpitz and Wilhelm were growing frustrated with a navy composed largely of torpedo boats and other expendable ships. Wilhelm grumbled that foreign navies were "far more modern and powerful than that of Germany, which consisted of a few old ships, almost without warfighting value." Tirpitz concluded that torpedo boats were of limited value against a blockade. Admiral Hollmann agreed, noting, "With coastal vehicles and torpedo-boats one can defend the coast; against a blockade only an offensive fleet can protect us."[23]

By the mid-1890s, Wilhelm and Tirpitz both wanted battleships, but for different reasons. Wilhelm often mentioned the prestige associated with a blue-water navy. Eckart Kehr observes, "The fleet preference of Wilhelm II reflected no insight into either the political or economic necessities of overseas power politics, but was mere games-playing." Tirpitz favored battleships for their fighting power. He argued, "a naval battle is a fight of one ship against another; the decisive technical factor is rather the concentration of force in the individual ship than the actual number of ships." In his memoirs, Tirpitz recounted, "I demanded sea-going vessels which could fight in the North Sea, and the struggle between the advocates of sea-going ships and those who supported the coast-defense scheme continued through all my activities." The push to shift German naval policy was under way.[24]

German Defense Policies Post-1897

Wilhelm remained frustrated with the pace of progress through 1896. He later reflected, "I insistently requested and warned [the fleet] must be strengthened in the first eight years of my reign," but these requests were "continually refused, and refused in ways which heaped scorn and ridicule upon me." Yet changes were afoot. The Kaiser appointed Tirpitz as state secretary of the Imperial Navy Office. One naval historian writes that Tirpitz replaced older leaders whose "ideas had perpetuated the navy's coastal defense role, a position that seemed outworn as German *Weltpolitik* developed during the reign of Wilhelm II." *Weltpolitik* (world policy) required a different set of defense policies. Tirpitz later described his mission as "transition to *Weltpolitik* and especially the creation of a German fleet." From 1897 forward, German defense policies shifted quickly. As German objectives evolved, the navy was refashioned for global sea control.[25]

Defense Objectives: Extensive

Wilhelm, Tirpitz, and Bernhard von Bülow—who became state secretary for foreign affairs in 1897—set about to reshape German defense policies. All three supported the concept of *Weltmacht*, or world power. Wilhelm first used the term in public in 1896, to describe his view that "the German Empire has become a world-empire." Bülow similarly asserted that Germans demand their "place in the sun." These views echoed those of the German people, who Admiral von Müller observed were "coming to accept an entirely different opinion of their ability and indeed their duty to expand than that expressed in [Germany's] naval and colonial policy so far." Indeed, Bülow counseled, "Only a successful foreign policy can help to reconcile, pacify, rally, unite." Thus, some officials thought it necessary for Wilhelm to "overthrow the status quo internationally in order to preserve it at home."[26]

Wilhelm believed that *Weltmacht* required a strong navy. In 1896, he stated, "Our own navy is still small, is in the budding stage. . . . We must become strong." Wilhelm insisted, "sea power and imperial power are so interdependent that the one cannot exist without the other." One of Wilhelm's advisers, Baron Holstein, said, "the Navy Question now takes precedence over everything. . . . The Kaiser wants a fleet like that of England—with 28 first-class battleships—and wants to direct his whole domestic policy to that end, i.e., to a fight." But many members of the Reichstag remained opposed. August Bebel warned, "To believe that . . . we could take up the cudgels against England, is to approach the realm of insanity. Those who demand it belong not in the Reichstag but in the madhouse."[27]

Wilhelm chose Tirpitz to rectify this situation. Tirpitz was selected in part because he had an uncommon ability to understand both military and political dynamics. Tirpitz "was generally viewed by the other admirals as an essentially political figure," writes Samuel Huntington. Indeed, the officer who suggested him for promotion commented that "an energetic man with a broad vision, . . . perhaps Tirpitz," was needed to rectify ignorance about "the purpose and tasks of the navy." He initially suggested that a crisis might be needed "to open the eyes of [Germany's] wrong-headed politicians. . . . It would dispose the nation to create a fleet." Yet, this proved unnecessary, as Wilhelm was able to pass his first naval law after threatening to launch a coup against the Reichstag.[28]

Wilhelm, Tirpitz, and Bülow were not satisfied. The naval law had funded a basic force, but a second law was needed for a true battlefleet. In 1899, Tirpitz insisted, "Great states become greater and stronger and small states become smaller and weaker. . . . Naval power is essential if Germany does not want to go under." Bülow speculated, "In every century there will be a great conflict, a major liquidation in order to re-allocate influence, power and territorial possessions on the globe. Are we just about to witness another redistribution of the earth . . . ?" If Germany was to prepare for such a war, Tirpitz warned that it was vital to use this "window of opportunity" to build up its navy. Wilhelm reflected this urgency during an infamous 1899 speech in which he proclaimed, "the sense of power and energy which the German people are capable of . . . can no longer continue without increasing our fighting strength upon the seas." Wilhelm urged, "The Fatherland is great and powerful, . . . proud of its greatness, . . . conscious of its inner worth. . . . Let it make the sacrifices which our position as a world-power demands."[29]

The second naval law passed, but only after two actions. First, the German Fleet Association was created to stimulate popular support for navalism. Its mantra was "For German strength and German tongue there must be room still on this earth!" Echoing Tirpitz, its charter noted the need to maintain "Germany's position among the world powers." One historian writes that "young Germans expressed a desire to expand beyond the Continent," and "Wilhelm II became the spokesman for this age." Second, German leaders had to commit that the navy would focus on defensive rather than offensive missions. Bülow insisted, "We have no intention at all of carrying out an aggressive policy of expansion. We intend only to protect the important interests which, through the natural course of events, we have acquired in all parts of the world." He warned, "in view of our naval inferiority, we must operate so carefully, like the caterpillar before it has grown into the butterfly." In another venue, Bülow argued, "We must never fail to insist that our naval construction has no offensive purpose behind it."[30]

Wilhelm and his advocates prevailed in 1900, when the Reichstag passed the second naval law. A pleased Tirpitz wrote to Bülow, "I should be content with the knowledge that I have been able to provide for you the tools you need for the development and expansion of Germany." Wilhelm triumphantly announced, "We have conquered for ourselves a place in the sun. It will now be my task to see to it that this place in the sun shall remain our undisputed possession." By this time, Germany had already signed a ninety-nine-year lease for Kiaochow and began to build Tsingtao into an economically successful colony. Wilhelm noted that the mission to China was "nothing more than the first expression of the newly united and newly arisen German Empire in its tasks beyond the seas." The effort to develop a German colonial policy in China was later identified by Bülow as "the first practical step on the way to *Weltpolitik*." Wilhelm announced, "in distant areas, no important decision should be taken without Germany and the German Kaiser." In another speech, he suggested, "the wave beat of the ocean knocks at the door of our people and forces it to demand its place in the world as a great nation."[31]

With colonialization and battlefleet construction under way, the Anglo-German competition began to take shape. The German admiralty warned, "If we wish to promote a powerful overseas policy and to secure worthwhile colonies, we must be prepared first and foremost for a clash with England or America." Admiral Müller noted that if a war occurred, Germany must "have the aim of breaking England's world domination so as to lay free the necessary colonial possessions for the central European states who need to expand." London watched and worried. The British military attaché advised, "Germany has a high mission to carry out with the right to Colonies for the expansion of its growing population and the hegemony of the world's trade." The British Admiralty assessed that the German fleet "has gone beyond the personal ambition of one or two men. . . . The expansion must go on until it meets a force stronger than itself." During a trip to England in 1908, Wilhelm asserted, "Germany must have a powerful fleet to protect that commerce, and her manifold interests in the most distant seas. Germany looks ahead. Her horizons stretch far away. She must be prepared for any eventualities."[32]

The cost of these policies was tremendous, even for the growing German economy. In 1906 and 1908, the Reichstag authorized new amendments to the naval laws. The 1906 amendment added large cruisers to the foreign fleet, as well as new torpedo boats. The 1908 amendment increased the replacement rate for battleships and initiated the construction of battle cruisers. These investments were needed because the Imperial Navy Office assessed that the British had "taken an immense step forward with the construction of the 3 *Invincible*-class cruisers." Bülow cautioned Wilhelm, "We cannot afford to engage in a Dreadnought competition with a far healthier England." British observers rightly calculated that Germany's "naval policy has outrun Germany's present economic development." Indeed, Bülow was struggling to obtain funding for additional construction. A frustrated Wilhelm chose Theobald von Bethmann-Hollweg to take Bülow's place.[33]

As World War I approached, Germany's extensive objectives were now plain for all to see. Wilhelm remarked to the U.S. ambassador, "Germany is now almost as rich as England. . . . What we want is an equal chance." Some officials in Berlin and London sought to slow the naval arms race. Bethmann-Hollweg was intent on improving relations with Britain. He would later note, "we must pursue a bold foreign policy, but in every diplomatic situation to rattle our swords when neither the honor, security nor future of Germany is at stake, is not only madly brave, it is criminal." London responded with the Haldane mission. Yet, Wilhelm believed that the "Haldane episode" was "engineered for the sole purpose of hampering the development of the German fleet." He complained that in other countries, "vast construction programs were carried out without eliciting one word of protest from England." Fearing a British trap, Wilhelm sought to build more battleships, cruisers, and torpedo boats, while also adding a substantial number of submarines. Frustrated with the failed negotiations, British Foreign Secretary Edward Grey remarked, "The German Emperor is ageing me; he is like a battleship with steam up and screws going, but with no rudder, and he will run into something some day and cause a catastrophe."[34]

Catastrophe was getting closer by the day. In December 1912, Wilhelm met his military leadership to discuss the prospects of war. General Helmuth von Moltke commented, "I regard a war as inevitable and the sooner the better." But Tirpitz requested a "postponement of the great struggle by 1.5 years." Navy leaders hoped that by "autumn of 1914," Germany's "naval armament will have achieved its purpose," which Tirpitz described as "political independence from England." Yet, Moltke worried, "the Navy would not be ready then either and the Army's position would become less and less favorable; the enemies were arming more rapidly than we do, as we were very short of money." The war was ultimately delayed, but not for long. In early 1914, Wilhelm prophesized, "Either the German flag will fly over the fortifications of the Bosporus or I shall suffer the same sad fate as the great exile on the island of

Saint Helena." As he foresaw, Germany's extensive objectives resulted in the Reich's collapse and Wilhelm's exile.[35]

Defense Strategy: Control

German leaders recognized that extensive objectives abroad would require a new defense strategy. Yet, German leaders were unsure what new strategy the navy should adopt. Two options were conceivable: offensive sea denial or offensive sea control. The former required commerce-raiding cruisers, while the latter required a fleet of battleships. According to Tirpitz, Wilhelm initially "intended to speak unreservedly in favor of a cruiser war." The decision was difficult, though, and one observer writes, "For the first nine years of his reign, he wavered between a battleship and a cruiser navy. He could change his mind from one to the other virtually overnight." Tirpitz insisted that cruisers could not be the "major aim for the development of a great naval power." He maintained that sea control should be Germany's ultimate aim because "the struggle for control of the sea is decisive and its major outcome will be achieved today as always through battle." But Wilhelm remained unsure.[36]

Tirpitz had already staked his claim to offensive sea control in 1895. His Directive IX stated that coastal defense and commerce raiding would no longer suffice; instead, Germany's fleet should prepare for battle at sea. Directive IX noted that Germany must "make its power tangible beyond its territorial waters. The worldwide protection of national trade and industry . . . are impossible without a fleet capable of the offensive." To that end, Directive IX contained a section titled "The Natural Purpose of a Fleet Is the Strategic Offensive," which stated, "only when sea supremacy is achieved can the enemy be forced to conclude peace." But opposition in Berlin was substantial. Army officers such as Alfred von Schlieffen worried, "Germany in a war against England unfortunately has no fleet which is strong enough to carry out the battle of destruction against the hostile fleet. . . . The rest of the task of the war will fall to the German army." Tirpitz fretted, "Without sea-power Germany's position in the world resembled a mollusk without a shell." Yet, he remained unable to win support for his ambitious plans.[37]

Wilhelm was finally convinced around 1897, when Tirpitz came home from the East Asia Squadron to lead the Imperial Navy Office. Wilhelm asked Tirpitz to "craft a program for the expansion of the navy," and Tirpitz set about doing just that. Several years earlier, Tirpitz had warned, "Germany will rapidly decline from its position as a great power in the next century unless the growth of these general sea interests is taken in hand energetically, immediately and systematically." Now Tirpitz had his chance to make his mark. He was remarkably successful at changing opinions in Berlin. An observer notes, "What had been the closely guarded plan of an inner cabal in January 1896 had become the wish of a substantial majority of the Reichstag by March 1898." The first naval law not only funded Tirpitz's approach but also explained, "Germany must have a battle fleet so strong that even for the adversary with the greatest sea power a war against it would involve such dangers as to imperil her position in the world."[38]

At the time, Wilhelm did not seek war with Great Britain. The navy insisted, "the French North Fleet and the Russian Baltic Fleet are our probable enemies." Indeed, Wilhelm hoped that a strong German fleet would make the Reich an attractive ally for Great Britain. He complained, "Only an evil will could interpret a fleet capable of defending the coastline as an instrument of malign intention." But the navy's new strategy put Germany and Britain on a collision course. Admiral Eduard von Knorr wrote, "The most important of our navy's tasks in war is to assure its unconditional command of the sea in the Baltic and in the North Sea to the Channel." A few years later, a confidential British memorandum warned that since "the whole of the German fleet is always within striking distance of our shores it is no longer safe to dispense with a modern and powerful fleet in Home waters." The British politician Benjamin Disraeli lamented, "The balance of power has been entirely destroyed, and the country which suffers most, and feels the effect of this great change most, is England."[39]

Those who were closest to Wilhelm soon recognized a change in his attitude. The Kaiser's mother commented, "Wilhelm's one idea is to have a Navy which shall be larger and stronger than the British Navy." Wilhelm insisted, "Only when we can hold out our mailed fist against his face, will the British lion draw back, as he did recently before America's threats." Bethmann-Hollweg said, "His fundamental idea is to break England's position in the world to Germany's advantage. For this he needs a fleet." And Bülow later recalled, "What Wilhelm II most desired and imagined for the future was to see himself, at the head of a glorious German Fleet, starting out on a peaceful visit to England. . . . It was his own and our misfortune that his words and his gestures never coincided with his real attitude in the matter."[40]

Many members of the Reichstag remained skeptical of the navy's new plan, but British actions provided the cover for a new naval law. In 1899, the British stopped two German commercial ships in pursuit of contraband headed to the Boers. Wilhelm and Tirpitz were overjoyed. Tirpitz reportedly exclaimed, "Now we have the wind we need for bringing our ship into port. The Naval Law will go through. Your Majesty must present a medal to the captain of the English ship in gratitude for having put through the Naval Law." Wilhelm later released the text of a telegram that noted, "I hope that events of the last few days will have convinced ever-widening circles that not only German interests but also German honor must be protected in distant oceans, and that to this end Germany must be strong and powerful on the seas." Wilhelm later recalled that he "ordered up champagne" and "drank joyously to the new law, its acceptance and the future German fleet." The navy finally had the political support to execute its new strategy.[41]

By this point, the strategic debate in the navy was largely over. Tirpitz bragged that the navy "has won the confidence of the Reichstag. . . . Naval proposals meet hardly any resistance." The Navy League had played an important part by inspiring "enthusiasm for the submission of a so-called major navy request." With public enthusiasm growing, Germany engaged in its first major overseas operation. Wilhelm sent a detachment to China and directed that it ensure that "no Chinese will ever again dare to look cross-eyed at a German." The risks remained substantial, however. Allied Supreme Commander Alfred von Waldersee commented on his way to China, "We should pursue world policy, if only I knew what that should be. For the moment it is only a slogan." Tirpitz observed, "We cannot avoid passing through the stages of a completely insufficient fleet and then of a mere defensive fleet. . . . Whether we will be able to realize the German Fleet Association's hope for an offensive fleet, it is impossible to foresee at the moment."[42]

Tirpitz soon began to develop a plan to confront the British for control of the seas. Yet, attacking the British fleet was risky, as Germany still did not match Britain's naval capabilities. Tirpitz warned, "Raising offensive perspectives at the present moment is to be regarded as irresponsible." Another observer commented, "Let us build ships and as many as we possibly can, but do not let us talk about them." In 1908, the German General Staff insisted, "Germany must follow offensive aims." But the navy was not ready. It warned, "we will not be able to wage an offensive war on the enemy coast with any chance of success, but will rather have to await the enemy in our own waters." In 1910, Admiral Müller stated, "We want a navy strong enough to knock about the English Navy sufficiently in case of attack so that other nations do not have to fear it any more. That is the present status of the fleets." The German Navy remained too weak to fight symmetrically, so its purpose was to act as a "risk fleet" to deter British action on the continent. Tirpitz explained that Germany "would have to pass through a danger zone," until it could truly confront the British in a battle for sea control.[43]

As World War I drew closer, many German officials insisted that the navy needed to be more than a risk fleet. Admiral August von Heeringen stated, "To maintain our morale our fleet needs a militarily feasible chance of victory against England." Yet, German leaders realized that they had not equaled the British fleet and that a fleet action would probably be suicidal. Even Tirpitz admitted, "The English navy is developing so strongly that the risk principle and thus the basis of our naval policy are in danger." Ironically, Directive IX had foreseen Germany's strategic challenge. The directive noted, "Enemy ships need not stay close to our coasts. ... Then our own fleet would have only the choice between inactivity, i.e., moral self-annihilation, and fighting a battle on the open sea." As one historian writes, Germany's "entire enterprise was an extreme example of a regional strategy of maritime control." But sea control was not yet attainable, so Admiral Eduard von Knorr proved correct that the navy was "confined to the strategic defensive." Germany had built a navy for strategic offensive and sea control; but by the time war broke out, it was too late to align German's strategy with reality. In the end, the battlefleet's longest foray was to Scapa Flow, where its captains scuttled their ships.[44]

Defense Investments: Sustainable

Germany's extensive objectives and desire for offensive sea control required a blue-water navy capable of long-distance power projection. No longer would commerce raiders or coastal combatants suffice. Instead, the navy desired battleships that could be sustained at sea. In the early 1890s, such ships were a figment in the imagination of a few German leaders. Wilhelm complained, "It now again becomes evident how foolish it was ten years ago to launch a colonial policy without possessing a fleet, and to develop this policy without keeping equal pace in the development of the fleet." But the German navy budget rose from 20 percent of the army budget in 1898 to over 35 percent in 1905 and 54.8 percent by 1911. The battlefleet soon became a reality.[45]

Shifting from coastal craft to sustainable battleships required a sizable investment in naval construction. Initially, Tirpitz pushed only for vessels that could operate in German's near seas. He advised, "The military situation against England demands battleships in as great a number as possible." But Tirpitz said the fleet should be "constructed that it can unfold its greatest military potential between Heligoland and the Thames." He ordered that ship designs "allow for a load of coal adequately large to enable them to operate off Brest or Cherbourg." Watching from the British Admiralty, Lord Selborne warned, "the German Navy was being constructed with a view to being able to fight the British Navy; restricted cruising radius, cramped crew quarters, etc., meant that the German battleships were designed for a North Sea fleet and practically nothing else." Tirpitz explained, "Commerce raiding and transatlantic war against England is so hopeless, because of the shortage of bases on our side and the superfluidity on England's side, that we must ignore this type of war against England in our plans for the constitution of our fleet."[46]

In 1898, the first naval law ushered in the era of the German battleship. The law authorized construction of nineteen battleships, eight armored cruisers, and forty-two other cruisers. Yet, Tirpitz wrote, "The task of the battle fleet is the defense of the coasts of the nation. Number and size of ships have been exclusively determined according to this principle. Against larger sea powers, this fleet has merely the significance of a 'sortie fleet.' " Tirpitz intentionally played down the sustainability of the fleet. He noted in his memoirs, "We therefore made it appear that by this first step we were not effecting anything more than Stosch's scheme for the foundation of a fleet. The whole procedure was not to appear as a break with the past. The coast-defense idea was mentioned, partly for the sake of its historical connection and partly to prevent ourselves being charged with offensive intentions."[47]

By the second naval law in 1900, there was no longer a need to hide the fleet's purpose. The law itself announced, "For the protection of sea trade and colonies there is only one means: a strong battle fleet." It authorized construction of thirty-eight battleships, twenty armored cruisers, and thirty-eight light cruisers, thirteen of which were intended for an overseas flotilla. The doubling of the number of battleships sent an unmistakable message. But it came at the expense of cruisers, torpedo boats, and submarines. Specifications also required greater coal capacity. The range of German battleships grew from 4,500 nautical miles at 10 knots in the early 1890s to 8,000 nautical miles at 12 knots (and 4,000 nautical miles at 18 knots on oil). Similarly, unarmored cruisers went from 2,810 nautical miles at 15 knots to 5,500 nautical miles at 12 knots (and an additional 1,000 nautical miles at 25 knots on oil). These were dramatic increases intended to permit distant sea control.[48]

Germany could have protected its coasts with less sustainable ships, such as submarines and torpedo boats. Indeed, Tirpitz had been one of the leading developers of the torpedo. But he remained skeptical of smaller craft, noting that they could "serve well in specific local and secondary purposes, but they will never bring about a great revolution." Wilhelm agreed, noting, "Our Baltic coast was practically defenseless. To protect it the fleet was necessary." He commented, "We needed our fleet for coast defense and the protection of our commerce; the lesser means of defense, such as U-boats, torpedo-boats and mines, are not sufficient for the purpose." This was contrary to the Admiralty's assessment: "we can hold the English fleet at our coast and subject it to the weakening effect of a blockade assignment ... [via] night attacks by our cruisers and torpedo boats against enemy battleships and cruisers, the results of which may significantly increase our chances in the decisive battle." Indeed, a German memo in 1902 assessed that the British could stand watch in the North Sea "to blockade [the Germans] from a distance and to avoid any offensive actions." Nonetheless, Tirpitz and Wilhelm had set their course and were unwilling to adjust.[49]

Critics of the battleship did periodically raise their voices. In 1907, Vice Admiral Karl Galster issued a pamphlet asking, "Which Type of Naval Armament Does Germany Need?," which supported a submarine or commercial war strategy. The liberal newspaper *Berliner Tageblatt* also expressed concern about the naval buildup. It noted, "The tasks of our fleet consist of the protection of our overseas trade, the safe-guarding of Germans abroad, and the defense of our coasts. It will never be able to fulfill the first two tasks, for the last, however, our forces suffice." Instead of the existing shipbuilding plan, the paper suggested, "An improvement of our coastal fortifications, the creation of a strong submarine arm and numerous mines are enormously more commendable for the purpose than the over-hasty construction of our fleet of capital ships which will hardly come to action against the British." Similarly, Bülow asked in 1908 "whether the best course would not be to specialize on improving our coast defenses, increasing our stock of sea-mines, and creating a strong fleet of submarines, instead of concentrating exclusively on increasing the number of battleships." He suggested, "The political situation would be very much facilitated for me if in our new constructions the large ships would not be given so much prominence and the emphasis would be placed on cruisers, also on torpedoes and on coastal fortifications."[50]

Yet, Tirpitz rejected this approach. He commented, "The U-boat is, at present, of no great value in war at sea." Tirpitz observed, "Naturally we would have little chance against a stronger opponent without submarine warfare; but without a battlefleet we would have no chance at all." One observer writes, "Tirpitz's dogmatism rendered him blind to the possibilities of the U-boat. He classified the submarine as a defensive weapon and a minor auxiliary to the battleship." Tirpitz was open, however, to more sustainable submarines. He explained, "I refused to throw away money on submarines so long as they could only cruise in home waters, and therefore be of no use to us; as soon as sea-going boats were built, however, I was the first to encourage them on a large scale." Years later, Wilhelm reflected, "Tirpitz believed that the types with which other nations were experimenting were too small, and fit only for coast defense. ... Germany must build seagoing submarines capable of navigating the open sea."[51]

As World War I neared, Germany had built a sustainable fleet of battleships. Wilhelm and Tirpitz were also developing sustainable submarines, yet this was a secondary priority. Funding for coastal defenses and commerce-raiding ships was negligible. Wilhelm had succeeded in building a fleet for long-distance sea control. The British Admiralty concluded, "The more the composition of the new German fleet is examined, the clearer it becomes that it is designed for a possible conflict with the British fleet." In 1908, Britain assessed that Germany had or was building twenty-eight battleships, eight coastal-defense ships, fifteen armored or protected cruisers, thirty-one small cruisers, eighty-one destroyers, forty-seven torpedo boats, and one submersible. Nonetheless, Germany still could not match the British fleet. Before the war, Tirpitz wrote, "a fleet of equal strength to England's was Germany's natural and single aim [which] could not be admitted in the past two decades." For all his efforts, the fleet was not yet sufficient when World War I broke out.[52]

Assessment

As this chapter has shown, German defense policies transformed rapidly between 1890 and 1910. A small group of German leaders shifted the Reich from limited objectives, a denial strategy, and less sustainable naval platforms to a power-projection navy capable of sea control using a sustainable battlefleet. As Prince Adalbert of Prussia had foreseen, "For a growing people there is no prosperity without expansion, no expansion without an overseas policy, and no overseas policy without a Navy."[53]

What are the potential explanations for Germany's shifting defense policies? Most structural and cultural explanations do not stand up to scrutiny because they cannot explain why Germany changed its approach so rapidly around 1897. Germany did mimic British naval policy, but that does not explain why Berlin pursued coastal defenses and commerce raiding beforehand. Geography does not explain why a continental state like Germany would shift so much investment from its army to its navy. Technological explanations also fail to explain this transition, since torpedoes and submarines were making sea denial more rather than less effective. In fact, Tirpitz helped develop many of these innovations himself. Cultural explanations also cannot explain why German policy changed so rapidly in just two decades.

As with the United States, explanations rooted in domestic politics and individual leadership appear to fit better. There is no doubt that German support for the navy changed around the turn of the century. However, this public support was stimulated in no small part by Wilhelm and Tirpitz through their encouragement of naval advocacy groups. It is notable that these organizations arose only after German leaders had already decided to reinvigorate the navy. Individual leadership was critical to this change. But here again there is conflicting evidence. When Wilhelm came to power in 1888, he explicitly rejected overseas adventures and colonies. To argue that Wilhelm drove many of the changes in the navy is therefore to acknowledge that something changed his mind about the importance of *Weltmacht* and naval power.

What altered the policies pursued by German leaders in the mid- to late 1890s? Wilhelm himself explained, "Germany had been poor, she was now growing rich." He announced, "We see the empire, although still young, growing strong within itself from year to year. . . . This is that world-empire which the German spirit strives for." Wilhelm's lieutenants echoed his newfound confidence. Tirpitz proclaimed, "The German people [were] nearing the zenith of maturity." Even after the war, Wilhelm reflected, "The general situation of the German Empire in the period before the war had become increasingly brilliant. . . . The curve of our development tended steadily upward." In short, German leaders' more extensive objectives were the result of their assessment that Germany had become a strong world power.[54]

Why did the Reich pursue a sea-control strategy and sustainable battleship fleet so doggedly, despite the growing danger of a conflict with Britain? The answer appears to lie in the nature of Germany's rise and the perceived requirement for overseas capabilities. German leaders could not simultaneously look abroad and purchase an unsustainable fleet capable only of defending Germany's coasts. British enmity was not desired, but it could not be avoided. After all, German observers worried that Britain sought "to sentence the other capitalist states, and especially the strong, young, and lusty German capitalist empire, to perpetual inferiority upon the seas and thereby preserve England's hegemony over the waves forever." As Paul Kennedy reflected, "At the root of the naval race lay two conflicting assertions about the contemporary strategic balance and the world order." Unfortunately, Wilhelm and Tirpitz could not foresee the outcome that was increasingly apparent to others. General Waldersee's final diary entry before his death noted, "I pray God that I may not have to live through what I see coming."[55]

In the end, multiple factors drove the changes in German defense policies from 1890 to 1910. But there is substantial evidence that the Reich's leaders built a new fleet because their assessment of Germany's relative power had changed. Wilhelm sought the fleet that Tirpitz called for when he acknowledged "the growing strength and dignity of the German Empire." This triggered a reconsideration of Germany's defense objectives, strategies, and investments. Thus, this case provides confirming evidence for Hypotheses 1, 3, and 5.[56]

CHAPTER FOUR

Britain's Apex

Is it contended that the weary Titan staggers under "the too
vast orb of her fate," and that we have not the strength to
sustain the burden of the empire? . . . Why should we shrink
from our task or allow the sceptre of empire to fall from our
hands thro' craven fears of being great?

—JOSEPH CHAMBERLAIN (1897)

THE NINETEENTH CENTURY MARKED the height of Pax Britannica.
After Napoleon's defeat at Waterloo, Great Britain's economy surged,
its colonies flourished, and its navy ruled the seas. This was a time of
unparalleled global reach and rapid territorial expansion for the British Empire. Britain acquired Egypt, Singapore, New Zealand, Hong
Kong, Afghanistan, and Burma. In addition, India was now under direct control of the British Crown, as were large and growing areas of
sub-Saharan Africa. In 1880, the British Empire accounted for 23.2
percent of world trade. France, the United States, and Germany lingered around 11.2 percent, 10.1 percent, and 9.7 percent, respectively. The British Empire and the British Isles were protected by the
world's leading navy. Until the 1880s, the British Navy's capital ships
nearly outnumbered the rest of the world's combined. In 1883, for

example, Britain maintained thirty-eight battleships, compared to nineteen for France, eleven for Germany, seven for Italy, three for Russia, and none for the United States or Japan. The British Empire was at its apex; it was without peer.[1]

Yet, circumstances changed rapidly as Britain's rivals united and industrialized. The United Kingdom and Ireland saw only 1.6–1.8 percent average yearly growth in manufacturing from 1881 to 1913. Meanwhile, manufacturing growth rose to 4.2–5.2 percent in the United States, 4.0–5.1 percent in Germany, 4.8–6.6 percent in Russia, and 2.5–3.5 percent in France. Leaders in London feared a coalition of hostile continental powers, particularly an alliance between France and Russia. But they soon came to view Germany as a greater menace. By the early 1900s, many British leaders were seized with the German threat and recognized the inevitability of the empire's decline.[2]

This chapter analyzes the decisions of British leaders as they came to grasp the reality of Britain's relative decline from 1890 to 1910. Perceived relative power theory makes three predictions about states that believe they have reached their apex and are transitioning from rise (Phase 2) to decline (Phase 3). Hypothesis 2 predicts a change in objectives from expansion to consolidation. Hypothesis 4 predicts a shift from offensive to defensive strategies. Hypothesis 6 predicts investments in less mobile systems. In short, perceived relative power theory suggests that if leaders believe their nations' are at their apex, they should transition away from power projection. Great Britain's defense policies did shift more toward consolidation, defense, and immobility around 1904. But many British leaders remained resistant to change, resulting in a somewhat slower and smaller shift in defense policies than expected. Explaining the timing and magnitude of Britain's defense policy reforms is critical to understanding the conditions under which the theory of perceived relative power applies.

British Defense Policies Pre-1904

Public concern about Britain's relative position emerged due to a series of successive shocks that began in the 1880s. Economic challenges rose, creating the sense that Britain was facing unprecedented headwinds, which would inevitably have military effects. As a result, Paul Kennedy writes, "The era of inexpensive maritime supremacy came to a sudden end in 1884," when British competitors began to build large naval forces. By 1886, the signs of British decline were becoming more apparent. The Royal Commission on the Depression of Trade and Industry reported that Britain could not maintain "the lead which [it] formerly held among the manufacturing nations of the world": "our supremacy is now being assailed on all sides." These shocks aroused concern about Britain's relative position. It took another two decades, however, before British leaders finally admitted that the empire had probably already reached its zenith. Meanwhile, Britain's objectives remained expansive, its strategy offensive, and its defense investments highly mobile.[3]

Defense Objectives: Expansive

The first signs of British decline emerged around 1884, when the *Pall Mall Gazette* highlighted concerns about French shipbuilding. These worries forced the government to spend an additional £5.5 million on naval ships, ordnance, and coaling stations. Meanwhile, France and Russia grew closer, compelling British leaders to consider having to fight both at once. The French and Russian navies would pose a particular challenge to the British position in the Mediterranean, especially if their forces were combined. Meanwhile, British concerns about Russian activities in Afghanistan and French endeavors in Africa mandated deployable ground forces. Concerns reemerged in 1888 when a second panic gripped London. "Confidence in the ability of the Navy was weakened by extensive building programmes in France and Russia," writes one observer, who notes that as a result, "a general overhaul of naval and military machinery was carried out." The Imperial Defence Loan of 1888 and Naval Defence Act of 1889 sought to rectify the navy's decline. To further bolster military power, fortifications were constructed around London. Britain also adopted a two-power standard mandating that the British Navy be at least as strong as the next two naval powers combined.[4]

Nevertheless, concern about Britain's relative position increased through the 1890s. In 1893, the *Daily News* wrote, "The panic mongers are abroad and venerable Admirals are joining juvenile politicians in their attempts to prove that the British fleet, if it has not already gone to the dogs, is at least on its way to them." Some observers suggested it was time for Great Britain to retrench. In 1895, Sir William Laird Clowes argued, "It is ridiculous to assert that our occupation of the Mediterranean brings us any corresponding benefit of a substantial kind." Instead, he suggested that Britain should focus primarily on Gibraltar and Suez, to enable it, "in case of necessity, to shut and bolt the two narrow doorways of this long passage." Rather than projecting power, Clowes and his supporters wanted to see Britain garrison key strategic choke points.[5]

Yet supporters of continued expansion persisted in pressing their case. Foreign Secretary Lord Rosebery argued, "It is said that our empire is already large enough, and does not need extension. That would be true enough if the world were elastic, but unfortunately it is not elastic, and we are engaged at the present moment, in the language of mining, 'in pegging out claims for future.' " The famed imperialist Cecil Rhodes was even more ambitious, suggesting, "The people of England ... have all become Imperialists. They are not going to part with any territory. . . . The English people intend to retain every inch of land they have got, and perhaps they intend to secure a few more inches." Rosebery similarly noted, "We have to consider not what we want now, but what we shall want in the future." Retrenchment also worried British leaders in India, who warned, "A defensive attitude in India would undoubtedly lead to very grave internal troubles. . . . It would destroy the confidence of the native army and civil population, and undermine our prestige and supremacy in the East." For these reasons, First Lord of the Admiralty Frederick Richards argued, "The only true policy lies in unquestioned superiority."[6]

As these sentiments demonstrate, the desire for empire would prove difficult to relinquish, even as British power waned. But by the late 1890s, British policy makers were forced to recognize that they could not simply continue business as usual. The historian Paul Kennedy dates "the decline in Britain's position as a world power" to "a little before the Diamond Jubilee year of 1897." Through the late 1890s, however, British leaders held fast to expansive objectives.

The British people became not less attached to Empire but more focused on how to confront potential challengers. Facing ominous relative power trends, British leaders brushed aside spending concerns from the Exchequer and forced through new defense funding. Thus, from 1897 to 1912, the navy budget averaged 5 percent yearly growth and the army 2 percent yearly growth.[7]

Despite this increased spending, the second Boer War was a disaster for Great Britain. Army expenditures increased from £17 million in 1887 to £94 million in 1901. The navy found itself struggling to maintain the two-power standard. The First Lord of the Admiralty Lord Selborne commented on the difficulty of the British position, "It is a terrific task to remain the greatest naval Power, when naval Powers are year by year increasing in numbers and in naval strength and at the same time to be a military Power strong enough to meet the greatest military Power in Asia." Germany now posed a serious threat, both on land and at sea. In 1901, Lord Selborne warned, "The Emperor seems determined that the power of Germany shall be used all the world over to push German commerce, possessions, and interests. Of necessity it follows that the German naval strength must be raised so as to compare more advantageously than at present with ours." To meet this challenge, British naval expenditures rose from £13 million in 1897 to £45 million in 1912.[8]

By 1904, however, pressure was mounting to decrease defense expenditures. Chancellor of the Exchequer Austen Chamberlain warned, "however reluctant we may be to face the fact, the time has come when we must frankly admit that the financial resources of the United Kingdom are inadequate to do all that we should desire in the matter of Imperial defence." As the German challenge intensified, British leaders raised difficult questions about relative power trends. But through at least 1904, few leaders in London showed any willingness to consolidate Great Britain's aims. If anything, British defense objectives looked as ambitious and expansive as ever. As Kennedy notes, this "did not denote the zenith of Britain's power, but constituted rather the defiant swan-song of a nation becoming less and less complacent about the increasing threats to its world-wide interests." British leaders prepared to meet their rising challengers head-on.[9]

Defense Strategy: Offensive

Expansive British aims required an offensive strategy to project power around the globe. Great Britain had three primary defense missions: protecting the British Isles, safeguarding the empire abroad, and acting on the European continent when necessary. All three required coordination between the army and the navy. Of the two, the army was seen as the more offensive force. Arthur Marder notes, "The navy was the defensive force of the empire. Its power, however strong, ended with the enemy's shore. . . . Once the success of the navy had cleared the sea for military transport, the army, the real offensive weapon of the nation, was set free for action."[10]

The British Army was postured for offensive missions overseas. Army officers argued that only they were capable of conquering new territory and repelling attacks on British holdings abroad. Furthermore, the army was required to be prepared to act on the European continent. Edward Grey would later describe the British Army as "a projectile to be fired by the Navy." But army leaders saw themselves as the empire's front line. One observer notes, "Throughout the long nineteenth century, Britain was engaged in more or less constant military actions in her colonies." Controlling local populations required the army and its local proxies to remain engaged around the world. The army therefore considered itself the backbone of the British Empire and its offensive arm. Commander in Chief General Lord Wolseley argued, "I know of nothing that is more liable to disaster and danger than anything that floats on the water."[11]

Meanwhile, the navy's most basic mission was defense of the British Isles. The continental powers had large populations and enormous standing armies, which Britain could not match. But unlike its continental neighbors; Britain had the luxury of a fleet for home defense. British naval strength prevented continental challengers from invading across the English Channel. As one expert wrote, "Should Great Britain be shorn of her Colonies, her existence would still demand a Navy of the strength it is to-day; the need for an Army, on the other hand, would disappear." Admiral Jackie Fisher was even more colorful, noting, "The Navy is the 1st, 2nd, 3rd, 4th, 5th, . . . *ad infinitum* Line of Defence! If the Navy is not supreme, no Army however large is of the slightest use. It's not invasion we have to fear if our Navy is beaten, IT'S STARVATION!" After all, the navy was needed to protect the food imports and continued trade on which Britain relied.[12]

The navy was not willing to accept a simply defensive role. Centuries earlier, the navy had "transformed from a short-range, Narrow Seas, almost a coastal-defence, force into a high-seas fleet capable of operating at long range as an ocean-going force." This fleet served as Britain's lifeline to its colonies. The head of the Colonial Defence Committee would later observe, "sea supremacy has been assumed as the basis of the system of Imperial defence against attack over the sea." Sea control required that Britain build a fleet capable of seeking out and destroying its opponent. An 1896 Directorate of Military Intelligence memo suggested that purely defensive dispositions in the Mediterranean "would chain [Britain's] vessels to the Italian waters, and deprive them of that mobility which is essential to the principles of [its] naval strategy." Naval records proclaimed, "British fighting policy [is] to take the offensive, and bring on action with the enemy at the earliest possible moment." In fact, Andrew Lambert writes that the 1889 Naval Defence Act shows that "Britain was re-asserting her sea control strategy." He suggests that Britain intended to "blockade her main enemy, France, with a fleet of ocean-going battleships capable of fighting on the open ocean, supported by a large force of cruisers." For this reason, Admiral Fisher wrote, "Our maritime frontier must be the territorial waters of the enemy." Thus, through the 1800s, the army and navy both embraced offensive strategies.[13]

It soon became clear, however, that emerging technologies might favor alternative strategies. France, for example, had adopted an approach that relied on sea denial and submarines. An 1899 assessment by the British naval attaché in France noted that after destroying British commerce, the French policy would seek to counter a British blockade through "successful attacks of torpedo and submersible boats, and possibly by fire from the shore batteries." Experts assessed, "the Channel is now studded with torpedo-boat stations, and this development of what is known as the 'Defense Mobile' has for its object to make it impossible for British battleships to blockade any of the French naval ports owing to the danger to which they would be exposed by torpedo-boats and submarines." Yet, British experts discounted this denial strategy. British intelligence insisted, "the French have done much to strengthen their position in the Western Mediterranean by means of fortified bases and torpedo boats, ... but it is difficult to believe that they can have in their present state a decisive influence."[14]

Some naval officers did ask whether a similar strategy could accomplish Britain's objectives. One reason to consider sea denial was that technological breakthroughs were being made on submarine development. Director of Naval Intelligence Admiral Louis Battenberg noted that the French "point out with pride that the existence of submarines as part of the defense mobile makes any attempt at invasion of French territory the act of lunacy. They are quite right and the argument cuts both ways." The Board of Admiralty's H. O. Arnold-Forster suggested, "The introduction of this new weapon, so far from being a disadvantage to us, will strengthen our position. ... If the submarine proves as formidable as some authorities think is likely to be the case, the bombardment of our ports, and the landing of troops on our shores will become absolutely impossible." Admiral Fisher noted that torpedo boats could "practically deny all passage of the Straits of Dover by night to merchant ships, and except in very clear weather, even to men-of-war."[15]

Yet, sea denial seemed to many British leaders an unnecessary and overly defensive strategy. The submarine and torpedo were unable to accomplish sea control, and thus they were initially seen by most observers in London as threats rather than opportunities. Admiral Edmund Freemantle cited Lord St. Vincent in noting that anyone who supported submarine development was "the greatest fool that ever existed, to encourage a mode of war which they who commanded the seas did not want, and which, if successful, would deprive them of it." Offense remained the chosen strategy. Paul Kennedy argues that Britain could not simply stand on the defensive: "Neither the British public, led by the Press to expect great deeds from the navy, nor the service itself, which has for years been preparing for *Der Tag*, were prepared to accept such a tame policy." In fact, in 1902, the Admiralty required "the word 'defense' not appear. It is omitted advisedly, because the primary object of the British navy is not to defend anything but to attack the fleet of the enemy." As Lord

Selborne advised, "We will never adopt any word or phrase implying defence. The word should be struck out of the Navy's vocabulary. Offence, always offence, and nothing but offence."[16]

Defense Investments: Mobile

Through the early 1900s, mobile forces were considered critical to all of Great Britain's objectives. The navy wanted mobility to attack enemy fleets. The army wanted mobility to permit its forces to move quickly to trouble spots around the world. Through at least 1904, British leaders remained committed to highly mobile forces, which they saw as necessary for global power projection.[17]

The British Army was focused on mobility because it needed to fight abroad. After all, its primary missions at the time were to fight on the European continent or to reinforce local groups elsewhere aligned with the British. From 1900 through 1903, the British Army invested vast sums in forces to fight the second Boer War. Even so, Sir Charles Dilke expressed concern that "the war was in part prolonged, because of [Britain's] difficulty as regarded horses, the greater mobility of the Boers." To rectify this and other problems, spending on the army rose to over £90 million. This expenditure was directed almost entirely to support the empire, rather than home defense.[18]

British naval policy was likewise focused on mobile forces, particularly battleships and cruisers. Experts argued, "The relative strength of Navies depends almost entirely on their relative strength in battleships." By this measure, Britain was easily the strongest naval power in the world, and barring a combination of several continental powers, it had little to fear in the near term. From 1895 through 1904, Britain dedicated an average of roughly 90 percent of its naval spending to battleships and cruisers, which were the most mobile of its forces. Funding was split between battleships and cruisers, in part to upgrade both ship types with better engines capable of sailing longer distances more quickly. Other elements of the fleet—flotilla craft and submarines—received only 10 percent of British naval spending over this decade.[19]

Advocates of less mobile systems did press their case. Tests in 1888 convinced one British observer that "torpedo-boats, if not capable of keeping the sea independently, under all conditions of

weather, would inevitably prove a cause of embarrassment and anx-
iety to an Admiral commanding a blockading fleet. ... They are
admirably adapted for purposes of defence." A decade later, advances in torpedo technology convinced the First Lord of the Admiralty that the torpedo was "a four-fold more dangerous weapon
of offence than it has previously been." Other naval leaders desired
submarines, arguing, "there is no function that the minefield might
fulfill that cannot be better performed by a mobile defence such as
a submarine." Initially, Director of Naval Intelligence Battenberg
warned that submarines' "radius of action is also very limited." But
by 1903, Battenberg said, "The establishment of submarine stations along the South Coast of England ought to go a long way to-
wards dispelling the ever-recurring fears of invasion."[20]

Nonetheless, the British Navy generally rejected reliance on
these smaller and less mobile craft. Admirals often associated immobile systems with weakness and defensiveness, neither of which
won much support at the time. Admiral Reginald Bacon recounted,
"Considerable prejudice has always existed against England developing torpedo craft, chiefly on account of the seductive formula
stating that torpedo craft were 'the arm of the weaker power.' "
Writing in 1897, First Lord George Goschen noted of the gyro-
scope (which was critical to effective torpedoes), "We as the stronger nation, and who have done so much to perfect existing systems,
are clearly sufferers from such a new invention." He explicitly described the submarine as "the weapon of the weaker power." The
same year, two British experts argued that mines were of use only
"to a weak naval Power whose commerce must be thrown over in
time of war." As a strong power with an offensive strategy, the British Navy rejected submarines, torpedo boats, and mines.[21]

Thus, until at least 1904, Britain continued to invest primarily
in mobile systems. In preparation to deploy quickly abroad, the
British Navy was focused on power projection with large mobile
combatants. Although there was some growing interest in torpedo
boats and submarines, they remained of little interest to British
leaders. As the historian Arthur Marder notes, the Admiralty believed that "the torpedo-boat was essentially the weapon of the
weaker naval powers, and not one to be cultivated by a great naval
power with an offensive naval strategy."[22]

British Defense Policies Post-1904

In 1904, France and Britain signed the Entente Cordiale, essentially neutralizing the threat from France and preparing the way for an alliance. Shortly thereafter, Russia suffered a severe blow as Japan won a series of naval engagements, culminating in the sinking of eight Russian battleships at the Battle of Tsushima. Japan, a British ally since the signing of the 1902 Anglo-Japanese Treaty, was left in a dominant position in Asia. Nearly overnight, British holdings in East Asia, India, the Middle East, Africa, and the Mediterranean were made more secure. No longer were British leaders forced to divide their attention between a number of potential competitors. Now the primary threat was clear: a rising Germany. Great Britain soon began to reassess its defense objectives, strategy, and investments.

Defense Objectives: Consolidative

By 1904, it was clear that British power was declining relative to that of Germany and that this trend was likely to continue in the years ahead. As France, Russia, and Japan fell from the list of likely threats, only Germany and the United States could pose a direct challenge to British supremacy. British leaders quickly put aside any rivalry with the United States to focus on Germany. Secretary to the Committee of Imperial Defense Charles Ottley warned Prime Minister H. H. Asquith, "The resources of this Country simply cannot compete with the resources of such a power as the American plus Germany. . . . We must renounce (as unattainable) the Two Power Standard vis-à-vis the U.S.A." Fisher agreed that "war between Great Britain and the United States is not a contingency sufficiently probable to need special steps to meet it." As Kori Schake has chronicled, "Great Britain chose to encourage and make possible [the United States'] continued success. Clear-eyed assessments of its own strategic position led Britain to enact policies that catapulted the United States into the first rank of great powers."[23]

Britain now turned its full attention to Germany. Admiral Fisher told King Edward in 1906, "Our only probable enemy is

Germany. Germany keeps her whole Fleet always concentrated within a few hours of England. We must therefore keep a Fleet twice as powerful concentrated within a few hours of Germany." But the problems were larger than the German fleet. Diplomat Eyre Crowe explained, "The building of the German fleet is but one of the symptoms of the disease. It is the political ambitions of the German Government and nation which are the source of the mischief." Leaders in London worried not only about Berlin's aims on the European continent but also about Kaiser Wilhelm's willingness to test the British Empire. Bernhard von Bülow had foretold, "If the British public clearly realized the anti-British feeling which dominates Germany just now, a great revulsion would occur in its conception of the relations between Britain and Germany." Now Bülow's prediction came true.[24]

The time had come for Great Britain to consolidate its holdings. This meant focusing more at home than abroad. Winston Churchill had noted in 1901, "As to a stronger Regular Army, either we had the command of the sea or we had not. If we had it, we required fewer soldiers, if we had it not we wanted more ships." At the height of the second Boer War, this argument won few adherents. But by 1903, with the war winding down, Secretary of State for War Arnold-Forster concurred, "I do not find that any definite instruction exists as to what is the exact purpose for which the Army exists, and what duties it is supposed to perform." The Admiralty capitalized, contending that "the Navy will entirely suffice to protect the United Kingdom from any attack or invasion." The influential Lord Esher argued, "The Navy can deal with Home Defence." Indeed, the army received less funding than the navy in 1904, after having been given nearly twice as much the previous year.[25]

Meanwhile, the British Navy refocused on the challenge from Germany. And it had just the man for the job—Admiral Jackie Fisher. In 1904, Fisher took over as First Sea Lord and unveiled a scheme to overhaul the navy. He acknowledged that Britain could not carry out a competition with Germany if its forces remained scattered across the world. Fisher warned, "We are weak everywhere and strong nowhere! We have dissipated our naval forces all over globe." He therefore recalled nearly all British capital ships to home waters. Fisher rejected the idea that "particular squadrons are for the protection of the lands they frequent" and instead insisted that they be prepared "for the destruction of the enemy's fleet wherever it may happen to be." As Nicholas Lambert writes, British leaders "instructed the armed forces to lower their strategic horizon. The Board of Admiralty at once complied by jettisoning commitments in the less vital regions of the globe and concentrating the fleet at home."[26]

Consolidating British objectives greatly simplified the navy's tasks. The Admiralty remained confident that it would remain superior to the German Navy for the foreseeable future. After all, Germany had several continental challengers that required it to maintain a large army. And the British Navy was now freed of many global responsibilities as well as the two-power standard. Fisher said, "[The British Navy's] present margin of superiority over Germany (our only possible foe for years) is so great as to render it absurd to talk of anything endangering our naval supremacy, even if we stopped all shipbuilding altogether." He insisted, "the Germans know it would be madness for them to provoke a war." Indeed, German observers commented that "in a future war our fleet cannot do better than to confine itself to the defensive if it does not wish to experience another Tsushima and disappear." In 1907, Fisher told King Edward that Tirpitz "has privately stated in a secret paper that the English Navy is now four times stronger than the German Navy! And we are going to keep the British Navy at that strength." Edward Grey and Lloyd George made clear to German Ambassador Paul Wolff Metternich that "every Englishman would spend his last penny on maintaining British supremacy at sea."[27]

Nevertheless, British leaders knew that Germany's power was rising and diluting Britain's lead. The navy would have to focus more seriously on its home defense mission. The Admiralty worried about three potential challenges: "1. Minelaying in the approaches to our harbours. 2. Torpedo attacks on our shipping, either at anchor or at sea. 3. The escape of commerce destroyers from German ports to prey on our trade." Yet, naval leaders dismissed these dangers as an "annoyance . . . not likely to do [Britain] any vital injury." One reason for this confidence was that British leaders believed submarines would not sink ships without prior warning. While later serving as First Lord of the Admiralty, Winston Churchill rejected the idea that "this would ever be done by a civilized Power." A British legal expert concurred that "no submarine would dare to touch a vessel without the proper visit and search being made. . . . The civilized world would hold up its hands in horror at such acts of barbarism as a submarine sinking its prey." Thus, the British Navy remained focused on the threat from German's growing fleet of surface combatants.[28]

As World War I drew closer, British aims became even more focused on protecting what Great Britain had won. Gone were dreams of further expansion. The question now was whether Britain could hold onto what it had won. The Admiralty warned, "The fact is that after a long peace each Power is prepared to fight for what it considers its legitimate aspirations. It will only yield when exhausted by war." War plans called for a cordon "from the coast of Norway to a point on the east coast of England." Yet some British leaders worried, "In case of war between this country and Germany, alone, neither nation has much opportunity of doing the other any vital injury, and if other nations did not intervene, the war might drag on indefinitely." In this case, it would be necessary to end the war by using force on the continent. The Admiralty noted, "To content ourselves with blockading German ports while the country of our ally was being overrun by German troops would be too humiliating a position to be accepted." Defense leaders therefore prepared to deploy the army to the continent to assist in the defense of France.[29]

British leaders consolidated their objectives when they realized that relative power trends were working against them. In particular, London grew increasingly concerned about the challenge from Berlin. British leaders took significant risk in East Asia and the Americas by permitting Japan and the United States greater authority in both regions. This permitted the navy to focus more on protecting the British Isles. As *The Standard* announced, "Because of that formidable and threatening Armada across the North Sea, we have almost abandoned the waters of the Outer Oceans. We are in the position of Imperial Rome when the Barbarians were thundering at the frontiers. The ominous word has gone forth. We have called home the legions."[30]

Defense Strategy: Defensive

For centuries, British leaders had preferred offensive strategies over defensive ones. Offensive approaches were encouraged by the navy's preference to seize the initiative and by perceptions that defense was a symptom of weakness. But changing power dynamics forced British leaders to embrace a more defensive strategy that better fit Britain's more consolidated objectives.[31]

As London awoke to the German threat, attention turned to Berlin's naval construction program. The German ambassador to Britain wrote in 1904, "The papers regard every step in the progress of our fleet as a menace to England. . . . The sight of the German fleet at Plymouth reminds Great Britain that she must be sufficiently armed to uphold absolutely her supremacy at sea." The British Navy had no intention of ceding sea control. The Admiralty insisted, "command of the sea is essential for the successful attack or defense of commerce, and should therefore be the primary aim." Command of the sea required the British Navy to confront the German fleet. In 1905, Admiral Fisher suggested to King Edward that the navy was ready to do just that. Worried about German naval construction, Fisher offered, "if you want to smash up the German Fleet, I am ready to do so now. If you wait five or six years, it will be a much more difficult job."[32]

The Admiralty still believed it held a substantial edge in naval power, which was compounded by France and Russia turning against Germany. Director of Naval Intelligence Charles Ottley advised in 1905, "Previous studies of the question of war against Germany have all been based on the assumption that Germany was supported by powerful maritime allies, such as France or Russia. . . . The situation is entirely different, and our maritime preponderance would be overwhelming." The navy therefore pushed for sea control and a decisive fleet engagement. Many members of the Admiralty continued to equate defense with weakness, noting that "the superior fleet will always take the offensive—will seek to attack and get a quick and final decision." British war plans stated, "They being the weaker Power at sea, will act strictly on the defensive, and our strategy must be directed to making them abandon this attitude and come out to attack us in a position of our choosing and under conditions agreeable to us."[33]

The navy was so confident in its supremacy that Secretary of State for War Arnold-Forster insisted, "If the Admiralty are right, then we need not maintain an Army for home defence, capable of resisting serious invasion. If the Admiralty are wrong, then no Army we can maintain will be sufficient to protect us from hostile attack. If we have command of the sea, we can prevent any invading Army landing. If we have not command of the sea, it will not be necessary for an enemy to land—it can starve us into submission." Therefore, British war plans insisted, "It is not necessary for us to risk a single man by operations on the coast" of the European continent. On the basis of the navy's dominance, Chancellor of the Exchequer H. H. Asquith argued against further naval spending. He noted, "Our naval supremacy is so completely assured that there is no possible reason for allowing ourselves to be hastily rushed into these nebulous and ambitious developments."[34]

But British concerns about the German Navy grew. Winston Churchill recalled, "Genuine alarm was excited throughout the country by what was for the first time widely recognized as a German menace" around 1909. He noted "a deep and growing feeling, no longer confined to political and diplomatic circles, that the Prussians meant mischief, that they envied the splendor of the British Empire, and that if they saw a good chance at [Britain's] expense, they would take full advantage of it." Newly promoted Prime Minister Asquith changed his position, noting, "Our naval position is at this moment, as I believe, one of unassailable supremacy, and such it must remain." He asked "why Germany should need, or how she can use, twenty-one Dreadnoughts, unless for aggressive purposes, and primarily against [Britain]." The British Navy sought additional funding for new warships. In Churchill's words, "The Admiralty had demanded six ships: the economists offered four: and we finally compromised on eight."[35]

British leaders simply would not accept a secondary position in the naval realm. While serving as First Lord of the Admiralty, Churchill explained, "The maintenance of naval supremacy is our whole foundation. Upon it stands not the empire only, not merely the commercial property of our people, not merely a fine place in the world's affairs; upon our naval supremacy stands our lives and the freedom we have guarded for nearly a thousand years." Foreign

Secretary Edward Grey warned, "If we alone, among the great Powers, gave up the competition and sank into a position of inferiority, . . .
we should cease to count for anything among the nations of Europe,
and we should be fortunate if our liberty was left and we did not become the conscript appendage of some stronger power." But even
substantial investments in the navy were unable to maintain the naval
balance without a major realignment of British forces.[36]

The clearest indicator of British retrenchment was the return of
its capital ships to home waters. From 1897 to 1912, the number of
British capital ships outside the Home Fleet fell from twenty-four
to two, while the number of capital ships in the Home Fleet rose
from eleven to thirty-three. Fisher later explained, "We cannot
have everything or be strong everywhere. It is futile to be strong
in the subsidiary theatre of war and not overwhelmingly supreme in
the decisive theatre." In Fisher's mind, the decisive theater would be
the North Sea. British strategy was clear: to maintain control of the
North Sea at all costs, even if that meant sacrificing British interests
elsewhere. In 1904, Fisher had noted, "Five keys lock up the world!
Singapore. The Cape. Alexandria. Gibraltar. Dover. These five keys
belong to England, and the five great fleets of England will hold
these keys!" By 1914, Britain's great fleet was protecting only the
North Sea, leaving smaller craft to "lock up" four of the five keys.
Fisher even began to openly express interest in using a French-style
"Defence Mobile," with torpedo boats and submarines protecting
these choke points. Thus, Britain's defense strategy had shifted from
offense to defense as its relative power declined.[37]

Defense Investments: Immobile

At the turn of the century, both the British Army and Navy were
postured to protect the empire by rapidly deploying to meet crises
abroad. But as the German threat became clear, British defense investments came under the microscope. The challenge for the Admiralty was to field a modern fleet despite the budgetary limits put
in place by the Exchequer. Meanwhile, the army sought to retain
whatever share of the budget it could, despite being Britain's offensive force. The result was a shift in resources to the navy, which
then invested in a less mobile fleet.

When Jackie Fisher became First Naval Lord in 1904, he initiated a series of far-reaching reforms. Fisher proposed that the navy be "restricted to four types of vessels, being all that modern fighting necessitates. (a) Battleships of 15,900 tons. 21 knots speed. (b) Armoured Cruisers of 15,900 tons. 25.5 knots speed. (c) Destroyers of 900 tons, and 4-inch guns. 36 knots speed. (d) Submarines of 350 tons. 14 knots surface speed." Thus, the navy shifted from a focus on capital ships to a more diverse fleet. These changes are evident in the development and acquisition of three types of vessels: (1) large surface ships, including battleships and cruisers; (2) smaller surface ships, such as destroyers; and (3) undersea systems, namely, submarines. Each class of vessel underwent substantial changes during this period.[38]

Fisher's first focus was on battleships and cruisers. He established a Committee on Designs that proposed the creation of a new battleship with greater speed, bigger guns, and enhanced armor—the dreadnought. The committee also proposed what came to be known as a battle cruiser, which had the armor and guns of a battleship but the speed of a cruiser. Fisher believed that only a large and well-armed cruiser could effectively scout the enemy fleet, as well fight alongside battleships in a fleet engagement. The tremendous cost of dreadnoughts and battle cruisers required sacrifices. Fisher decided to retire over one hundred old ships, which he viewed as having little military value, in light of their high upkeep and manning costs. The savings from selling and retiring these vessels allowed Fisher to show a budgetary decrease despite his expensive procurement plans. Yet, opposition was substantial. Respected experts like the naval architect Sir William White raised the danger of putting "all one's naval eggs into one or two vast, costly, majestic, but vulnerable baskets." However, this was not Fisher's plan.[39]

Fisher also embraced a second type of ship: the destroyer (a term he coined himself). Fisher warned, "To build battleships merely to fight an enemy's battleships, so long as cheaper craft can destroy them, and prevent them of themselves protecting sea operations, is merely to breed Kilkenny cats unable to catch rats or mice. ... What use is a battle fleet [against a fleet] possessing no battleships, but having fast armoured cruisers and clouds of fast torpedo craft?" As commander in chief of the Mediterranean, he had sought to use torpedo destroyers to counter the growing small-boat threat to British bases and the fleet. First Naval Lord Walter Kerr had been critical, writing, "He is using them in a way which it is properly the role of gunboats and 3rd class cruisers to fill." By 1904, however, Fisher had assumed Kerr's role as First Naval Lord, and he pushed ahead with two types of destroyers. Coastal service destroyers would deal with foreign torpedo craft. Oceangoing destroyers would be "designed to accompany fleets in all weathers, anywhere and to any part of the world."[40]

Fisher's third area of investment was the submarine. Initially, he had called them "weapons of the weak," but now Fisher noted that "they loom large as the weapons of the strong. . . . Is there the slightest fear of invasion with them even for the most extreme pessimist?" The submarine advocate Reginald Bacon concurred that large ships should "never be allowed" to approach ports defended by submarines. The Admiralty advocated using submarines in daylight and torpedo craft at night to deny "the waters in turn to the enemy, thereby neutralising these areas for offensive operations." Political leaders bought in, despite earlier critiques that submarines were too immobile. Prime Minister Balfour commented, "I wish we had more submarines. . . . They are, after all, cheap." Churchill likewise noted the "better value for money out of the small craft." The costs were growing, however. Selborne warned Fisher, "I should like to build more destroyers or torpedo-boats and more submarines, but the total for new construction cannot be increased."[41]

Where could more money be found for shipbuilding? Fisher made his view known that additional funds should come from the army: "If we are not safe from invasion then make us so. Spend money on submarines, destroyers, etc., but don't waste money on an armed mob." The navy now suggested that it should take over port defense. The Admiralty had previously insisted that fortifications were "a better form of local defense, as a rule, than stationary ships." Now navy leaders suggested that "submarines and torpedo-boats could take the place of submarine mines." Fisher noted, "Thirty years ago the Admiralty adopted the policy of entirely disowning any responsibility with regard to the defense of coasts and harbours. . . . But times have so changed." One of his disciples proposed "transference of the whole of the Garrison Artillery from Army to Navy." Prime Minister Balfour assured Fisher that Britain would go ahead with "the substitution of submarines for mines, and the defense of places like Malta, Gibraltar and Bermuda by submarines." Coastal defenses around Britain, however, remained largely under the army's control. But the navy's new interest in immobile defenses was clear.[42]

British leaders increasingly questioned the army's value. Balfour wondered whether colonial defenses "might not be made almost impregnable at a small cost by strengthening the naval defenses, and whether, in this case, the existing garrison might not be reduced?" Secretary of State for War Richard Haldane commented in 1906, "We live on an island, and our coasts are completely defended by the Fleet." The Haldane Reforms that followed ushered in a major change in the British Army, namely, the creation of a smaller force capable of only limited offensive operations abroad. The reforms restated the army's strategy in defensive terms. The army's new mission was "to protect the distant shores of that Empire from the attacks of the invader." The reforms did acknowledge that Britain might need to land troops on the European continent to help defend France. But this was seen as a secondary concern. Balfour later explained, "If you drilled every man in this country to the picture of perfection now possessed by the German Army, ... what would it avail you if the sea was not free and open to bring to these shores raw material and the food upon which we depend?" Therefore, from 1904 onward, the navy—Britain's defensive force—won out for funding over the army.[43]

There was substantial opposition to Britain's more defensive approach. Fisher's frequent critic Charles Beresford later criticized those who suggested that "the main fleet is to remain in harbour because the fleet is in danger at sea! ... Nelson would turn in his grave." Reginald Custance warned that "naval opinion is and has been for years saturated with the ideas of defense." Others in the Admiralty called for "a second Trafalgar, a great fleet action, in which [Britain's] superior strength in ships will assure ... victory." Winston Churchill periodically expressed similar views, suggesting that "vigorous offence against the enemy's warships wherever stationed, will give immediately far greater protection to British traders than large numbers of vessels scattered sparsely about in an attitude of weak and defensive expectancy." The historian Arthur Marder suggests that Beresford and his supporters saw the submarine, in particular, as "merely a defensive weapon, and therefore unsuitable for use in an offensive fleet like the British."[44]

Yet, Fisher's logic largely won out. He noted, "The battleship of olden days was necessary because it was the one and only vessel that nothing could sink except another battleship. Now, every battleship is open to attack by fast torpedo craft and submarines. . . . A battle fleet is no protection to anything, or any operation, during dark hours, and in certain waters is no protection in daytime because of the submarine." Fisher pressed his case, asking, "What is the use of battleships as we have hitherto known them? NONE!" Other members of the Admiralty pushed forward Fisher's ideas. Admiral Reginald Bacon pressed home the importance of torpedo boats, noting, "the battleship is no longer the ultimate power on the sea: it may be sunk by the smallest vessel afloat." First Lord of the Admiralty Reginald McKenna called "destroyers and submarine flotillas . . . the true defense against invasion." Admiral Mark Kerr reinforced this view when he observed, "It is impossible that the capital ships can escape the attack of the flotilla either by day or night. It is apparent, therefore, that capital ships are only of value in the open sea out of the radius of action of the flotilla." Indeed funding rose for both flotilla craft and submarines in the years after 1904, primarily at the expense of cruisers.[45]

Some naval historians, most notably Nicholas Lambert, believe that a fundamental change was afoot immediately prior to World War I. Lambert argues, "Fisher developed a new theory of sea power—the concept of 'flotilla defense.' This was a sea-denial strategy intended to protect the British Isles from the possibility of invasion in the absence of the main fleet." He argues that the Fisher intended to compete asymmetrically with Germany by launching a surprise submarine-building plan. One piece of evidence is that Fisher wrote to the famous naval theorist Julian Corbett in June 1914 and expressed frustration that a British naval officer had made the submarine's value too clear to the Germans. Fisher hoped Germany would lavish money on large battleships "that will be securely blockaded by [British] submarines, as the Mediterranean and the

North Sea will be securely locked up." Thus, it is possible that Fisher intended to adopt an even more defensive strategic approach using immobile systems.[46]

Regardless of the veracity of this claim, it is clear that British strategy shifted substantially in the decade prior to World War I. Table 7 depicts British defense spending from 1895 to 1913. Two changes are evident. The first is a decrease in spending on the army from 1904 onward. The second is a decrease in spending on cruisers—the most mobile ship in the fleet—in favor of battleships and largely immobile flotilla craft and submarines. Together, these shifts suggest that Fisher and his adherents transitioned Great Britain toward a set of less mobile systems. Great Britain did continue to invest in a number of mobile systems, but overall the changes put in place around 1904 brought about a more defensive and less mobile posture. With this in mind, Lord Esher advised in 1912 that British naval strength should be measured by "(1) personnel; (2) submarines; (3) destroyers; (4) large armoured cruisers; (5) armoured cruisers; (6) battleships—in that order." Gone was Britain's exclusive focus on offensive sea control. More defensive and less mobile systems had won an increasing share of British attention and investment.[47]

Assessment

Great Britain reached its apex in the late nineteenth century when Russia, France, the United States, and Germany started to rapidly industrialize. But until 1904, many leaders in London believed they could stall or reverse these power trends. When the reality of Britain's relative decline finally sunk in, British leaders consolidated their objectives, adopted a more defensive strategy, and invested in less mobile systems.

Gone was talk of expanding the empire. Now the focus was on simply holding onto what Britain had conquered. Winston Churchill described the mood in Britain in early 1914: "We are not a young people with an innocent record and a scanty inheritance. We have engrossed ourselves, in time when other powerful nations were paralysed by barbarism or internal war, an altogether disproportionate share of the wealth and traffic of the world. We have

Table 7. British Defense Spending (1895–1913)

	Naval construction expenditure (%)				Gross naval expenditure (£)	Gross army expenditure (£)
Year	Battleships	Cruisers	Flotilla craft	Submarines		
1895	54	33	12	—	21,264,377	18,471,518
1896	35	45	20	—	23,886,177	18,997,917
1897	41	47	11	—	22,547,844	18,481,661
1898	50	42	9	—	26,145,598	20,209,526
1899	52	37	11	—	28,478,842	20,901,675
1900	46	43	11	—	33,302,260	44,107,399
1901	43	53	4	—	34,994,553	92,424,671
1902	37	50	11	3	35,525,731	94,165,905
1903	38	52	8	2	40,503,873	70,248,523
1904	39	49	9	3	41,696,313	39,653,034
1905	41	47	5	7	38,175,045	31,559,638
1906	37	50	9	5	35,693,850	29,129,574
1907	47	36	13	4	33,950,169	28,365,987
1908	57	21	15	7	34,775,752	26,716,612
1909	47	27	21	5	37,385,460	26,338,073
1910	45	33	20	2	43,903,499	26,624,098
1911	51	30	15	4	46,793,789	26,922,908
1912	55	24	16	6	48,742,182	27,328,810
1913	59	21	15	6	52,920,960	27,633,380
Average 1895–1904	44	45	11	1	30,834,557	36,225,311
Average 1905–1913	49	32	14	5	41,371,190	27,846,564

Source: Data compiled and reproduced from Nicholas A. Lambert, *Sir John Fisher's Naval Revolution*, Studies in Maritime History (Columbia: University of South Carolina Press, 1999), 306; Jon Tetsuro Sumida, *In Defence of Naval Supremacy: Finance, Technology, and British Naval Policy, 1889–1914* (Boston: Unwin Hyman, 1989); Bernard Mallet, *British Budgets 1887–88 to 1912–13* (London: Macmillan, 1913), 504.

got all we want in territory, and our claim to be left in the unmolested enjoyment of vast and splendid possessions, mainly acquired by violence, largely maintained by force, often seems less reasonable to others than to us." By the early 1900s, British leaders realized that they would have to scale back their ambitions and consolidate control of the possessions that mattered most.[48]

As British leaders consolidated their objectives, they adopted more defensive strategies. The British Army, which was long viewed as the empire's offensive force, shrunk in size. The army sacrificed much of its budget to fund naval procurements. Thus, the navy's share of defense spending rose from 42 to 62 percent from 1887 to 1912. Meanwhile, the navy came back home, bringing nearly all its capital ships back to the North Sea. This was not an easy transition. Indeed, naval leaders continued to talk about the importance of offense in operations and tactics. But the British Navy was on the strategic defense, trying mainly to "bottle up" the German Navy. Foreign Secretary Grey explained, "the Navy is our one and only means of defence and our life depends on it and upon it alone."[49]

Meanwhile, naval investments slowly shifted away from mobility, since defense did not require it to the same degree. British spending on cruisers decreased and was supplanted in part by spending on flotilla craft and submarines. While 45 percent of naval construction was devoted to cruisers before Fisher came into office in 1904, only 32 percent went toward them afterward. Meanwhile, flotilla craft and submarines increased from 12 to 19 percent of spending. This was in line with Fisher's belief in the "vast impending revolution in naval warfare and naval strategy that the submarine will accomplish!"[50]

It is important to note, however, that the magnitude and timing of Britain's shifting defense policies were somewhat smaller and slower than might have been expected. Indeed, British leaders took decades to accept that the British Empire had peaked. In economic terms, Britain was already declining rapidly in the 1880s, but it was not until two decades later, during the second Boer War, that many political leaders and the general public accepted this reality. Moreover, British defense policies did not shift entirely toward a garrison fortification approach. Both the army and navy exhibited some of these changes, but they did not adopt them wholesale (unlike the French during the interwar period, described in chapter 5). Perceptions of relative power shifts differed greatly among British elites, and this slowed down and moderated defense reforms.

Perceived relative power theory therefore explains the direction of change in British defense policies from 1890 to 1910. But two intervening variables played a critical role in the timing and magnitude of these changes. First, British strategic and organizational culture favored expansive aims, offense strategies, and large surface combatants. As Director of Naval Intelligence Reginald Custance wrote in 1902, "Naval opinion has been and is now under the influence of the traditions of the Napoleonic wars, when we had such a great superiority over the forces opposed to us." Naval leaders clung to the status quo and worried that any decision to abandon offensive traditions and prestigious weapons would undermine the navy's bureaucratic influence. Large offensive weapons, such as the dreadnought, may also have been preferred because they fit the navy's view of itself as master of the seas and permitted more flexibility in operations. Second, Britain's geographic position still mandated the ability to project naval power. An island nation like Britain was reliant on trade for survival. Moreover, the alliance with France required the ability to land troops on the European continent. And the British Empire still needed defending. Fortifications could not protect British sea lines of communication or allow transport of the army during war. Thus, even discussing defense created worries about sacrificing interests and alliances abroad. As a result, retrenchment aroused much opposition and had to be carried out more slowly than perceived relative power theory would have otherwise suggested.[51]

In summary, Britain's experience with relative decline aligned with many of the predictions of perceived relative power theory. This case generally accords with Hypotheses 2, 4, and 6. But it diverges in the timing and magnitude of British defense reforms. British leaders were slow to recognize their nation's relative decline, and many of its leaders held fast to existing policies. Thus, geographic and cultural explanations played important roles in moderating British behavior and slowing some of the reforms predicted by perceived relative power theory. This case therefore provides important insights into the conditions under which the theory holds. As Lord Bolingbroke observed, "The precise point at which the scales of power turn . . . is imperceptible to common observation. . . . They who are in the sinking scale . . . do not easily come off from the habitual prejudices of superior wealth, or power, or skill, or courage, nor from the confidence that these prejudices inspire."[52]

CHAPTER FIVE

France's Apex

What dominates everything are the awful threats that hang
over France. . . . Alone, exhausted, ruined, without
government, without compass, living from day to day,
haphazardly. The future is terrifying. I believe German
revenge inevitable, unavoidable and close.

—MARSHAL HUBERT LYAUTEY (1921)

FRANCE EMERGED TRIUMPHANT FROM World War I, but its victory
came at tremendous cost. The French Republic lost 1.4 million men
in the war—10.5 percent of its active male population. Moreover,
much of the war occurred in northeastern France, which accounted
for half of French coal, iron, steel, and cotton production. By the
end of the war, 7 percent of French territory had been damaged,
and coal and steel production had fallen by 37 percent and 60 percent, respectively. As Winston Churchill later remarked, "Victory
was to be bought so dear as to be almost indistinguishable from defeat." French leaders therefore drove a hard bargain at Versailles.
They sought reparations for France's devastation and constraints on
Germany's ability to wage war in the future. Allied leaders physi-

cally controlled much German territory and received a large proportion of its economic production in the form of reparations.[1]

But demographic and economic trends were in Germany's favor. The French diplomat Jules Cambon lamented, "France victorious must grow accustomed to being a lesser power than France vanquished." In 1922, Prime Minister Raymond Poincaré warned of "the truly frightening prospect of Germany economically hegemonic and capable of realizing all the objectives it would have gained had it won the war." Over the next two decades, population growth rates differed substantially. In 1920, France's population was 39 million compared to Germany's 43 million. By 1938, however, Germany had 26 million more people than France. In the early 1920s, France fielded a 350,000-man standing army, as compared to 100,000 for Germany. By 1938, the German Army was estimated at 850,000. Meanwhile, French industrial production declined 24 percent from 1929 to 1938, while German production increased 16 percent. By the late 1930s, Germany was producing 351 million tons of coal compared to just 47 million tons for France. France's decline occurred over only two decades. A French officer asked, "Can it be that France has had her day like Athens, Rome, Spain or Portugal in the past? Is it Germany's turn now?"[2]

This chapter analyzes French defense policies from 1918 to 1938, as leaders in Paris came to terms with the Republic's relative decline. Perceived relative power theory makes three predictions about states that have reached their apex and are transitioning from rise to decline. Hypothesis 2 predicts a change in objectives from expansion to consolidation. Hypothesis 4 predicts a shift from offensive to defensive strategies. Hypothesis 6 predicts a redirection of investments from mobile to immobile systems. In short, perceived relative power theory suggests that states at their apex should transition from power projection toward garrison fortification. Indeed, this is evident in the French case. As the Republic's relative power waned, French leaders consolidated their objectives. They shifted from an offensive to a defensive strategy. This defensive strategy relied not on mobile forces but on largely stationary units and fortifications, particularly the Maginot Line. French defense policy changes may not have succeeded in rebuffing the eventual Nazi invasion, but they do align with perceived relative power theory.

French Defense Policies Pre-1927

Despite the devastation imposed on France by World War I, the Republic emerged in position of relative strength. Germany had been beaten and had lost people and territory. It was saddled with massive war reparations. And both Great Britain and the United States initially appeared committed to avoiding a resurgence of German militarism. Through the mid-1920s, the German economy struggled under the weight of reparations, territorial losses, and depression. France's relative position appeared secure, and French leaders were determined to maintain their upper hand. As a result, through at least 1927, most French leaders embraced expansive objectives, offensive strategies, and mobile investments.

Defense Objectives: Expansive

Before World War I, various interest groups within France pushed for colonial expansion. According to the scholar Anthony Adamthwaite, "Expansionist pressures in the late nineteenth and early twentieth centuries came from soldiers, businessmen and missionaries." After the war, however, the focus shifted to Europe. The challenge for French leaders was to exploit their relative strength. They sought to slow Germany's economic resurgence in order to prevent Berlin from launching another bid for mastery of Europe.[3]

Ensuring that the postwar settlement would both rebuild France and constrain Germany was the top priority. Massive economic reparations and territorial adjustments were viewed as necessities. Both measures weakened Germany while strengthening France, in both relative and absolute terms. French negotiators therefore insisted on enormous reparations. Although their initial demands were not met, France won 52 percent of all German reparations to the allies. Germany also lost all its overseas possessions and over 13 percent of its territory on the continent. France gained Alsace and Lorraine and parts of Togo and Cameroon and occupied the Rhineland. Defending France's considerable demands, Prime Minister Georges Clemenceau explained, "After expending the greatest effort, and suffering the greatest sacrifices in blood in all history, we must not compromise the results of our victory."[4]

French leaders also sought to impose restrictions on the German military and strengthen alliances with Germany's neighbors. The German Navy had already been scuttled at Scapa Flow, but France and Britain also prevented Germany from fielding naval vessels above ten thousand tons. The German Army was limited to one hundred thousand men, although France failed to force Germany to adopt a conscript army that might have proven more difficult to reconstitute. All fortifications east of the Rhine were to be dismantled. In addition, Germany was prohibited from retaining or constructing military aircraft. Meanwhile, France entered into alliances with Belgium in 1920, Poland in 1921, Czechoslovakia in 1924, Romania in 1926, and Yugoslavia in 1927. And Paris sought continued commitments from London, Washington, and Moscow to jointly meet any future German threat. France was expanding its activities throughout Europe, at Germany's expense.[5]

Yet cracks quickly emerged among the allies. Paris's hard line on reparations, territorial concessions, military constraints, and economic reintegration damaged ties with London and Washington. Collective security mechanisms, such as the League of Nations, required German cooperation. So U.S. and British leaders pushed for early German reintegration into the international community, despite French opposition. Tensions rose among the allies. Herbert Hoover articulated the view of many observers in Washington and London when he stated, "France always goes through this cycle. After she is done and begins to recuperate, . . . she gets rich, militaristic and cocky; and nobody can get on with her until she has to be thrashed again."[6]

French leaders were not satisfied that reparations, territorial concessions, military limitations, renewed alliances, and institutional arrangements would contain the German threat. Ferdinand Foch, who had accepted the German surrender, said of Versailles, "This is not peace. . . . It is an armistice for twenty years." Although France was strong relative to Germany in the immediate aftermath of the war, the German population was growing quickly. Clemenceau warned, "The Treaty means nothing if France does not agree to have many children, . . . for if France renounces large families, we will have taken all the guns from Germany for nothing." In 1920, a French industrial expert foretold, "Our enemy, regardless of all treaties, will certainly find a way of reconstituting its military power. Given the density of its population, we will be able to field equal numbers against it only by drawing heavily . . . on our allies."[7]

By the early 1920s, Germany's inability to pay reparations created a political struggle among the allies. British and U.S. leaders hoped to lessen the burden on Germany by decreasing the size and pace of reparations. On the other hand, France and Belgium—desiring the funds to rebuild their economies—wanted to use military force to ensure German compliance. French leaders urged an occupation of the Ruhr region, Germany's manufacturing heartland. Military officers had long advocated an occupation of the entire Rhineland, with Foch arguing, "If we do not hold the Rhine permanently, no neutralization, or disarmament, or any kind of written clause can prevent Germany . . . from sallying out of it at will." The French diplomat Jacques Seydoux explained, "It is a violent solution, but it will settle everything. We will become the masters of Germany, independent of England, and an industrial power of the first rank." By 1922, Paris believed Berlin was testing the allies' resolve by cutting off timber (and later coal) deliveries. Under pressure from Paris and Brussels, the Inter-Allied Commission announced that Germany was in default, and France and Belgium moved to occupy the Ruhr.[8]

The occupation demonstrated that France was strong relative to Germany. French leaders were so determined that some British counterparts began to worry more about Paris than Berlin. Lloyd George exclaimed, "France is full of the idea that she is going to control, overwhelm and keep under Germany. . . . It is only France who could give us trouble now." Other foreign officials were more sympathetic. John Maynard Keynes, who had represented Britain at Versailles, defended the French by noting that "it was essential to rectify the situation unilaterally created by the occupation and the devastation of northern France. The occupation of the Ruhr restored that equilibrium." Immediately thereafter, Germany experienced hyperinflation and economic stagnation. The allies established a committee to find a solution. The resulting Dawes Plan restructured German reparations and ended the allied occupation of the Ruhr. French control over the Ruhr ended in 1925, ushering in reduced reparations.[9]

As the 1920s continued, it became clear that France's relative position would erode. Political and economic limitations shrunk the French Army and diminished its ability to invade Germany. Foreign Minister Aristide Briand announced in 1925, "We will not go beyond our zone. . . . We are possessed by no spirit of conquest. . . . We should be acting in a criminal fashion if we entertained the least ulterior motive of dragging our country into bloody adventures in pursuit of a conquest that we couldn't even digest." In 1927, Minister of Colonies Jean Fabry attempted "to organize the army in such a fashion that its standing units would be capable of immediate action" against Germany. But less than two years later, the historian Judith Hughes writes, "the terms of the discussion had changed. . . . With one-year military service and the evacuation of the Rhineland impending realities, the point at issue for Fabry was no longer what the active army might initiate but rather how it should be equipped to withstand a German attack." Thus, French leaders began to shift from a strategy of imposing their will on Germany to one of consolidation.[10]

Defense Strategy: Offensive

Through the mid-1920s, France adopted an offensive strategy in line with its expansive aims. French leaders had settled on an offensive strategy before World War I, with devastating results. Although some pushed for defensive approaches to force allied intervention, these calls fell on deaf ears. The aftermath of World War I rekindled the debate about defensive strategies, particularly given the prevailing view that defense had proven superior to offense. Yet, French leaders continued to embrace offensive capabilities in the immediate aftermath of the war. French leaders did not believe that they could simply defend against an attack; they wanted to maintain the ability to be proactive. Clemenceau framed the French predicament by noting, "America is far away and protected by the ocean. England could not be reached by Napoleon himself. You are sheltered, both of you; we are not." France could not simply hide from threats.[11]

With Germany diminished, France found itself in a position of strength. French leaders therefore developed a series of offensive war plans. Plan T, Plan P, and Plan A all called for offensive action against Germany. Fortifications were considered, but mainly to provide avenues for a French offensive into Germany. They would also form a backstop against a German attack, allowing time for mobilization and enabling a counteroffensive. But General Adolphe Guillaumat reflected prevailing views when he commented, "It is dangerous to let the false and demoralizing notion spread that once we have fortifications the inviolability of our country is assured." Instead, the Frontier Defense Commission suggested that fortified regions could act "as a real instrument of maneuver at the disposition of the command-in-chief."[12]

An offensive strategy required mobile units capable of invading Germany. Merely defensive approaches were rejected. Guillaumat argued, "The Wall of France is a dream. . . . It would be better to build a strong army capable of going on the offensive." According to one observer, "Even Marshal Foch did not dissent. Indeed, throughout the discussions of defensive works, he sided with Guillaumat and consistently saw fortifications as offering support to the army's maneuvers." Marshal Émile Fayolle wrote in 1925 of the need for "forces capable of decisive strikes into Germany such that Germany will be required to maintain the mass of her forces in face of [France] and to fight on her territory." The Treaty of Versailles would not carry out itself; French soldiers had to be prepared to impose the terms on an unwilling Germany.[13]

It would have been logical for the hard-learned lessons of World War I to have convinced France to choose a defensive strategy throughout the 1920s. But this is not what happened. As Elizabeth Kier notes, "Although the memory of World War I was etched in France's collective memory, the French army did not leave World War I convinced that the only possible doctrinal orientation was a defensive one reminiscent of the trench warfare in northern France." Barry Posen chronicles how "French civilians did not complete their drift to an overwhelmingly defensive doctrine until the end of the 1920s." As Kier explains, "Not until the late 1920s did the advocates of a continuous line of fortifications dominate the debate; until then, a more offensive conception for the use of fortified regions held sway."[14]

Defense Investments: Mobile

France learned the difficulty of attacking well-fortified positions in World War I. Those memories gave French leaders ample reason to abandon mobile forces. General André Beaufre commented, "We had been haunted by the tenacity of the German machine-guns, and the impossibility in which we found ourselves of breaking the enemy front." A French tactical manual made clear that "firepower had given a remarkable strength of resistance to impro-vised fortifications." Yet, the French Army continued to invest in mobility after the war. Kier notes, "It was only later, in the late 1920s and especially the 1930s that the lesson of World War I be-came dominant."[15]

In the early 1920s, with France in a strong position relative to Germany, mobile French forces seemed the logical investment for two reasons. First, the postwar environment required an army that could force Germany to pay reparations. Second, mobility permit-ted more flexible and offensive operations, which were the army's preference. In 1920, French infantry regulations announced, "In-spired with an offensive spirit, . . . infantry and its supporting forces will never let themselves be stopped by the fear of incurring a few losses, which it would be . . . chimerical to hope to avoid completely." General Edmond Buat insisted, "The appearance of the motor on the battlefield once again gives mobility and move-ment its full importance." And Foch warned that without a mobile force, fortifications would not "be the umbrella that will protect the country."[16]

The Germans were also exploring mobile forces. General Hans von Seeckt commented in 1921, "The whole future of war-fare appears to me to be in the employment of mobile armies, rela-tively small but of high quality, and rendered distinctly more effective by the addition of aircraft." This would eventually lead to German blitzkrieg tactics, but French leaders were not ready to adopt combined-arms warfare utilizing tanks and mechanized in-fantry. Instead, André Maginot suggested in 1923 that France pur-sue "protective operations of limited range, carried out with prudence." As Posen notes, "The French always stressed firepower over maneuver. The requirement for a heavy firepower offensive with a massive preliminary bombardment fostered a slow and deliberate style of warfare. New techniques and machines were fitted to this model."[17]

How did France plan to make use of its mobile forces in the early 1920s? General Maurice Gamelin identified the need "to prepare, at the edge of the frontier, a mobile force and to ensure its rapid transfer into Belgium." Marshal Philippe Pétain also called for "a mobile force near the frontier and to make sure of its swift advance into Belgium." This was a notable position from the general who "attributed his success in stopping the enemy advance mainly to the fortress ring of Verdun." France kept mobile units near the Belgian and German borders in part to ensure that any fighting occurred outside French territory. A repeat of World War I was unacceptable—France refused to see its people and territory devastated again.[18]

But as the 1920s advanced, French politicians grew increasingly concerned about Germany's resurgence and worried that a mobile French force would be insufficient. Fortifications now seemed more prudent. French leaders initially tried to frame fortifications as mobile weapons. Maginot envisioned "extremely mobile defensive organizations, . . . a kind of fortification on wheels." In the years ahead, however, defensive strategies and immobile forces would win the day. After all, French attacks into German territory seemed less plausible as funding evaporated for a large, well-trained French Army capable of offensive action. Thus, as 1927 approached, French leaders were preparing to embrace a decisive shift away from mobile forces.[19]

French Defense Policies Post-1927

France's power relative to Germany declined through the mid-1920s, but it was not until roughly 1927 that Germany's resurgence appeared unavoidable. Germany's economy was beginning to recover as its population swelled. Meanwhile, Great Britain and the United States proved unwilling to force Germany to pay its full share of reparations. In 1927, the Inter-Allied Commission was abolished, eliminating the primary mechanism for ensuring German compliance with the Treaty of Versailles. French leaders felt abandoned by their erstwhile allies, left alone to face a strengthening Germany. It was now impossible to avoid the conclusion that relative power dynamics were turning against France. Meanwhile, domestic forces also pushed the army toward a new and more defensive posture. Thus, French leaders scaled back their ambitions and adapted their strategy and investments accordingly.

Defense Objectives: Consolidative

The shift in French defense policies that began in the late 1920 was embodied by André Maginot. Maginot had been wounded at Verdun and later went on to serve as minister of war. He was determined to prevent another round of fighting on French territory. Speaking before parliament, Maginot proclaimed, "We are always the invaded, we are always the ones to suffer, we are always the ones to be sacrificed. . . . After all we have suffered, we have the right to demand certainties." But those certainties evaporated around 1927, when the dissolution of the Inter-Allied Commission eliminated France's primary tool for restraining Germany. Maginot warned, "it is going beyond the possibilities of human nature to expect our people to rebuild the regions that remain exposed to the risks and calamities of a new invasion."[20]

French leaders shelved more substantial aims and focused instead on consolidating France's position and defending its territory. In 1927, the conservative politician Michel Missoffe advised of the need "to defend the frontier . . . in an efficient fashion, for three or four months, and to give the country time to attain its full potential, both at home and in the colonies, of men, of armaments, and of provisions." No longer would France retain a large standing army, which was already proving difficult politically. Politicians such as Édouard Daladier warned of the dangers of a large army, noting, "we do not want any professional shock Army, more dangerous than one could believe for the security of the country." Instead, France would have to make do with a smaller and less-well-trained force. This army would be capable of limited defensive maneuvers but not major offensive actions. Gone were hopes of imposing France's will on Germany or coming to the aid of allies to the east.[21]

As France consolidated its objectives, concerns grew abroad. France chose not to fortify its border with Belgium. Minister of War Paul Painlevé explained in 1928, "we cannot build up impregnable defenses in the faces of our friends the Belgians." Yet France's allies were not reassured. Leaders in Paris committed that France would "earmark most of her mobile forces for a defensive maneuver into Belgium." After all, Pétain contended, "The northern frontier can only be defended by advancing into Belgium." But this would redirect a German invasion through Belgium. This was no oversight; it would avoid the destruction of French territory. Posen notes, "The main goal was to get others to share the costs of French defense. Until such cooperation could be assured, French military doctrine would aim to limit possible damage to France and to the French Army." Fighting in Belgium might also force Britain into the war. Thus, British leaders viewed French actions as a "deliberate inducement to compel [Britain] to intervene on land in order to safeguard an area which [the British] have regarded as vital for centuries." Some scholars therefore suggest that the Maginot Line's purpose was "to incite the Germans to invade through Belgium ... to alienate England and to lead the Belgians to intervene."[22]

French leaders were willing to tolerate allied anger. In 1930, the Young Plan further reduced the German payment schedule, and the return of the Rhineland was shifted from 1935 to 1930. Maginot called it "a veritable crime against the country." He later explained, "the fortification of the north-eastern frontier is essential to replace the protection that was afforded us by the occupation of the Rhineland." Jean Fabry acknowledged, "fear of another invasion ... dominates all France's military policy." Prime Minister Édouard Herriot warned in 1932, "I am convinced that Germany wishes to rearm. . . . We are at a turning point in history. Until now Germany has practiced a policy of submission. . . . Tomorrow it will be a policy of territorial demands backed by a formidable means of intimidation: its army."[23]

Why did France not invade Germany in the early 1930s, before relative power trends worsened? Army Inspector General Maxime Weygand himself asked, "Why not a preventive war? Today France still has military superiority. Soon she will have lost it." But few French leaders were willing to entertain the notion. One reason is that many believed France was still "the dominant military power in Europe in the air as well as on land." Prime Minister Daladier commented, "If Germany continues to rearm, France will increase its armaments so as to maintain its current superiority." Gamelin insisted that France had "a considerable margin of superiority over Germany": "We will see how long it will take for the Germans to catch up with the 20 billion we have spent on armaments!" French leaders hoped they could uphold more limited aims without an invasion. Maginot said, "As a people we threaten nobody. We have undertaken never to commit an act of aggression against anybody. We wish only to live in peace."[24]

An offensive against Germany was rejected. Even after Adolf Hitler was sworn in as German chancellor, French leaders pushed for negotiations at the Geneva Disarmament Conference. The French military attaché in Berlin noted that this would at least "have postponed the outbreak of a war." Unfortunately, Hitler withdrew from the conference and the League of Nations. With Germany rearming, France consolidated its aims. Daladier hoped only that "France retains its position among the great states." Pétain commented on "the profound feeling of the population which wishes to live in peace behind solid frontiers." French decline was now evident. Adamthwaite writes, "1934 was the last year in which the military chiefs freely acknowledged that the balance of forces favored France." Herriot said France "could no longer regard herself as a great power of sufficient military strength or human resources to maintain her position in central and eastern Europe and bring effective support to her allies." The diplomat Alexis Léger admitted that "France could only react to events, she could not take the initiative."[25]

Germany, on the other hand, was taking the initiative. Hitler was reconstructing his military. In 1935, he reasserted control over the Saar. In 1936, Hitler remilitarized the Rhineland. He commented, "If the French had then marched into the Rhineland we would have had to withdraw with our tails between our legs, for the military resources at our disposal would have been wholly inadequate for even a moderate resistance." By 1936, however, the French were unwilling to contemplate a new conflict. Fabry admitted, "from the point of view of material, Germany is on the verge of surpassing us." France was suffering from a weakening economy and a financial crisis. The U.S. embassy cabled to Washington, "France wants peace, fears war, does not conceal that fear, and will be forced to take the consequences."[26]

French leaders abandoned hopes of constraining Germany. Yet French strategy was thrown further into disarray when King Leopold III returned Belgium to neutrality by revoking the Franco-Belgian Treaty. The French minister of war asserted, "Have no fears. . . . We shall make sure the North will never be invaded and occupied again. Our frontier shall be inviolable." And Popular Front leader Léon Blum insisted, "France does not tremble in the face of war." The unavoidable reality, however, was that German military manpower was increasing rapidly. Yearly conscription classes were over 450,000 men for Germany and under 200,000 men for France. France was losing allies, while Germany expanded its population, territory, and military. In 1936, the French Higher Military Committee was informed that "Germany was on the point of overtaking [France] outright." Herriot warned that if negotiations with Germany failed, "There would be only one recourse left, . . . an armaments race. . . . Germany's chances, with its dense population, with its heavy industry . . . Imagine what the relative situation of the two countries would become."[27]

By 1938, French leaders recognized the shadow of war. Daladier predicted, "we risk becoming, after the Czechs, after the Poles, the prey of the Reich." Gamelin asked whether "France wishes to renounce its status as a European Great Power and abandon to Germany hegemony of not only central but all of eastern Europe." He warned Daladier that France must resist Germany or risk becoming a "second class power" within a decade. A French diplomat similarly commented that France "cannot retreat any more": "we have reached the extreme limit at which the slightest hesitation, the weakness would bring disaster." But French leaders had no appetite for initiating a conflict. U.S. Treasury Secretary Henry Morgenthau asked, "Who, in France, would have imagined in 1930 that in less than 10 years this great democratic nation would become a second-rate power."[28]

As World War II approached, conflict with Germany appeared unavoidable. But Georges Bonnet admitted, "If France declared war against Germany her position would be weaker than at any time since 1919." Germany fielded 1,400 bombers, 342 dive-bombers, 1,000 fighters, and 500 reconnaissance and scout planes. This compared to just 175 bombers, 54 dive-bombers, 700 fighters, and 400 reconnaissance and scout planes for France, plus a British force of 220 bombers, 130 fighters, and 50 reconnaissance and scout aircraft in France. France, therefore, "found herself in the war she had dreaded for so long, with no allies but Britain and Poland, Belgium neutral and the Maginot Line incomplete be-tween Longwy and the sea, her Army strong on paper but weak in fact, her Air Force hopelessly outclassed, and the nation di-vided." Five days after the war began, Premier Paul Reynaud ad-mitted to Churchill, "We are beaten; we have lost the battle." France's slow decline took decades, but its final defeat took only days.[29]

Defense Strategy: Defensive

French strategy was offensively oriented through most of the 1920s but shifted rapidly after 1927. This is not to say that defen-sive strategies were entirely ignored earlier. After the Franco-Prussian War, General Séré de Rivières noted the possibilities of "a barrier stretching from Calais to Nice." Military leaders again argued for defensive approaches and fortifications in the aftermath of World War I. Indeed, France initiated a study of defensive orga-nization, which was later presented by the Frontier Defense Com-mission. But leaders such as Ferdinand Foch and Joseph Joffre "were unwilling to translate this experience into an endorsement of defensive over offensive tactics and operations."[30]

It was not until the late 1920s that defensive arguments truly gained ground. In 1927, France launched an Organizing Commis-sion for Fortified Regions. In 1928, the French Army stated, "The military organization of the country has as its essential objective the safeguarding of the integrity of the national territory." Over the next decade, France adopted five defensive war plans, named Plan B, Plan C, Plan D, Plan E, and Plan F. French leaders systematically abandoned offensive notions and chose to emphasize the defensive value of fortifications. Posen notes, "Stationary, defensive, attrition warfare, waged in the company of a powerful coalition, was both the French fear and the French aim."[31]

Scholars are divided on the cause of this defensive shift. Elizabeth Kier argues that domestic and organizational constraints altered the army's ambitions. She notes, "the French army's endorsement of a defensive doctrine after 1929 is partly attributable to its being part of [a] larger package that allowed the army to retain what it most treasured, a small (and relatively autonomous) professional force." She suggests that Paris was weak relative to Berlin throughout the interwar period, so she discounts the possibility that the balance of power was responsible for the shift in French strategy. As evidence, Kier notes that a 1920s report suggested, "An offensive conception is the only one that would permit us to compensate for the inescapable causes of our weakness, which result from the inferiority of our population and industrial strength." Kier concludes, "The French army switched to a defensive doctrine long before Germany began to rearm. ... The French army did not connect the rise of German power with the adoption of a defensive doctrine."[32]

The argument presented here focuses not on relative power levels but on perceived relative power trends. French perceptions of relative power trends deteriorated rapidly in the late 1920s. This in turn drove French leaders to abandon their more expansive objectives and offensive strategy. It is true that this change predated German rearmament, but by the late 1920s, relative power trends were evident as demographic realities took hold, reparations declined, occupation ended, and alliances withered. French leaders recognized these changes at the exact moment that they began to consider more defensive strategies. The historian Judith Hughes notes that "discussions of military policy in 1928 and 1929 were suffused with such an awareness. Even those who for a decade had been staunch advocates of safeguarding their country's armed strength now echoed the defensive commonplaces of the ideological opponents."[33]

The strategic logic of a more defensive approach aligned with domestic constraints. France's manpower shortage had worsened its military position. In 1930, General Antoine Targe admitted, "Only a professional army could go beyond our frontiers. . . . A militia army is apt for the defensive at prepared positions, but is not apt for maneuver." As a result, French "forces were capable of exclusively defensive action." Posen explains, "The French Army accepted a defensive doctrine because it reduced uncertainty in three ways. First, it helped the army protect what it perceived to be a vulnerable political position. ... Second, a defensive doctrine would allow the army to fight the kind of battle it had learned to fight. ... Third, French officers distrusted the military skills and morale of one-year conscripts." Hughes notes, "The French had relinquished the notion of maintaining on active service a superior military force, and while this shift in power justified and stimulated the construction of fortifications, concrete bastions could not reestablish the preponderance that had existed in the immediate postwar years."[34]

France's defensive strategy had several elements. Fortifications would strengthen French defenses by helping to "protect the frontiers against a surprise attack, ... protect the frontiers during the vital three weeks needed for mobilization, ... provide a core for resistance and ... ensure the integrity of the nation and its industrial potential." But France still needed an army capable of waging a defensive campaign. A retired French officer argued, "The part played by the passive defense of the frontier must always be much less than that of the active defense. ... Let's remember that, much more than the expensive permanent works of fortification, success in the event of war will be found once again in a good all-round preparation of the army." Unfortunately, by the mid-1930s, the French Army was not up to this task.[35]

A defensive strategy had serious implications for France's allies. French leaders refused to expend their limited resources to build fortifications on the French-Belgian border. Maginot noted, "it is not possible decently to construct a strong defensive system opposite the territory of this friendly nation." Yet, this would inevitably draw Germany into Belgium. The Frontier Defense Commission acknowledged, "The fortified regions might possibly, or even probably, divert the attack toward Belgium." Yet, this seemed a better choice than allowing Germany to invade France directly. The École Supérieure de Guerre noted that a defensive strategy would "elicit military contributions from France's allies at a minimum cost to France." The Belgian ambassador to Paris warned against using "Belgian bodies alone to oppose the march of Germany" and suggested that it would be imprudent for France to leave its "northern door wide open." But Gamelin privately insisted, "If one considers the devastation that a modern battle entails in the region where it takes place, isn't this argument even more convincing?"[36]

Meanwhile, the Ardennes also went unfortified. French General Charles Lanrezac had earlier said that the Ardennes was "imminently suitable for the defensive and for ambushes": "you will not enter into this region and if you do you will not return from it." Military experts believed that the Ardennes was "un-tankable." Pétain himself noted in 1934, "Beginning at Montmédy are the Ardennes forests. They are impenetrable. . . . The enemy will not deploy there. If he should, we shall close the pincers as he emerges from the forests. This sector, therefore, is not dangerous." French weakness in this sector would later allow Hitler to bypass the Maginot Line and strike directly into the heart of the small, immobile, and poorly trained French Army.[37]

By 1935, the offensive had been bled from the French psyche. General Louis Maurin wondered, "Would we be mad enough to advance beyond this barrier upon goodness knows what adventure!" He would later ask, "How can anyone believe that we are still thinking of an offensive, when we have spent billions on setting up a fortified barrier." In 1936, Gamelin insisted, "The Quai d'Orsay must understand that the present organization of our army is such that, without mobilization, we can occupy our defensive lines, stop an attack, but any offensive action in enemy country is out of the question." This left Paris unable to respond when Berlin remilitarized the Rhineland. French generals told political leaders, "The idea of sending quickly into the Rhineland a French expeditionary force, even if only a token force, was a chimera." Churchill later reflected, "If the French government had mobilized, there is no doubt that Hitler would have been compelled by his own General Staff to withdraw, and a check would have been given to his pretensions which might well have proved fatal to his rule."[38]

This failure prompted French leaders "to conduct a kind of stock taking in the second half of 1936," in the words of the historian Robert Young. The main critic of the defensive approach was

Charles de Gaulle. De Gaulle recognized the need for mechanized forces. He commented that "modern offensive techniques are alone capable of effectively collaborating with an ally in peril." Martin Alexander writes, "De Gaulle envisaged two parallel paths of development for the army. The first demanded a massive expansion of mobile automotive forces and their permanent peacetime establishment as a trained and homogenous shock force. The second was the manning of this battle group or 'ready force' solely by professional career soldiers." Yet De Gaulle's offensive dreams were unpalatable to political leaders. Gamelin noted that French politicians "conceived of only a war thrust upon [France], therefore a defensive one." Daladier underscored the point, saying, "We shall make defensive war. We will not have the French people slaughtered."[39]

The French Army did not change its strategy even after watching Polish defenses fail in 1939. French General Paul Armengaud observed the German onslaught and warned, "It would be mad not to draw an exact lesson" about France's vulnerability. But others commented, "We did not ask for this war. . . . Now that the Polish question is liquidated we have gone back to our lines. What else did you expect?" And General Maxime Weygand took the opposite lesson, that "greater strength [was] required for attack than for the defense, particularly with the help of modern defensive weapons." So did General Narcisse Chauvineau, who remained insistent that "for the attack, three times as much infantry, six times the artillery and fifteen times the ammunition are necessary than for the defense." Hitler, on the other hand, was confident of victory, announcing, "I shall maneuver France right out of her Maginot Line without losing a single soldier." When the invasion finally came, Weygand lamented, "We have gone to war with a 1918 army against a German Army of 1939."[40]

Defense Investments: Immobile

With France's defensive strategy in place, the French Army began to shift toward an immobile posture after 1927. France's embrace of immobile investments flowed directly from the consolidation of its objectives as Germany rose. Maginot argued, "concrete is better . . . and is less expensive than a wall of chests" for stopping an invasion.

Investments in the Maginot Line were huge, crowding out spending on mobile forces. The biggest forts cost roughly 150 million francs, with middle-sized forts costing 50 to 90 million francs and smaller outposts 5 to 20 million francs. All told, approximately 375 million francs were devoted to the Maginot Line from 1927 to 1929, 750 million between 1929 and 1934, and another 750 million from 1934 to 1938.[41]

Defensive fortifications evolved rapidly during this period. Early plans saw fortifications as a jumping-off point for a counter-invasion. Minister of War Paul Painlevé commented in 1928, "Our scheme is a combination of two plans. The first is a sort of continuous front line, an organized trench system of concrete and steel, whilst the second is a series of regional strongholds." The French Army planned to use more mobile forces "to compensate for what, by definition, the Line lacked—mobility." Three types of forts would be created, with the largest housing twelve hundred soldiers. Those forts included guns as large as 135 millimeters, hidden in steel turrets sunk into the ground. But as more of France's funds went toward pouring concrete, there was little money left for mobile forces and still not enough to fortify the entire front. Jean Fabry argued that "no part of French territory should be undefended against invasion." But facing severe resource constraints, the army chose to prioritize the Franco-German border.[42]

By the early 1930s, French leaders had all but abandoned the concept of mobile forces. Gamelin noted, "Everything has changed. It is no longer a question of mobile equipment, but instead, the organization of a barrier." De Gaulle warned in 1934 that a passive and defensive army would be "surprised, immobilized and outflanked." But a mobile force would have required greatly increased spending, which was politically impossible. Daladier flatly refused, noting, "Financial considerations must take precedence over military policy. A balanced budget is the best guarantee of national security." Meanwhile, the German military developed its new shock tactics. In 1935, General Maurin explained that France might suffer a rapid "breakthrough by armored and motorized units moving through the breach at hitherto unknown speed and dislocating [French] mobilization centers whilst the enemy air forces . . . sealed off the battle zone to prevent the arrival of [French] reserves." But by this point, there was no appetite for investments in new mobile forces, which did not fit France's new defensive strategy. Instead, French leaders suggested that even more money be spent on fortifications.[43]

This is not to suggest that France entirely abandoned mobility—indeed it retained large numbers of tanks—but the clear focus of its military investments was immobile fortifications. Gamelin remarked in 1936 that evidence from Spain showed that German tanks had been "fit only for the scrap-heap" and insisted, "it is our doctrine which is correct." He maintained, "You cannot hope to achieve real breakthroughs with tanks. The tank is not independent enough. It has to go ahead, but then must return for fuel and supplies." French instructions warned, "it cannot be emphasized too strongly that today the antitank weapon is to the tank what the machine gun was to the infantry during the World War." Gamelin concurred that "the antitank weapon has caused the renunciation of [large tank units]": "just because the Germans have committed an enormous error does not mean we must do the same." Daladier noted that in Spain, tanks were "pierced like sieves," and the war "had seen the crumbling of immense hopes based on certain machines." He claimed, "our fortified works are sufficiently equipped to halt a sudden attack even on Sunday."[44]

Not only were the French caught off guard by the effectiveness of the tank, but they were also ill prepared for aerial warfare. French plans suggested, "The Maginot Line will play a leading part, therefore, in the defense against aerial attack. But it will be reinforced by a veritable Maginot Line in the air." Yet, Air Minister Pierre Cot exclaimed, "We will end up by having the weakest air force because we have spent so little." When war came, France had only 1,254 aircraft to 3,228 for Germany. Even worse was the operational use of the French Air Force, which was left largely separate from the ground forces. A 1937 instruction advised, "It is convenient to leave to the Air Force commanders the initiative for launching their attack." The Germans, on the other hand, closely integrated the Luftwaffe with their ground forces, creating a true combined-arms capability. French leaders did not think doing so was necessary, since they expected to wear down the Germans by repelling their attacks on static French fortifications.[45]

By the late 1930s, French leaders had entirely abandoned mobility. In 1936, Minister of War Fabry noted, "Germany is on the verge of surpassing us; thus our superiority rests . . . on our fortifications." Unfortified areas, including in northern France, would be abandoned at the outset of a conflict. General Émile Ricard later explained, "effective protection for this part of the front would have demanded an effort truly disproportionate to the means we possessed." Instead, French forces prepared to move into Belgium and build field fortifications there in the event of a conflict. French immobility carried even into North Africa, where a "chain of forts, protected by lines of trenches, ensures the protection of the French African frontier."[46]

French and German assessments of the benefits of mobility diverged during this period. Hitler was confident that warfare had changed, noting, "The next war will be quite different from the last world war. Infantry attacks and mass formations are obsolete. Interlocked frontal struggles lasting for years on petrified fronts will not return." Meanwhile, the French inspector-general of tanks remained optimistic that France could prevail "even supposing that the present fortified lines were breached or outflanked." Another member of the French General Staff commented, "the tank is finished as an offensive weapon." Instead, the French Army invested in infantry and artillery. A 1937 instruction directed that the infantry be "entrusted with the principal duty in battle. Protected and accompanied by its own guns and by the guns of the artillery, and occasionally preceded by combat tanks and aviation, etc., it conquers the ground, occupies it, organizes, and holds it."[47]

Believing in the benefits of immobile fortifications, France helped its eastern allies construct limited defenses. In Czechoslovakia, the defenses were particularly substantial. German General Erich von Manstein said, "had Czechoslovakia defended herself, we would have been held up by her fortifications, for we did not have the means to break through." Hitler too noted, "When after Munich we were in a position to examine Czechoslovak military strength from within, what we saw of it greatly disturbed us; we had run a serious danger." When attacking France, Germany therefore sought "a solution elsewhere" rather than directly attacking the Maginot Line. The Ardennes provided the solution. The

French were not so badly outnumbered as to make victory impossible. When war finally came, Germany mobilized 135 divisions against France, which fielded 94 divisions (alongside 10 British divisions). But the German forces included 10 armored divisions, compared to only 3 for the French. Germany's victory was thus enabled by the lack of fortifications in the Ardennes, the poor quality of the troops located there, and the few mobile forces available to reinforce gaps in the line.[48]

After the war, Marc Bloch reflected, "If we were short on tanks, aeroplanes, and tractors, it was mainly because we had put our not inexhaustible supplies of money and labor into concrete. . . . We had been taught to put our whole trust in the Maginot Line . . . only to see it turned, and even pierced, on the Rhine for the simple reason that it had been allowed to stop short on our left flank." British General Alan Brooke commented "that the French would have done better to invest the money in the shape of mobile defenses such as more and better aircraft and more heavy armored divisions rather than to sink all this money into the ground." Thus, as Stanley Hoffmann concluded, "The declining Third Republic was blamed for its growing short-sightedness and isolation, its devotion to a policy of defense behind an illusory fortified barrier." As Hughes explains, "from the outset fortifications were a confirmation of the army's weakened state, a sign of the altered military balance between France and Germany."[49]

Assessment

France learned the value of defensive approaches in World War I and went into World War II with a defensive strategy. It would be only natural to assume that French leaders maintained a defensive approach throughout the interwar period. For most of the 1920s, however, France embraced offense. As Adamthwaite notes, "It is not true to say that the French army had no offensive plans against Germany. Until 1926, military planning provided for a strong attack against Germany, using the Rhineland as a springboard. The decision to build fortifications was not taken until the end of 1927."[50]

Many structural and cultural explanations struggle to account for the rapid changes in French objectives, strategy, and investments that occurred in the interwar years. Domestic and organizational explanations have therefore attracted substantial interest. Elizabeth Kier argues, "French civilians responded to domestic, not international, threats." Eugenia Kiesling finds that the army was pushed to adopt a defensive strategy because it "had to create the safest possible doctrine, one designed to win a defensive war, using the short service conscript army that French citizens were willing to provide." But critics such as Douglas Porch insist that this "ignores the possibility that France's doctrine may have been a rational response to France's external circumstances." Michael Desch also concludes that "French military doctrine clearly reflected Europe's changing balance of power. . . . The reasons France made the fateful strategic decisions it did actually had little to do with the domestic political crisis of the Third Republic." And even Kier admits, "France's position in the international system changed from the 1920s to the 1930s."[51]

The evidence presented here supports the theory that changes in French defense policies were caused in large part by changing perceptions of relative power trends. This shift correlated directly with French defense reforms. As Kier herself notes, "There does seem to be a powerful correlation between German power and French doctrine. When Germany was relatively weak in the 1920s, the French army had an offensive orientation; when Germany was strong in the 1930s, the French army had a defensive doctrine." France adopted an offensive strategy for multiple reasons, but the central driver was a strategic logic rooted in perceptions of relative power. Leaders in Paris viewed France as strong relative to Germany in the first half of the interwar period and prioritized maintaining the ability to force Berlin to abide by the Treaty of Versailles. A defensive approach reliant on massive fortifications could not accomplish this goal.[52]

By the late 1920s, however, France was forced to consolidate its objectives and adopt a defensive strategy and immobile investments. General Victor Bourret commented, "Our moral position, our political, geographical, demographical and financial position, made not only aggression but even the initiative in attack absolutely impossible. . . . The army corresponding to our policy could only be one organized for an initial defensive." Adamthwaite assesses that "France lacked the inherent stamina needed to sustain a great power role." Daladier lamented, "there could be no greater tragedy than to see one's country, through a falling birth rate, the slowing down of production, disordered finances and the undermining of its currency, running the risk of sinking to a second class power." By 1937, an estimate of "world war potential" suggested that Germany controlled 14.4 percent, the United Kingdom 10.2 percent, and France just 4.2 percent. The French politician Yvon Delbos admitted, "it was clear that France was no longer strong enough to maintain the status quo in Central Europe."[53]

Thus, this case provides evidence for Hypotheses 2, 4, and 6. French leaders recognized the Republic's decline relative to Germany, but they were unable to devise policies that could deter or defend against the German onslaught. France's time in the sun had passed. Other factors played a role as well, including the army's sclerotic, anti-intellectual, and stove-piped culture, which played a major part in France's stunning defeat. In announcing the French surrender, Pétain commented, "Less strong than we were 22 years ago, we also had fewer friends. Too few children, too few weapons, too few allies: these are the causes of our defeat."[54]

CHAPTER SIX

Japan's Decline

In the first six to twelve months of a war with the United
States and Great Britain I will run wild and win victory upon
victory. But then, if the war continues after that, I have no
expectation of success.

If we should go to war against the United States we must
recognize the fact that the armistice will have to be dictated
from the White House.

—ADMIRAL ISOROKU YAMAMOTO (1941)

JAPAN WAS ONE OF the world's fastest rising powers for much of the
early twentieth century. After winning the Russo-Japanese War,
Japan joined World War I's victors and acquired German territories
in East Asia. Over the next several decades, Japan engaged in "perpetual expansion of the perimeter of defense," in the words of the
historian Louise Young. The Imperial Army pushed for territorial
expansion, but the Imperial Navy came to believe this would trigger
a war with the United States. Japanese officials worried that the empire would lose a prolonged war, since they assessed that the United
States had ten times Japan's war-production potential. H. P. Will-

mott writes that the navy appreciated "the realities of power and Japan's strength" but nevertheless concluded that since "war was inevitable, . . . it was better that war came sooner rather than later."[1]

When war came, Japan's initial successes could not disguise the relative power imbalance. Japan built four million tons of shipping during the war but lost nearly nine million tons. This cut its merchant fleet from over six million tons in 1941 to just under two million tons by 1945. Japan built 16 aircraft carriers, 2 battleships, 9 cruisers, 63 destroyers, and 126 submarines during the war but lost 12 aircraft carriers, 4 battleships, 23 cruisers, 61 destroyers, and 59 submarines in 1944 alone. Meanwhile, the U.S. Navy commissioned 18 fleet carriers, 9 light carriers, 77 escort carriers, 8 battleships, 13 heavy cruisers, 33 light cruisers, 349 destroyers, 420 destroyer escorts, and 203 submarines. As Japan's leaders had foreseen, the empire could not compete with the scale of U.S. manufacturing, particularly given Japan's restricted access to oil, ore, and rubber.[2]

This chapter examines Japanese defense policies from 1935 to 1945. During this time, Japanese leaders perceived two shifts in the empire's relative power. Many leaders in Tokyo believed that Japan was a strong and rising power through the early months of World War II. But after the battles at Midway and Guadalcanal in 1942, it became clear that Japan was declining. And by 1944, it was apparent to Japanese leaders that the empire was weak compared to the United States. This case assesses Japanese defense policies during both of these shifts, focusing primarily on the second transition, during which Japan declined from a position of strength to one of weakness.

This case is in some ways unique because it is the only one that involves changes in both relative power trends and levels and also occurs amid a world war. Perceived relative power theory makes three claims about states moving from Phase 3 to Phase 4. Hypothesis 1 predicts a shift from extensive to limited objectives. Hypothesis 3 predicts a change from control to denial strategies. And Hypothesis 5 predicts investments in expendable systems. Thus, Japan should have jettisoned its power-projection strategy around 1942 and adopted an area-denial strategy around 1944. Indeed, Japanese leaders reshaped their defense policies in ways that largely align with these predictions. That this transition occurred rapidly amid a major war helps to establish the conditions under which perceived relative power theory holds.

Japanese Defense Policies Pre-1942

Japan's emergence as a regional power in the late nineteenth century represented the fastest ascendance of an Asian power in centuries. Before the Meiji Restoration, Japan had been a relatively weak and inward-looking state, invading the Asian continent only twice. Yet Japan's insularity evaporated as its power rose. Michael Barnhart argues, "Japan pursued the status of a great power through expansion abroad and reform at home." After signing the Anglo-Japanese alliance in 1902 and triumphing over Russia in 1905, Japan found itself the strongest power in Asia. Determined to continue this rise, one nationalist wrote, "If the sun is not ascending, it is descending. . . . Japan must conquer Korea, Manchuria, and Russia's Kamchatka peninsula or else be conquered itself." Thus, many leaders in Tokyo saw "expansion as a prerequisite for self-defense," as Jack Snyder writes. Yet these efforts came at a cost. By 1934, Foreign Minister Kōki Hirota warned the Japanese Diet, "The path of a rising nation is always strewn with problems." Indeed, the years ahead would be difficult. Through 1942, however, Japanese leaders still believed Tokyo was relatively strong. As a result, they adopted extensive objectives, a control strategy, and sustainable military investments.[3]

Defense Objectives: Extensive

Beginning in the early 1900s, Japanese leaders believed they were in a relatively strong position. Japan embraced the Meiji-era slogan "rich country, strong army," and its leaders exhibited a "growing recognition of the relationship between imperial expansion and national power." This led Japanese leaders to espouse goals that were ambitious in both scope and scale. In particular, Tokyo sought to exercise substantial authority over a considerable colonial empire. Japan adopted extensive defense objectives, ruthlessly exercising its authority across East Asia.[4]

Through the 1930s, many leaders in Tokyo were optimistic in their assessment of relative power levels and trends. Japanese conquests on mainland Asia accreted more power to Tokyo. But Japanese leaders worried that they did not have reliable access to sufficient amounts of oil, ore, and rubber. Fearing another war with Russia or a conflict with the United States, the Japanese sought access to resources abroad. After all, "neither the home islands nor the empire in Formosa, Korea, and south Sakhalin could provide resources sufficient for waging modern war. The control of richer territories, such as China, was imperative." The Marco Polo Bridge incident provided the rationale for "a comprehensive productive power expansion plan." In the mid-1930s, Lieutenant General Sadao Araki urged a total mobilization plan. Soon the Imperial Army was enlarged to 41 divisions and 142 air groups. Critics worried that Japan's extensive objectives would prove too costly. Major General Kanji Ishiwara, for example, predicted that China would be for Japan "what Spain was for Napoleon, . . . an endless bog." Indeed, within a year, there were one and a half million Japanese troops in China. But Japanese leaders persisted.[5]

The response from abroad was critical. President Franklin Roosevelt asserted that "the epidemic of world lawlessness is spreading" and suggested "a quarantine . . . to protect the community against the spread of disease." But Imperial Japan would not be contained. In 1938, the government nearly doubled military spending compared to the prior year. Meanwhile, Hachirō Arita, originator of the Greater East Asia Co-Prosperity Sphere, called for Japanese access to resources "in territory from which she could not be cut off by belligerent action of third powers." At the time, Japan relied on foreign imports for 88 percent of steel, 90 percent of petroleum, 99 percent of wool, 100 percent of cotton, 100 percent of rubber, and nearly 100 percent of alloy metals. The United States accounted for roughly 25 percent of Japanese imports and exports, including 78 percent of its oil imports. At the time, Manchuria accounted for 14 percent of Japan's trade, Kwantung-leased territory for 12 percent, and the rest of China for 10 percent. Arita hoped these and other Japanese colonies could supply Japan in a conflict.[6]

By the early 1940s, Japan's extensive objectives abroad put it on a collision course with the United States. Japan signed the Tripartite

Pact with Germany and Italy. Then Japan occupied French Indo-China. In response, U.S. ambassador to Japan Joseph Grew testified, "the time had come to consider, not whether we must call a halt to Japan's expansion, but when." The State Department concluded, "Japan's aim is to create an economic empire in the Far East which will be self-sufficient and capable of resisting the application of sanctions by any power or group of powers." To forestall this possibility, sanctions were enacted in the hope that Japan would be unable to arm itself. Secretary of State Cordell Hull advised Roosevelt, "speak softly ... while simultaneously giving by our acts in the Pacific new glimpses of diplomatic, economic, and naval 'big sticks.' " Roosevelt provided a glimpse of the United States' financial power when he issued an executive order freezing Japanese assets in the United States. The State Department asserted that it was "in a position to wreck completely the economic structure of the Japanese Empire."[7]

U.S. policies only reinforced Japan's drive for autarky. Hideki Tojo later commented, "the economic blockage resorted to constitutes a measure little less hostile in character than armed warfare." Japanese ambassador Kichisaburo Nomura warned, "If the United States refuses to sell us oil and other supplies, we must get them elsewhere." As Harold Feis writes, "the oil gauge and the clock stood side by side." Nomura asked Hull why the United States, "advocating as she does the Monroe Doctrine and holding as a matter of fact the leadership of the American continent, should interfere so much in Asiatic affairs." By 1941, however, 62 percent of Americans wished "to keep Japan from becoming more powerful, even if this means risking war."[8]

Tojo and other military leaders preferred that Japan fight sooner rather than later. They thought that Japan was relatively strong but that its warfighting ability would decline if it could not secure the resources necessary to make war. General Rikichi Tsukada urged, "We just can't maintain the status quo, so there is only one conclusion: we must go to war. ... This is the moment!" Admiral Osami Nagano, chief of the Imperial Japanese Navy General Staff, warned, "With each day we will get weaker and weaker. ... Thus our only recourse is to forge ahead!" He insisted, "If we do not fight now, our nation will perish. But it may well perish even if we do fight. It must be understood that national ruin without resistance would be ignominy." Admiral Hirayasu Fushimi lamented, "If war breaks out, Japan will lose all that has been achieved since the beginning of the Meiji Era. But it seems that there is no way to avoid war." Tojo likewise insisted, "There are times when we must have the courage to do extraordinary things—like jumping, with eyes closed, off the veranda of the Kiyomizu Temple."[9]

Civilian leaders were more divided. Prime Minister Fumimaro Konoe urged caution in the face of the United States' material superiority. Kōichi Kido, Lord Keeper of the Privy Seal, also reckoned, "war with the U.S.A. would offer little chance of our victory, so we had better reconsider it." But Tojo responded, "Your view is too pessimistic. You know our weak points too well. . . . America has her weaknesses too." Indeed, many Japanese thought the United States was strategically and culturally encumbered. Back in Washington, Ambassador Nomura wrote, "America is confronted with the European war on one hand, and the Pacific question on the other, but she has yet many strategically weak points." A 1935 Japanese War Ministry pamphlet noted that "Western nations" had developed "individualistic" civilizations that would limit their fighting abilities. Furthermore, Admiral Nobutake Kondo later commented, "we had some information which indicated our superiority to the potential enemy in skillfulness of operations." As Lieutenant General Torashiro Kawabe stated, "We believed that our spiritual convictions and moral strength could balance your material and scientific advantages." In short, many Japanese leaders "believed that mechanical inferiority could be covered by the troops' efficiency and the men's mental strength." These factors were included in relative power assessments.[10]

Military leaders hoped to knock the United States out of the war early or at least to construct an impermeable defensive perimeter. Admiral Nagumo advised, "If we assure our strategic position from the start, by attacking all the important points and seizing them before America is ready, we can tilt the balance in our favor." Finally, after years of discussion and debate, the Imperial Conference endorsed this plan on September 6, 1941. The Emperor concluded, "Concerning the prospects of the negotiations with America I fear that, to my great regret, we are now confronted by the worst stage." He decided that there was "no alternative but to take the initiative in operations." Later, just days before the attack on Pearl Harbor, the Emperor questioned whether Japan's "material strength . . . will stand a protracted war or not." He asked his military commanders, "Will you win a great victory? Like the Battle of Tsushima?" Yet he was told that this was not possible. The Emperor commented, "Then the war will be a desperate one." When he asked how long the war would take and noted that the army had promised that the invasion of China "would only be three months," Army Chief of Staff General Hajime Sugiyama responded, "China is bigger than we thought." The Emperor noted, "The Pacific is also big." On December 1, 1941, Kido, the Emperor's closest adviser, recorded simply, "at last war of Japan on the U.S.A. was decided." He wrote, "our country is going to enter upon war against America and Britain, the two greatest powers in the world."[11]

Ambassador Grew had cautioned that Japan was "capable of sudden and surprise action" and had "a determination to risk all." He had warned of the potential for an "all-out, do-or-die attempt, actually risking national hara-kiri." And Secretary of State Hull had told Secretary of War Stimson of the failure of negotiations and stated, "I have washed my hands of it, and it is now in the hands of you and Knox—the army and the navy." Yet the United States was still surprised by Japan's audacity. The strike on Pearl Harbor had its intended military effect. Although U.S. carriers were out of port, the battleship losses crippled the U.S. Pacific Fleet, and Japan lost just 29 aircraft compared to 150 aircraft for the United States. Nomura wrote, "The competency and boldness of our naval officers and sailors as demonstrated in the surprised attack on Hawaii and the sinking of the two British battleships have startled the world."[12]

Japanese optimism peaked in the six months that followed. Japan took only days to capture Guam, land in the Philippines, seize Wake Island, and invade Thailand and British territories in Asia. Ten days after the war began, Japanese forces were on the march and winning on every front. According to one account, "The Japanese had expected to suffer between twenty and thirty percent ship losses in the conquest of the Dutch East Indies. In fact, only twenty-three warships, and all these of classes below that of destroyer, had been sunk." One observer writes, "Encouraged by these results, the Japanese leaders decided to speed up their strategic advances, instead of consolidating their conquests as they might have been expected to do. This meant continued enlargement of their defense perimeter through new conquests." Japanese successes resulted in "victory disease."[13]

By early 1942, "the Japanese people were intoxicated with the idea that their nation was invincible." Paul Dull notes that "victories had come so fast and with so few losses that they actually outpaced the planning of the Imperial General Headquarters and the staffs of the Army and Navy." Japanese leaders extended their original plans as "victory fever made such steps seem not only possible, but inevitable." Admiral Matome Ugaki wrote, "the future is filled with brightness." Japanese assessments of relative power had reached their zenith, and Japan's aims were at their maximum in both scope and scale.[14]

Defense Strategy: Control

Japan's extensive objectives mandated a strategy oriented around territorial and maritime control. The desire to expand Japanese control to form a defensive position was a continuation of long-standing policy. In the decades prior to World War II, the Japanese colonial expire was enlarged by force and treaty, growing to include Formosa, Korea, South Sakhalin, various South Pacific islands, Manchuria, and other areas. Tokyo required a strategy that could maintain control of these locations and ensure that resources from these colonies flowed back to Japan.

Japan's extensive aims therefore required control of the sea. To obtain it, one historian notes, "the Imperial Navy was committed to a doctrine of the offensive battle with the U.S. Pacific Fleet." The naval strategist Tetsutarō Satō identified the "advantage of an ocean-oriented aggressive (offensive) defense over a static land-oriented defense. . . . Control of the surrounding seas was all that mattered." The scholar Jisaburo Ozawa writes that Japan's approach was "to control the command of the sea in the Orient in order to secure the traffic between the Asia continent and the southern district. To invade Guam, . . . to invade the Philippines, . . . expecting to have the decisive sea battle somewhere from the Nansei Islands down to [the] east of the Philippines." Then Japan would shift to the strategic defensive to protect its position. Over time, Japanese leaders hoped to "seize key objectives and then use the power of the defense to defeat American counterattacks, which in turn would lead to a negotiated peace." Both strategies would require the control of territory, but the early approach would be offensive while the later effort would be more defensive.[15]

Admiral Nagano said he hoped Japan could "establish a strategically impregnable position." With this in mind, the Combined Fleet instructed in 1941, "Strategically important points shall be captured, expanded in area and strengthened in defensive forces in order to prepare for a prolonged war." In the first six months of the war, Japan gained nearly one and a half million square miles in territory. By early 1942, Japan had "gained control of the sea in the Southwest Pacific." James Wood writes that "Japanese forces had seized all the essential objectives needed to establish a new and expanded National Defense Zone. Losses had been minimal." Consolidating control and shifting to the defense had been Japanese strategy; but as the empire won battle after battle, Tokyo's aims continued to expand, and its strategy remained offensive. Vice Admiral Shigeyoshi Miwa pushed to expand the perimeter, noting, "We want to invade Ceylon; we are not allowed to! We want to invade Australia; we cannot! We want to attack Hawaii; we cannot do that either! All because the army will not agree to release the necessary forces." The attack on the Aleutian Islands and the ensuing operation against Midway, for example, went beyond Japan's initial war plans.[16]

As Japan struggled in 1942, however, the empire was forced to adopt a more defensive strategy—although one still predicated on maintaining territorial and maritime control. Japan lost many aircraft and pilots at Midway and in the Coral Sea. The navy had opted to train only a small number of pilots, since the navy had assumed that "it would fight a short, decisive war." Meanwhile, army leaders desired "time to consolidate the advantages they had already obtained—to fortify the territory they had captured and build a political and military structure capable of withstanding a long war." The army chief of staff warned, "the ratio of armament between Japan and the United States will become more and more unfavorable." A continued offensive "could only aggravate Japan's already difficult logistics problems and her number-to-space troubles." Therefore, Japan "was forced to take a defensive position geographically." Tojo declared, "measures shall be taken by seizing opportunities to expand our acquired war gains, and by building a political and military structure capable of withstanding a protracted war." But by mid-1942, Japan was shifting from a strategy of offensive control to one of defensive control.[17]

Defense Investments: Sustainable

Around the turn of the twentieth century, Japan invested in the traditional tools of power projection. The statesman Kinmochi Saionji warned, "The reason that Japan maintains her world power status is that she holds that baton of command with England and America. If Japan loses her grip like France and Italy, how will she develop as a world power?" Japanese leaders built a large army that could be sustained abroad for years. And the navy jettisoned its coastal-defense role and built an oceangoing battlefleet. Gone was the focus on the torpedo boat; now the navy began to build battleships that could be sustained through an engagement. Investments in sustainable systems would remain Japan's preference through 1942.[18]

Despite the similarity of Japan's ships to those of other great powers, the empire struggled to compete symmetrically. The Washington Naval Treaty restricted Japan to 60 percent of U.S. and British battleship and carrier construction. Moreover, the treaty imposed a ten-year building moratorium on battleships, each of which was limited to thirty-five thousand tons. The London Naval Treaty then applied the 60 percent limit to Japanese heavy cruisers, with a 70 percent ceiling for light cruisers and destroyers. This was deemed insufficient for Japan's aims. The naval strategist Satō concluded that a defending fleet needed 70 percent of the attacker's strength, based on research conducted at the Japanese Naval Staff College. Assuming that Japan could sit on the defense after an initial strike, leaders in Tokyo sought this margin. By 1937, Japan had withdrawn from the treaties and commenced unrestricted naval development. By 1941, Japan had amassed 10 battleships, 38 cruisers, 9 aircraft carriers, 112 destroyers, and 64 submarines. With this fleet in place, Imperial Navy estimates placed its relative strength vis-à-vis the U.S. Navy at exactly 70 percent.[19]

The Imperial Navy was composed specifically for "the annihilation of the United States Fleet." The Navy General Staff "divided their strategy into two parts: the attrition stage and the decisive battle." Attrition would bring the United States down to parity, but a decisive battle would still have to be fought to force a negotiated settlement. The desire for a decisive battle led to a focus on large surface ships over smaller vessels. Through the 1930s, Japanese leaders debated whether to invest in battleships or aircraft carriers. In 1934, the navy instructed, "battleship divisions are the main weapon in a fleet battle and their task is to engage the main force of the enemy." With this in mind, plans for the seventy-thousand-ton *Yamato* battleship were drafted. One scholar explains, "The demands of offensive action were for high speed, good maneuverability, long range and heavy payload; the demands of defensive warfare were for ruggedness of construction, the ability to take punishment, armor and heavy fire power. Defensive needs had been sacrificed to secure optimum performance in the attack."[20]

Aircraft carrier advocates did eventually gain traction. Early on, aircraft carriers had been seen as "playing a defensive role." This limited their value in the mind of many Japanese admirals. But as Mark Peattie observes, "despite the deeply rooted fixation of the Imperial Japanese Navy on warships as the decisive weapons of naval war, the navy's air war in China brought home to nearly all its leadership the tremendous offensive potential of aerial weapons." Furthermore, "fleet maneuvers made obvious the offensive potential of carrier aviation. ... Thus, Japanese navy leaders became convinced of the needs for more carriers." The vulnerability of battleships to aerial attack became apparent. Captain Takijiro Onishi observed, "Because battleships are fragile under enemy attack, it is wrong to make them the navy's main force. For our naval armament we should shift from battleships to land-based air power." In 1935, Admiral Yamamoto advised, "the practical value of battleships has declined," and asserted, "They retain their symbolism as an indicator of naval power. . . . Think of it is as a decoration."[21]

By the mid-1930s, "carrier aircraft had come to be viewed as instrumental in attacking capital ships themselves." Engineers designed carriers for "speed and ease of handling" to aid in offensive actions. And as Japan constructed larger and faster carriers, it also increased the size and payload of its carrier-based aircraft. Yet, unfortunately for the Imperial Navy, the naval treaties had limited the size and protection of Japanese aircraft carriers. As a result, a Japanese carrier "was splendid in projecting power at great distance but significantly inferior to its American counterpart in warding off an enemy counterstrike. . . . It could throw a punch but couldn't take one." For example, the *Kaga* went to sea with only sixteen fighter aircraft for defense, as opposed to forty-five torpedo bombers and thirty dive-bombers for offensive action. To make things worse, Admiral Nobumasa Suetsugu, commander in chief of the Combined Fleet, noted, "The Japanese Navy at present lags manifestly behind the American Navy in aviation and communications."[22]

Despite the Imperial Navy's shortcomings, Japan had a robust fleet of aircraft carriers and battleships at the outset of World War II. The navy's capital ships were designed to be sustained through a decisive battle, although they were oriented for offensive rather than defensive engagements. More expendable platforms, such as escort vessels and submarines, were to play a lesser role and accomplish secondary objectives. The navalist Atsushi Oi writes that defensive missions such as anti-invasion and shipping protection were given "slight importance." Submarine development focused on more sustainable long-range boats. Rear Admiral Nobumasa Suetsugu's first submarine division "was molded to support his vision of far-ranging offensive submarines," rather than more expendable, short-range systems for commerce raiding. Doctrinal innovations were also "directed toward fleet operations, not commerce raiding."[23]

Japan's battlefleet was oriented around sustaining offensive operations through early 1942. Japanese carrier aircraft had much greater range than their U.S. counterparts. U.S. aircraft searched up to 360 miles from their carrier, while Japanese aircraft ranged up to 560 miles away. Similarly, U.S. aircraft attacked at ranges around 250 miles, but their Japanese counterparts struck at distances up to 350 miles. These capabilities proved useful at Pearl Harbor and in the strikes that followed. But Japan's early successes evaporated as Midway and Guadalcanal sapped Japanese strength. Japan soon had to do away with its focus on sustainable systems. Unable to compete symmetrically with the United States, Japan would embrace expendability—to the horror of many people abroad.[24]

Japanese Defense Policies Post-1942

From 1942 onward, Japanese leaders perceived their power to be declining. Japan's worsening position was impossible to ignore as the empire's losses mounted. Initially, this resulted in a shift from power projection to garrison fortification. But by 1944, most leaders in Japan saw the empire as weak compared to the United States. Japanese leaders further scaled back Japan's objectives, strategy, and investments to accord with reality. By 1944, Japan adopted an area-denial approach. Leaders in Tokyo were forced to accept limited objectives, a denial strategy, and investments in expendable systems. The most difficult of these decisions was the pursuit of "special attack units"—those assigned suicide missions. Emperor Hirohito would later reflect, "The Special Attack operations were truly impossible to bear in terms of our natural human feelings but Japan having been put in an impossible position, those unreasonable measures were all that was left to us." Japan simply could not overcome the relative power disparity with the United States.[25]

Defense Objectives: Limited

Japan's early victories were short-lived. By the middle of 1942, the army and navy were struggling both in mainland Asia and in the Pacific. Meanwhile, Japan's need for a quick and decisive victory was becoming even more pressing. Japanese oil consumption exceeded expectations, while fields in Borneo, Java, and Sumatra produced just over half their prewar levels. Japanese oil reserves therefore disappeared in just two years. With this in mind, Admiral Yamamoto became "convinced that he must destroy the United

States fleet in 1942." Navy leaders suggested a plan to draw out the remainder of the U.S. Pacific Fleet by attacking Midway Island. Yamamoto hoped to "succeed in drawing out the enemy's carrier strength and destroying it in decisive battle." The Combined Fleet was ordered to Midway. But the United States' clandestine decoding of Japanese naval and diplomatic codes led to a shocking loss. This marked the beginning of Japan's military decline. Evan Thomas writes that the defeat "spelled the end of Yamamoto's efforts to sink the U.S. Navy before America became too strong for Japan. From now on, Japan would be on the defensive, slowly retreating across the Pacific."[26]

As the tide turned, Japanese leaders "withdrew to an inner defense line." A key point in this defensive line was Guadalcanal. Paul Dull writes, "Just as Midway was the turning point in the war at sea, Guadalcanal would be the turning point in the war on land." U.S. General Alexander Vandegrift noted this shift when he commented before the invasion of Guadalcanal, "we land in the first major offensive of this war." On the other side, Colonel Sako Tanemura wrote, "Today there is the impression that Japan is on the verge of rise or fall. . . . The fake pride of Imperial Headquarters is forcing us to wage the Decisive Battle on Guadalcanal." That battle proved unwinnable for Japan, in large part due to the logistical requirements. Although the Japanese fought desperately, only 20 percent of the supplies sent from the stronghold at Rabaul reached Japanese troops on Guadalcanal. Facing reality, Major General Kenryo Sato advised Tojo to withdraw from Guadalcanal, noting, "We have no choice. Even now it may be too late. If we go on like this, we have no chance of winning the war. . . . It will end up as a battle of attrition of our transports." The Emperor's imperial rescript after Guadalcanal led him to thank the navy for its "brave fight" but to warn that the situation would "become more and more difficult." Japan was forced to withdraw and consolidate its position.[27]

Guadalcanal and Midway signified the end of Japan's expansive aims and the extent of its power projection. Willmott notes, "The months from April to June 1942 represent the period when the imbalance of power that had previously favored the Japanese shifted." Now Japan had to adopt a war of attrition using a garrison-fortification approach. But the army was overstretched and struggling on multiple fronts. Meanwhile, the navy was running short on ships, aircraft, and pilots. The navy lost 38 percent of its aircraft in 1942 and 63 percent in 1943. These losses amounted to 7,820 aircraft—more than three times the number Japan had at the beginning of the war. Meanwhile, Japanese merchant shipping fell from 3,112,400 tons in April 1942 to 2,629,300 tons in February 1943. While the United States built 331 destroyer escorts in the first two years of the war, Japan built none. Admiral Nobutake Kondō would therefore note that Japan "had to aim at destroying the majority with the minority."[28]

As Japan declined, leaders in Tokyo attempted to consolidate their aims. By late 1942, it was clear that a staunch defense was the empire's only hope. Japanese leaders still hoped they could defend the remainder of the empire, but even this proved increasingly difficult. By early 1943, "only in Burma were faltering offensive operations still under way. . . . Victory fever had subsided, but the samurai spirit had not; now a determination to yield no more territory without making the enemy pay a tremendous price came to pervade Japanese strategic thinking." Japanese hopes were damaged further when Admiral Yamamoto was killed in April 1943. Amid domestic strife a decade earlier, Yamamoto had been seen as so important that he was sent to sea "purposefully because he would have been assassinated if he had stayed in Tokyo." Now, Admiral Miniuki Koga took over as commander in chief of the Combined Fleet. Upon assuming command, Koga noted, "There was only one Yamamoto and no one is able to replace him. His loss is an insupportable blow to us."[29]

Consolidating Japan's objectives meant forgoing any hope of additional expansion. But even this was not sufficient to stem Japan's decline. In 1943, the Emperor chastised Tojo, saying, "You keep repeating that the Imperial Army is invulnerable, yet whenever the enemy lands you lose the battle. You've never been able to repulse an enemy landing. Can't you do it somewhere?" Soon it became necessary to adopt limited objectives, even where Japan was still in control. The initiative was with the United States and its allies. Late in 1943, the allies decided to blockade Japan, capture advanced bases nearby, conduct strategic bombing from the second island chain, and then follow two routes to the Japanese home islands. The momentum had unmistakably shifted. Japanese leaders realized that the "defense perimeter could not be maintained at the extent originally planned." At the outset of the war, the Emperor had approved war plans despite the fact that "no long-term, concrete plan for guiding the war through its protracted stage existed." Now leaders in Tokyo recognized Japan's weakness but could do little to reverse it.[30]

By 1944, it was clear that Japan was no longer just declining but was now weak compared to the United States. The stronghold of Rabaul, Japan's chief fortified location in the South Pacific, became the focus of much attention. Tojo ordered, "Rabaul must be held without fail. It is the key to our barrier in this region," but he admitted to commanders, "Unfortunately, I cannot do much for you just now." Chihaya writes, "Japan, especially the Japanese Navy, did everything possible to reinforce Rabaul, . . . to pour into Rabaul as many weapons, ammunitions, and planes as possible until in February 1944 Japan at last was forced to give up maintaining the Rabaul area." Japanese leaders set a new "absolute" defense line from the Ogasawara Islands through the Marianas Islands to western New Guinea. This line "would be defended to the death." The Japanese commander in Saipan directed, "positions are to be defended to the bitter end, and unless he has other orders, every soldier must stand his ground." Nearly thirty thousand Japanese would die on the island over just three weeks. The U.S. figure was a little over three thousand killed. Even Japan's limited hopes of slowing the U.S. advance across the Pacific were proving impossible. By April 1945, Prime Minister Kantarō Suzuki openly noted that the United States was in an "advantageous position." This recognition of Japan's relative weakness was accompanied by even more limited goals in the last year of the war.[31]

Defense Strategy: Denial

As Japan's power declined and its leaders' aims contracted, Tokyo shifted from a control strategy to a denial strategy. Early in the war, the difficulty of exercising total control had been made clear by the Doolittle raid on Tokyo. Commenting on the attack, Admiral Matome Ugaki said, "Our homeland has been air raided and we missed the enemy without firing a shot at him." One scholar notes that Doolittle "forced the Japanese high command to face up to the reality that their conquests could not be secured, that the safety of the homeland could not be guaranteed, and that the peoples of Southeast Asia could not be reconciled to Japanese rule unless and until the Americans were defeated."[32]

But as Japan's efforts to control East Asia failed, it became apparent that much of Japan's strength had already been spent. Initially, Japan shifted from "mobile to positional warfare," adopting a defensive control strategy. But even a defensive control strategy proved untenable. The fall of Saipan made clear Japan's transition from strength to weakness. Saipan's loss prompted Tojo to remark, "Japan is threatened by a national crisis without precedent." Ugaki commented, "how unsuccessfully we have fought since the defeat at Midway! Our strategy, aimed at invasion of Hawaii, Fiji, Samoa, and New Caledonia as well as domination over India and the destruction of the British Eastern Squadron, has dissipated like a dream." Tojo had failed, and the cabinet was replaced. Kuniaki Koiso was appointed both prime minister and army minister, while Mitsumasa Yonai became navy minister. Masanori Ito writes, "Japan advanced too far beyond her strength, or, to use a military term, had exceeded the offensive terminal point, ... the ideal point for the offensive force to hold, rest, and strengthen its lines of communication, supply, and reinforcements." As a result, Samuel Tangredi comments, "After having achieved conquests in China, Indochina, Indonesia, and outlying islands, Imperial Japanese forces shifted to an anti-access strategy in order to ensure that outside powers could not reverse the gains."[33]

It is notable that Japanese leaders only adopted a denial strategy when they perceived that their relative power had declined to a point of weakness. Before the war, denial strategies had been viewed so unfavorably that "the Japanese Navy placed little importance on commerce-destruction warfare." As a result, submarines were not prepared for commerce raiding. Toward the end of the war, however, Japan began to emphasize submarine warfare. Submarines, long an afterthought in Japanese naval strategy, were coming to the forefront, but there were too few for them to make a decisive difference. Meanwhile, some Japanese leaders began to advocate suicide operations. In July 1943, Rear Admiral Kameto Kuroshima requested use of volunteer suicide attacks, but "the navy and army high commands refused to consider such a drastic step. They were proud and spirited men who still believed that they could defeat the Allied forces in regular combat." Some worried that "a sure-death aerial weapon like this will have a grave impact on military discipline." The future prime minister Kantarō Suzuki, a retired admiral, insisted, "Using men in a situation where there is no chance of survival is not a proper military operation. The Japanese Navy has always opposed such undertakings."[34]

Yet Japan's weakness made a denial strategy its only option. By 1944, "frustrated pilots began to urge the use of suicide tactics." Admiral Onishi noted, "there is only one way of assuring that our meager strength will be effective to a maximum degree. That is to organize suicide attack units." Captain Eiichiro Jyo, commander of the *Chiyoda* light carrier, wrote, "No longer can we hope to sink the numerically superior enemy aircraft carriers through ordinary attack methods. I urge the immediate organization of special attack units to carry out crash dive tactics." Vice Admiral Kimpei Teraoka wrote in his diary, "Ordinary tactics are ineffective. . . . We must be superhuman in order to win the war." Japan was forced to adopt suicide tactics "in a desperate effort not to achieve victory but to ward off defeat." To encourage combat, "Japanese servicemen were taught to believe that if they died in battle, especially if they died heroically, they would instantly become 'gods,' and join the guardian spirits of the nation at Yasukuni Shrine." Those killed in suicide operations would be given promotions of two ranks upon their death.[35]

The shift from a control strategy to a denial strategy accelerated as Japan's position declined. Admiral Ugaki commented that Japan had to be like a sumo wrestler and conserve its strength by "pushing out" or "outwitting" opponents rather than competing with them strength-on-strength. The symmetric strategy that envisioned a battle for control between two great militaries had failed. The question now was how long Japan could use an asymmetric strategy to deny U.S. forces control of East Asia.[36]

Defense Investments: Expendable

As Japanese strength declined and leaders in Tokyo adopted a denial strategy, they turned increasingly toward expendable systems.

With few other options, Willmott writes that Japan embraced "forces they regarded as expendable; submarines and aircraft were considered cheap craft, capable of relatively quick and easy replacement." The Imperial Headquarters had previously assigned targets that were beyond the round-trip flying range of its pilots. And midget submarines had been used at Pearl Harbor, killing most of their operators. But these efforts were different from the special attacks that followed. Before Pearl Harbor, Admiral Yamamoto had rejected most midget submarine attacks, only giving permission for operations "on condition that the midgets could be recovered." These systems differed from suicide boats, which were expressly "designed for one-way trips."[37]

The first officially planned suicide attack occurred near New Guinea on May 27, 1944. The next kamikaze aircraft attack took place on October 13, 1944, and continued almost daily for the next month. Thousands of attacks were conducted using a variety of aircraft, some designed specifically for suicide attacks and others converted for that purpose. Suicide attacks were framed as Japan's best defense. In fact, kamikaze ("divine wind") were named in reference to a typhoon that destroyed Kublai Khan's invasion fleet in 1281, an incident that had saved Japan and "prevented foreign barbarians from violating Japan's sacred soil." Pilots were instructed, "Japanese air strength in the Philippines is too hopelessly depleted to oppose the enemy effectively by orthodox methods of attack. The moment calls for the employment of crash-dive tactics." Another wing commander announced the special attack units by reflecting, "Without taking extreme measures against the enemy, we will not be able to go on. We must do something that is unique in the annals of military history. Otherwise we will be ground down and destroyed as a nation."[38]

Throughout 1944, many forms of special attack craft were devised. This included 850 piloted bombs, or "Ohka," which were constructed with ranges of roughly fifteen nautical miles. Nine Ohka attacks occurred in November 1944, followed by eleven in December and twelve in January 1945. By March 1945, Japan had twenty-one hundred aircraft remaining, but few pilots and crews. Of these aircraft, three hundred were on Formosa, four hundred on Honshu, six hundred on Kyushu, and eight hundred in the Tokyo area. To increase their effectiveness, over four hundred special attack aircraft were constructed, with ranges as high as one thousand miles. In the end, 3,913 kamikaze pilots died. They incurred over 12,000 dead and 36,000 wounded U.S. service members. Japan also attempted to build missiles similar to the German V-1, choosing to pilot these aircraft rather than leave them unguided. However, these designs never proceeded to the production stage.[39]

Although special attack aircraft were the most well-known, many other special attack units were created. As Richard O'Neill notes, "In March 1944, the Imperial Japanese Army's Warship Research Institute at Himeji, near Kobe, was directed to devote considerable effort to the development of 'special (attack) boats'; in other words, suicide boats." Suicide boats proved an effective replacement for minefields around the first island chain, since only four minelayers were available. The boats had a warhead of roughly six hundred pounds, typically rigged to explode upon impact or be detonated by a pilot. These vessels had short ranges, roughly one hundred nautical miles when fully fueled. The need for these boats "was provoked by the inability of its aircraft, in the face of Allied superiority, to strike effectively at the most vulnerable element of the Allied amphibious landing forces—the landing ships." Over one thousand of these boats were deployed to the Philippines alone in 1944. In addition, Japan also produced over four hundred midget submarines. Some had ranges of up to one thousand nautical miles on the surface and could be deployed from submarine tenders. Japan also constructed piloted torpedoes with warheads that detonated on impact. Some of these torpedoes had ranges up to nearly fifty nautical miles. Roughly four hundred were constructed, as well as a number of surface ships and submarines capable of carrying the torpedoes, known as *Kaiten*. In a statement that demonstrates their perceived importance, one of the first questions asked by the U.S. commander in Manila at Japan's surrender negotiations was, "Are the *Kaiten* still at sea?"[40]

A U.S. operations booklet published in 1945 noted that the damage caused by suicide attacks far exceeded that caused by conventional attacks. Kamikaze attacks from the air reportedly sunk 22 ships in the Philippines, double the number sunk by conventional air attacks. At Leyte Gulf, the battleship *Yamato* received final orders instructing, "Fuel for only a one-way passage will be supplied. This is a special attack operation." On Okinawa, nearly half of the 6,300 sorties flown against the invaders were suicide attacks. All told, these attacks sunk 11 destroyers and damaged 10 battleships, 7 carriers, 5 cruisers, 61 destroyers, and over 100 other ships. Nearly 1,500 special air attacks were conducted by both the navy and army from April through June 1945, resulting in 11 U.S. ships being sunk and 102 damaged. The Strategic Bombing Survey following the war found, "The Japanese increased their ratio of results achieved to losses by adopting Kamikaze tactics. This was a measure of desperation, but the results obtained were considerable and, had they been much greater, might have caused us to withdraw or to modify our strategic plans."[41]

Japanese leaders only turned to "special attacks" in 1944 after deciding they were "Japan's last hope." Until this point, a veteran pilot insisted, "The right way is to attack the enemy with skill and return to the base with good results. A plane should be utilized over and over again. That's the way to fight a war. The current thinking is skewed." But a Japanese commentator notes, "given our desperate situation near the end of the war, there was nothing else we Japanese could do." The Japanese military was so weak that it could no longer contest control of the air, land, and sea. For example, army pilots at the beginning of the war had 500 hours of training while navy pilots had 650 hours, but this fell to just 100 hours at the end of the war. As a result, "the pilots themselves began to feel that if they were going to die on carrier decks, it would be much better to die crashing the decks of enemy carriers." With this in mind, a kamikaze pilot noted, "To us at the time, a suicide air force was a very natural thing, nothing more than a means of self-defense toward the end of the war." One scholar reflects that these tactics were "futility itself, and it bespoke the desperation of Japan and her fighting forces." U.S. Admiral William Halsey noted that beginning in 1944, "the Americans fought to live; the Japanese fought to die."[42]

Assessment

Japan's rise took decades, but its collapse transpired over just three years. Until the summer of 1942, many Japanese leaders believed Japan was a strong and rising power. But after Midway and Guadalcanal, most leaders in Tokyo admitted that Japan was declining. And beginning in the summer of 1944, it was evident that Japan was relatively weak compared to the United States. Japan's objectives, strategies, and investments changed rapidly as these realities became clear to Japanese leaders.

Most alternative explanations struggle to explain Japan's defense policies in this period. The distribution of capabilities changed rapidly during the war, but technology for suicide attacks existed long before these tactics were adopted. Suicide attacks might have proven highly effective had they been used at Pearl Harbor, both from an operational perspective and for demonstrating Japan's will to fight. Yet Japanese leaders disregarded these operations early in the war. Meanwhile, although the battle lines changed substantially, the basic geographic factors remained unchanged throughout the war. And Japanese culture also remained largely stagnant. Indeed, Atsushi Oi suggests that the "policy of surprise and offensive matched the Japanese national temperament very well. . . . To sit in a defensive position without fighting is very detrimental to the maintenance of Japanese morale." Yet this is what Japan did after 1942. And although domestic politics changed during the war, there is little to suggest that domestic interest groups were particularly influential in encouraging the use of suicide attacks.[43]

Perceived relative power theory explains the timing and direction of Japan's changing defense policies. At the start of the war, there was a sense in Tokyo that Japan was ascending while the United States was stagnating. By early 1942, Japan had succeeded in pushing British and U.S. forces out of the western Pacific. Japan therefore doubled down on its power-projection efforts. Its objectives were extensive, its strategy offensive, and its investments in sustainable systems. But as a U.S. Navy memorandum had correctly predicted, Japan's capabilities would "gradually decline which must eventually result in her eviction from the Asiatic continent and her decline as a world power." By late 1942, Japan was forced to shift toward a garrison-fortification approach. As Japan grew weaker, its leaders consolidated their objectives and favored the defensive.[44]

By 1944, Japanese leaders sought only limited objectives and shifted toward a denial strategy and expendable systems. David

Evans and Mark Peattie write, "the fortunes of the Japanese navy turned so disastrously by the end of 1943" that "few strategies, tactics, and technologies devised in the interwar years had any relevance in the last year and half of the war." Combat losses and wartime resource constraints no doubt limited Japan's military options. Admiral Takeo Kurita urged his subordinates, "The war situation is far more critical than any of you can possibly know. Would it not be a shame to have the fleet remain intact while our nation perishes?" One Japanese naval officer noted, "the major battles in 1944 and 1945, when [the navy] lost its striking capability, were like a boxing match between a big, muscled boxer, full of energy, and completely exhausted and emaciated players." By the end of the war, the Japanese navy had lost 334 warships and 300,000 personnel. The prediction of U.S. Chief of Naval Operations Admiral Harold Stark proved correct: "You may have initial success . . . but will grow weaker as time goes on. . . . We shall crush you."[45]

Why were Japanese leaders so confident of success before the war? First, the prospect of a Nazi victory over the Soviet Union, to say nothing of Great Britain, appeared to be a real possibility when Japan decided to go to war. Willmott explains, "The Japanese considered war in the Pacific in exactly the same light as the earlier wars against China and Russia around the turn of the century—a war that they could initiate and then limit in its conduct and aims. In global terms, the Japanese plans depended on the Anglo-Americans being engaged in two theaters, Europe and the Far East, and unable to mount effective responses in either area." Although Kido told the Emperor in 1941, "we are not strong enough to fight the U.S.A. and the Soviet at the same time," this suggests that he thought Japan stood a chance against the United States alone. Indeed, Richard Overy argues that either an outright Japanese victory or a favorable negotiated peace was a strong possibility: "There was nothing preordained about Allied success."[46]

Second, U.S. production in 1939 was lower than it had been in 1929. As one expert noted, "Japanese leaders feared American power, but they had to make decisions against the background of fitful and sluggish American production in the thirties, a decade when Japanese output doubled." While the United States struggled through the Depression, Japan engaged in what has been called

"Keynes in a uniform." The navy swelled from just over 80,000 personnel in 1928 to 429,000 by 1942. In 1938, Japan had 162 ships in the Far East, compared to 141 for the United States and 34 for Britain. In addition, Ambassador Nomura wrote in June 1941 of "the underestimation of the strength of the Japanese air force." Japan had an advantage of 1,102 aircraft to 973 for the United States and only 98 for Britain. In the short term, Japan was in a position of strength. Overy argues, "No rational man in early 1942 would have guessed at the eventual outcome of the war. . . . The situation for the Allies—and the coalition only emerged in December 1941, not sooner—was desperate, demoralizing."[47]

Third, Japanese leaders truly thought they might knock the United States out of the war early. Experts in Tokyo expected the navy's strength ratio to fall from 70 percent in 1941 to 65 percent in 1942, 50 percent in 1943, and 30 percent in 1944. But they were willing to take this risk. Barnhart argues, "For Japan, there were, in essence, only two alternatives to war with the United States. On the one hand, Japan might have given up all attempts to achieve self-sufficiency. . . . On the other hand, Japan might have actually achieved self-sufficiency with a great Asian empire and defied the West to overthrow it." Japan's bid for mastery of Asia failed, but Japanese leaders were willing to take this risk, since they "faced the stark alternatives of conquering or starving." As General Douglas MacArthur reflected, "There is practically nothing indigenous to Japan except the silkworm. . . . They feared that if those supplies were cut off, there would be 10 to 12 million unoccupied people. Their purpose, therefore, in going to war was largely dictated by security."[48]

The reasons that Japan lost the war in the Pacific are many, but the changes in Japanese defense policies appear to have been driven largely by one factor: assessments of relative power. Therefore, this case aligns closely with Hypotheses 1, 3, and 5. As Emperor Hirohito acknowledged in his understated way at the end of the war, "We declared war on America and Britain out of Our sincere desire to ensure Japan's self-preservation and the stabilization of East Asia. . . . The war situation has developed not necessarily to Japan's advantage." Indeed, Japan's relative decline not only caused Japan to lose the war but also triggered changes in its defense policies.[49]

CHAPTER SEVEN

Russia's Decline

In the latter half of the seventies—something happened that
was at first sight inexplicable. The country began to lose
momentum. . . . A country that was once quickly closing on
the world's advanced nations began to lose one position after
another.

—MIKHAIL GORBACHEV, *Perestroika* (1987)

FROM 1950 TO 1980, Soviet growth consistently exceeded that of
the United States. Edward Luttwak comments, "By the beginning
of the 1970s, it seemed that the Soviet Union could indeed look
forward to the day when it would become the world's greatest
military power, and its only truly global power." In the early 1980s,
U.S. estimates put Soviet defense spending 25 to 45 percent higher
than that of the United States. Soviet numerical advantages
were substantial, leading Ronald Reagan to highlight the danger of
a "window of vulnerability" in which the Soviet Union could
threaten Western interests. A Soviet leader commented, "What
should the Soviet Union fear? Only its own impotence, relaxation,
laxity."[1]

Yet the Soviet Union's deep internal contradictions proved inescapable. The booming Soviet economy eventually slowed, falling from 11.4 percent growth in the early 1950s to 4.3 percent growth by the late 1970s. The Soviet Union's relative national production peaked in the late 1970s at around 55 percent that of the United States. Observers warned that without new ideas and energy, the Soviet Union would "cease to be a great power" and become a "backward, stagnating state and an example to the rest of the world how not to conduct its economic life." Meanwhile, the Soviet military struggled technologically, and its allies remained much weaker than those of the United States. As a result, when Mikhail Gorbachev became general secretary of the Communist Party in 1985, he concluded that Soviet power had been declining since the late 1970s. By 1986, Gorbachev warned, "We're at a turning point—and have based our strategy on this realization. ... We see more clearly than anyone that drastic change is necessary." The Soviet Union was indeed at a turning point, one that resulted in its collapse just five years later.[2]

This chapter examines Moscow's defense policies from 1980 to 2000. During this time, Soviet (and then Russian) leaders came to realize that they were experiencing relative decline. After the collapse of the Soviet Union in 1991, Russian leaders were forced to accept that they were in a position of weakness compared to the United States. Perceived relative power theory makes three claims about states transitioning from perceived strength to weakness. Hypothesis 1 predicts a shift from extensive to limited objectives. Hypothesis 3 predicts a change from control to denial strategies. And Hypothesis 5 predicts investments in expendable systems. This chapter chronicles this shift away from power projection, but it notes a significant lag in Moscow's embrace of a denial strategy and investments in expendable systems. Russia's new leaders acknowledged their disadvantageous position and adjusted their objectives accordingly, but they saw few serious threats in the early 1990s. It was not until the late 1990s that leaders in Moscow perceived a serious external threat that prompted them to reconfigure strategy and investments. Thus, this case helps to identify the conditions under which perceived relative power theory holds.

Soviet Defense Policies Pre-1991

Throughout the 1980s, Soviet relative power declined. Economic problems were accompanied by a series of unforeseen political shocks. In 1985, the Soviet Union lost its third general secretary in less than three years. Soon afterward, the 1986 Chernobyl disaster demonstrated Soviet technological limitations. Then the 1988 Armenian earthquake raised questions about the Communist Party's competence. Meanwhile, the Soviet military struggled in Afghanistan, while Ronald Reagan strengthened the U.S. military. All these factors accentuated concerns about Soviet decline, leading to support for "new thinking." With this mandate, Mikhail Gorbachev attempted to open the Soviet economy, reform its political structures, and shift from a confrontational stance to a cooperative relationship with the West. These changes were profound, eventually leading to the consolidation of Soviet aims and the embrace of defensive approaches. But as expected, Soviet objectives abroad remained extensive, and Moscow continued to pursue a control strategy and investments in sustainable systems until the early 1990s.[3]

Defense Objectives: Extensive

The 1980s were a period of uncertainty for the Soviet Union. General Secretary Leonid Brezhnev had previously trumpeted Soviet economic, technological, and military strength. His "Brezhnev doctrine" directed that the Soviet Union intervene to forestall Western efforts to convert communist countries to capitalism. But the Warsaw Pact economies were declining; their total gross domestic product of $1.4 trillion amounted to less than half of the $2.9 trillion produced by the NATO economies. Defense-related expenses accounted for 40 percent of the Soviet budget. These dynamics drove Anatoly Chernyaev to worry, "If we do not undertake a real change in our military policy, the arms race aimed at our economic exhaustion will continue." By 1980, even Yury Andropov, the longtime KGB head and architect of the Afghanistan invasion, commented, "The quota of interventions abroad has been exhausted." The next year, he convinced Brezhnev not to invade Poland to stem the Solidarity movement. This marked the beginning of the end of the Brezhnev doctrine. By 1982, Brezhnev told military leaders to make better use of resources, given the Soviet economy's decline and its struggles in Afghanistan.[4]

But Brezhnev's health was also declining. Upon his death, Andropov took over. He worried that the United States sought "to ensure a dominating position in the world." Ronald Reagan had endorsed "a peacetime policy of applying the maximum economic pressure on the Soviet Union, directly through trade policies and the denial of advanced technology, and indirectly by developing new weapons that would make existing Soviet inventories obsolete." In 1983, Reagan gave his famous "star wars" speech, challenging the Soviets to keep pace with U.S. defense spending. Foreign Minister Andrei Gromyko warned, "Reagan and his team have taken up as their aim to destroy the socialist camp." Andropov initially argued, "the future belongs to détente," but soon abandoned these hopes. He and other members of the Soviet leadership became increasingly convinced that "major internal changes were needed in the USSR."[5]

By 1984, Andropov was dead too. His replacement, Konstantin Chernenko, lasted just over one year in office before he died as well. Others in the Politburo also perished around this time, including Premier Alexei Kosygin in 1980, Chief Ideologue Mikhail Suslov in 1982, and Minister of Defense Dmitry Ustinov in 1984. The party was decaying. One Soviet insider called this "a very dangerous period when the ruling circle cannot fully appreciate what it is doing and why." Thus, by 1985, many Soviet leaders believed it was time for someone more energetic. Mikhail Gorbachev, the youngest Politburo member, was the pick. Gorbachev's youth was contrasted with that of his predecessors in a popular joke: "What support does Gorbachev have in the Kremlin? None—he walks unaided."[6]

When Gorbachev took office, Soviet political and economic problems were unmistakable. He recognized their severity because he had been the Central Committee Secretary for Agriculture, providing a view of stagnating food production. With resources increasingly strained, Gorbachev warned military leaders that they would face strict resource limits. He critiqued the costly misadventure in Afghanistan and argued for pulling forces out, although he noted that "complete surrender of positions is unacceptable." Gorbachev's task became more difficult after the Chernobyl meltdown in 1986. He reflected that Chernobyl "was graphic evidence, not only of how obsolete our technology was, but also of the failure of the old system." Within months, Gorbachev won agreement to extricate Soviet forces from Afghanistan, explaining that success in foreign policy "lies in the healthy conditions of Soviet society and the economy." The Soviet Union's plan for 1986 to 1990 set an optimistic goal of 4.1 percent growth, but growth averaged only 3.7 percent per year from 1986 to 1989 and then crashed in 1990. Meanwhile, Gorbachev urged the Politburo to support arms control, including the Intermediate-Range Nuclear Forces Treaty. Without such agreements, he worried the Soviet Union would "be pulled into an arms race that is beyond [its] capabilities": "and we will lose it, because we are at the limit of our capabilities."[7]

Despite the Warsaw Pact's relative economic decline, its military spending was nearly even with that of NATO. But Soviet estimates indicated that the Warsaw Pact was spending two and a half times more of its relative gross national product on defense, just to stay even with NATO in spending. The Soviet Union contributed nearly 93 percent of this amount, leading the economist Oleg Bogomolov to warn, "Guns and rockets, unfortunately, are in abundance—instead of butter." Indeed, the 1986 to 1990 plan called for a 40 percent rise in military spending, which exceeded the 22 percent expected increase in economic output. One reason for high Soviet military spending was the need to match U.S. innovation. Marshal Nikolai Ogarkov, chief of the General Staff, argued that U.S. investments in conventional weapons—particularly stealth aircraft and precision munitions—marked the beginning of a military-technical revolution, so Ogarkov and others sought funding to counter the U.S. buildup. At a 1986 Politburo meeting, Gorbachev complained, "Ogarkov is very upset. He demands more and more. At a time when 25 million people here live below the officially proclaimed minimal living standard."[8]

Gorbachev knew what few others did, that the Soviet budget was in trouble. He later recollected that this was "the greatest 'secret'": "our budget was full of holes." As Gorbachev explained, "Money was drawn from the savings of the citizens and by raising the internal debt. Meanwhile, it was officially proclaimed that the revenues always exceeded the expenditure and that all was very well balanced." As a result, real military expenditure was 40 percent of the budget and 20 percent of gross national product, rather than 16 percent and 6 percent, as typically quoted. The Soviet Union would have to "either reconcile itself to military superiority of the U.S.A. and its allies . . . or face economic upheavals under the onus of increasingly costly military competition." Gorbachev now began putting real pressure on the military to scale back its spending and alter its objectives. The historian David Holloway notes, "Gorbachev treated the military carefully in the early years of *perestroika*. It was only after the January 1987 Plenum of the Central Committee that the armed forces came in for detailed criticism."[9]

Later in 1987, Gorbachev published *Perestroika*. He explained, "*perestroika* has been largely stimulated by our dissatisfaction with the way things have been going in our country in recent years." He aimed to spur "real economic independence" without ending central planning, but he needed to cut defense spending to do so. The Politburo now recognized "the obvious failure of economic reform to get going and the radicalization of public opinion." Gorbachev later noted, "We were feeling 'underground tremors,' even though society was expecting happy and swift changes and did not yet sense what cataclysms lay in store." When asked how to break Soviet international isolation, Georgy Arbatov advised immediate withdrawal from Afghanistan, unilateral reductions of Soviet forces in Europe, and the return of the Kuril Islands to Japan. Soon Gorbachev proposed a full withdrawal from Afghanistan. Then he announced a reduction of five hundred thousand troops, ten thousand tanks, eighty-five hundred artillery pieces, and eight hundred combat aircraft from the European theater.[10]

But even this could not stem the flow of bad news. In 1988, reported crime increased 17.8 percent, violent murders 14 percent, and robbery 43 percent. Then the Armenian earthquake killed twenty-five thousand people. Gorbachev announced a 14.2 percent budget cut and 19 percent decrease in defense procurement. Prime Minister Nikolai Ryzhkov stated that Soviet defense spending would be 9.3 percent of Soviet gross national product, but U.S. estimates placed it closer to 16 percent (compared to 7 percent for the United States). As Soviet troubles accumulated, Gorbachev held summits with Reagan and George H. W. Bush, as well as the first Sino-Soviet summit in twenty years. Despite this external outreach, Brent Scowcroft commented that "Soviet priorities seemed only to narrow." Declining power forced Soviet leaders to consolidate their aims. As the Soviet Union declined, its leaders focused increasingly on internal reforms. Yet Moscow was plagued by rapid inflation, a collapse in growth, and rising emigration. Inflation rose 7.3 percent in 1987, 8.4 percent in 1988, 10.5 percent in 1989, 53.6 percent in 1990, and at least 650 percent in 1991. Simultaneously, growth plummeted from 2.4 percent in 1989 to –15 percent in 1991. Meanwhile, emigration rose from 8,000 in 1986 to 235,000 in 1989, with polling showing that 12 percent of residents would leave the Soviet Union if they could.[11]

Perceptions of weakness triggered debate about Moscow's ambitions abroad. The Brezhnev doctrine was officially dead, replaced by what Gennady Gerasimov called the "Sinatra doctrine": "every country decides on its own which road to take." Gorbachev agreed to "unconditional respect for the principle of freedom of socio-political choice, the de-ideologization and humanization of international relations, the subordination of all foreign policy activities to international law, and the supremacy of universal human interests and values." Adviser Anatoly Chernyaev wrote, "what awaits us is the disintegration of the state and something resembling chaos." Soviet identity disintegrated as fault lines emerged among different nationalities, religions, and linguistic groups. After all, only Ukraine and Belorussia shared traditional religions and languages with Russia. Soon Estonia and Lithuania declared sovereignty. Then the Berlin Wall was torn down. The next year, Germany was unified. By 1990, the question was not whether the Soviet Union would end but when and how. Chernyaev recorded, "The centrifugal tendencies set in motion by Gorbachev ... are spinning out of control. We have only weeks, maybe just days left—it could all collapse at any moment. A wholesale transformation of the entire system appears imminent." By the end of 1990, Gorbachev told Boris Yeltsin that "attempts to weaken and undermine the Union" had caused "a stage beyond which collapse of the country would begin." The next year, the Soviet Union disappeared.[12]

Defense Strategy: Control

Despite the Soviet Union's declining position, its military stuck to a strategy of control. Control was necessary to accomplish the Soviet Union's extensive objectives in the Warsaw Pact and beyond. Power projection had been the calling card of the Soviet military for decades, but the military now shifted from a strategy of offensive control to one of defensive control. This process accelerated as Soviet decline became more evident.

Soviet military strategy had long been predicated on the need to rapidly penetrate enemy lines and exploit offensive advantages. Military leaders argued, "the active, offensive character of strategic operations is a most important principle of waging war." Soviet writers noted, "the enemy cannot be considered fully beaten until the time when his territory is occupied and he is deprived of the possibility of continuing the conflict." Thus, through Brezhnev's tenure, the Soviet military focused on three operational themes: exploiting advantages early in a war, conducting rapid ground offensives, and utilizing mobile forces. Each of these aspects emphasized the importance of offense. Soviet military leaders pushed back forcefully against defensive thinking. Ogarkov argued that more mobile capabilities were needed and that purely defensive approaches would fail. Minister of Defense Ustinov and Marshal Vasily Petrov emphasized the importance of sudden maneuvers to offset the United States' deep-strike capabilities.[13]

But as the 1980s progressed, political leaders—especially Gorbachev—forced the military to adjust its strategy. One of Gorbachev's advisers wrote, "Any major political power—in tandem with major social transformations or with changes in the military or political situation—has to undertake military reform from time to time. . . . And now a radical reform is imperative once again." In 1986, Gorbachev launched a three-part plan to cut defense spending. First, he sought arms-control and disarmament agreements to limit spending on strategic forces. Second, he pushed the military to pursue only "reasonable sufficiency" of forces, rather than parity. Defense Minister Dimitry Yazov redefined Moscow's defense objectives accordingly, noting that "the Soviet Union does not strive for superiority." Third, Gorbachev insisted that the military adopt a defensive form of warfare, which would require fewer resources and present less of a threat to NATO. Michael MccGwire writes that some people in Moscow blamed tensions with the West on the Warsaw Pact's "offensive posture facing NATO" and "responded by developing a defensive doctrine." These proposals amounted to a wholesale reexamination of Soviet strategy.[14]

Recognizing that neither superiority nor parity was realistic, Gorbachev stated, "Our country is for withdrawing weapons of mass destruction from circulation and limiting military potential to the limits of reasonable sufficiency." Sufficiency and defensive approaches were inextricably linked. In the words of one observer, Gorbachev ordered the military to "abandon the offensive strategy of reaching the English Channel in several days and to work out a new military doctrine based on 'strategic sufficiency' and defensive posture." Yazov said the Warsaw Pact desired "to reduce, on a mutual basis of course, military potential to such a level that neither side, while assuring its defense, has the forces or means enabling it to mount offensive operations." Yazov defined sufficiency as "having precisely the magnitude of armed forces necessary to defend oneself against an attack from outside." Gorbachev noted that he desired forces "sufficient for repulsing any possible aggression but inadequate for conducting offensive action." These efforts were intended to lower tensions, avoid an arms race that the Soviet Union could not afford, and win a propaganda victory against the West.[15]

The push for sufficiency met resistance. William Odom notes that "defensive doctrine" clashed with the "subconscious hegemony" and "conscious articulation" of long-standing Soviet combat philosophy. Gorbachev was steadfast, however, arguing, "If we won't budge from the positions we've held for a long time, we will lose in the end. We will be drawn into an arms race that we cannot manage. We will lose, because right now we are already at the end of our tether." By 1987, Soviet doctrine was restated, acknowledging that defense was "the main form of military operations." The 1987 Soviet low-level tactics manual contained twice the number of pages on defensive operations as it had in 1984, including new sections on "preparation of defense" and "disengagement from battle and withdrawal." For the first time in decades, spending rose on Soviet strategic defenses (particularly surface-to-air missiles and fighter-interceptor aircraft). The Warsaw Pact now called its doctrine defensive and explained, "in today's circumstances the use of the military way of resolving any disputed question is inadmissible." Supporters of defensive strategies published a book suggesting that Lenin had declared that socialist states "wage only defensive wars." Gorbachev trumpeted this change, saying, "Soviet military doctrine is ... unequivocally defensive. In the military sphere we intend to act in such a way as to give nobody grounds for fears, even imagined ones, about their security."[16]

Meanwhile, the Soviet position continued to deteriorate. The United States had adopted the so-called Second Offset, which relied on new technologies such as stealthy aircraft and highly accurate long-range cruise missiles to hold at risk Soviet forces deep in its own territory. Some Soviet leaders argued that they did "not possess the required means" to sustain parity. Yazov lamented, "The member states of NATO had a higher gross domestic product than those of the Warsaw Pact and were increasing their military expenditure. Considerable advances in military technology had been made in the West." By 1988, Gorbachev told the Politburo, "without substantially cutting military expenditures we cannot solve the problems of *perestroika*." He suggested, "Let's make a thorough analysis of what a strong modern army is, what ensuring security means, what the quality of security consists of. And when we know how much all this costs, we can cut out the rest."[17]

Gorbachev announced unilateral cuts to Soviet forces. He stated, "All remaining Soviet divisions on the territory of our allies will be reorganized. They will be given a different structure from today's which will become unambiguously defensive, after the removal of a large number of their tanks." The number of tanks per division was decreased from 328 to 260, and tank regiments were removed from motorized-rifle divisions. Gorbachev explained, "we have adopted a defensive doctrine and our armed forces are undergoing profound changes: the structure of our forces in Central Europe is changing—we have reduced the number of tanks per division, we are withdrawing airborne and amphibious equipment, repositioning our strike aircraft to the second echelon and so on."[18]

Gorbachev tried to strengthen relations with the West but met substantial opposition. Gorbachev suggested that he and Reagan

"agree on how to eliminate imbalances and asymmetries and reduce armed forces and weapons." He proposed a reduction of five
hundred thousand troops and that "conventional forces on both
sides would be restructured to become purely defensive and unsuited for offensive warfare." Yet when the Soviet Union signed the
Intermediate-Range Nuclear Forces Treaty in 1987 and the Treaty
on Conventional Armed Forces in Europe in 1990, neither
"received the wholehearted support of the General Staff." Gorbachev commented that "various forces—mostly connected with
the military-industrial complex—attempted then to undermine
improvements in Soviet-American relations." Many military experts remained unconvinced about the virtues of arms control and
"defensive defense." Soviet military experts worried that the Soviet
Union was now weaker than NATO in tanks (a two-to-three ratio),
artillery (three-to-four), and helicopters (four-to-five). Alexei Arbatov wrote, "the same elements can perform either offensive or defensive operations depending on the combat mission." U.S. leaders
were hesitant as well, with experts warning, "NATO planners
should not forget that the change from an 'offensive' to a 'defensive' doctrine was purely nominal, a change in words and nothing
more. . . . Doctrine remains much the same as in earlier periods."[19]

Despite this opposition, Gorbachev continued his push for a
defensive control strategy. He asked, "Why do we need such a big
army?" And he noted, "Attempts to achieve military superiority are
preposterous." After all, "The weak side may simply explode all its
nuclear charges, even on its own territory, and that would mean
suicide for it and a slow death for the enemy. This is why any striving for military superiority means chasing one's own tail. It can't be
used in real politics." The strategic shift from offensive control to
defensive control had largely won the day by 1990, but whether
military investments would follow was a separate question.[20]

Defense Investments: Sustainable

As Soviet leaders came to grips with relative decline, they were
forced to rethink their investment in power-projection forces. Sustainable systems continued to be seen as the most important assets.
But mobile systems—such as tanks, aircraft carriers, and aircraft—

became less critical. Through the 1980s, military investments increasingly shifted from mobile and sustainable systems to less mobile but still sustainable forces.

In the late 1970s, Soviet doctrine sought to rapidly bring multiple units to the point of attack, with echelons of follow-on forces attacking consecutively. U.S. operational concepts, such as "Air-Land Battle," sought to hold these forces at risk. U.S. capabilities, most notably stealth aircraft and cruise missiles, provided the United States with the ability to strike deep and accurately into Soviet territory. In 1978, Ogarkov suggested that Soviet forces adopt new strategies, tactics, and technology to deal with these "revolutionary" U.S. capabilities. Marshal Andrei Grechko wrote, "The battle between armor and antitank missiles has now shifted to the scientific research laboratories, the proving grounds, and industry." But others rejected Ogarkov's premise that a new type of warfare was emerging. Marshal Hamazasp Babadzhanian commented, "there are no objective reasons to speak of a demise of the tank troops, of how the tank has allegedly ceased to be viable on the battlefield." Dima Adamsky explains that resistance to new and sophisticated concepts of operations was due partially to the fact that they were "beyond the political, economic, and cultural capacity of the Soviet state."[21]

Another common response to Ogarkov was that nuclear weapons were more important than conventional capabilities. A Soviet spokesman stated, "Nuclear missile weapons have . . . become the main indicator and element in the military potential of the great powers." The Soviet Union still retained an edge in many types of nuclear weapons, with over six hundred intermediate-range ballistic missiles and three thousand nuclear-capable aircraft in Europe. Yet, Ogarkov wrote, "Soviet military strategy assumes that world war may begin and continue for a certain time with the use of only conventional weapons." In 1981, Brezhnev argued, "It is dangerous madness to try to defeat each other in an arms race, to count on victory in nuclear war. . . . Whatever strength the attacker may have and whatever means of starting a nuclear war he may choose, he will not achieve his aims. Retaliation is unavoidable. That is our essential view." Soviet leaders agreed to renounce the first use of nuclear weapons, and they issued a public pledge to that effect in

1982. Foreign Minister Gromyko announced that the Soviet Union "unilaterally assumes the obligation not to be the first to use nuclear weapons."[22]

How would the Soviet Union respond to a U.S. conventional attack? A battle erupted between advocates of traditional ground and air forces and those supporting Ogarkov's notion of reconnaissance strike complexes. Ogarkov suggested in 1983, "Inertia of thought and stubborn, mechanical unthinking attachment to old ways are dangerous in present-day conditions. . . . Bold experiments and solutions are necessary—even if it means discarding obsolete traditions." In 1984, he warned that Soviet conventional capabilities were lagging, requiring a substantial modernization program. In 1985, Marshal Sergey Akhromeyev wrote that Soviet adversaries were pursuing "conventional weapons with better destruction, range, and accuracy, . . . controlled and automated modes of high-accuracy weapons." Yet, ground-force commander Marshal Vasily Petrov responded, "tanks are still the main strike force of the Ground Forces even today—a reliable shield in defense, a telling sword in attack." Marshal O. A. Losik agreed: "massive employment of tanks . . . [increases] the mobility and strike power of the Ground Forces." In 1987, a military spokesperson stated, "nuclear weapons are increasingly becoming an instrument which it would be irrational to use."[23]

Nevertheless, political leaders forced the military to reconsider its reliance on mobile forces. To implement "non-offensive defense," some experts proposed "reduction of armaments with more clearly pronounced offensive functions: tanks, long-range artillery, tactical strike aircraft, tactical missiles, combat helicopters, and pontoon bridge facilities." They also advised "disbanding some major armored and mechanized forces together with their logistics support units, air armies and missiles groups, and redeploying others to areas farther removed from the forward edge so that they could perform the function of an operational reserve for the defense, and not that of an attack to mount a surprise offensive." In 1987, *Pravda* published a statement asserting that the Warsaw Pact would "never, under any circumstances, begin military actions. . . . They have no territorial claims to any state either in Europe or outside of Europe." As *perestroika* continued, Gorbachev became bolder, going after not just military spending but the defense industry itself. He complained, "We're in this fix thanks to the priority awarded the defense industry. But if we don't succeed, there won't even be sufficient funds for defense in the future."[24]

The massive changes being forced on the Soviet military drew criticism. Alexander Prokhanov said, "Today, the Soviet Union is weaker than ever before. . . . The Army today is being destroyed like so many columns in an Afghan ravine, . . . turning the Army into a motionless, demoralized mass." Indeed, from 1988 to 1990, half of Soviet tanks were removed from Europe. But the Warsaw Pact maintained substantial capabilities in the European theater. In 1988, the Soviets had rough parity in numbers of active ground forces (around 2.3 million each), reserve ground forces (4.3 million each), and attack aircraft (both around 2,400) in the European theater. Moreover, the Warsaw Pact held at least a three-to-one advantage over NATO in artillery pieces (37,100 to 11,100), anti-aircraft missiles (12,859 to 2,250), and fighters/interceptors (4,942 to 1,079), as well as a roughly two-to-one advantage in main battle tanks (52,200 to 22,200), armed helicopters (1,630 to 780), and bombers (700 to 323). Minister of Defense Sergey Sokolov wrote that the Soviet Union desired "cutting of military potentials to the level necessary and sufficient for defense, and the complete elimination of nuclear and other types of weapons of mass destruction from the strategic balance."[25]

Gorbachev's "new thinking" prevailed. By 1990, Soviet forces had been reduced by 265,000 personnel, 9,320 tanks, 50,000 artillery pieces, 835 combat aircraft, and 40 warships and submarines. The Conventional Armed Forces in Europe Treaty limited tanks and artillery to 20,000 each, armored combat vehicles to 30,000, helicopters to 2,000, and aircraft to 6,800. These cuts were deepest to the most mobile forces, setting in stone Gorbachev's more defensive approach. Yet leaders in Moscow remained committed to sustainable systems. Soviet leaders were careful to maintain capabilities for defensive control, even as they sought to shift away from mobile forces. In fact, by 1990, even if the Soviet Union had wanted to launch an offensive, it did not have the systems that would have been required. Soviet leaders had maintained extensive objectives, a control strategy, and sustainable systems while shifting toward more of a garrison-fortification approach to defend consolidating Soviet objectives.[26]

Russian Defense Policies Post-1991

Soviet leaders recognized the signs of relative decline in the 1980s, but few expected the "voluntary dismantlement of Soviet military power" that occurred after the Berlin Wall fell. Boris Yeltsin later commented, "The Soviet Union could not exist without the image of the empire. The image of the empire could not exist without the image of force. The USSR ended the moment the first hammer pounded the Berlin Wall." By late 1989, Azerbaijan had declared sovereignty; Estonia, Georgia, and Lithuania followed in March 1990; Latvia in May; Russia, Moldova, and Uzbekistan in June; Belorussia and Ukraine in July; Armenia, Tajikistan, and Turkmenistan in August; Kazakhstan in October; and Kyrgyzstan in December. By March 1991, the Warsaw Pact's military components were formally disbanded. In August, a failed coup against Gorbachev hastened Boris Yeltsin's rise. In December, Yeltsin signed the creation agreement for the Commonwealth of Independent States, effectively dissolving the Soviet Union. Several weeks later, Gorbachev resigned. Upon stepping down, he announced, "When I became head of state, it was already obvious that there was something wrong in this country. We had plenty of everything: land, oil, gas and other natural resources. . . . Yet we lived much worse than people in other industrialized countries and the gap was constantly widening." Within days, the Soviet Union ceased to exist, and Russia's defense policies took a new direction.[27]

Defense Objectives: Limited

The Soviet Union's disintegration forced leaders in Moscow to limit their objectives. The new Russian state controlled less territory and included many fewer people than its predecessor. Moreover, the Russian Federation suffered from political and economic instability, which further depleted its military. By the end of the 1990s, Russia's gross domestic product was less than one-tenth that of the United States, placing it not even in the world's top ten countries. Russia had lost its European allies by the end of 1991.

The following year, the economy went into freefall, reducing per capita income by nearly one-third. Over the next decade, the military shrunk by 80 percent, from five million personnel to one million. Meanwhile, conflicts broke out in several former Soviet republics. Leaders in Moscow reassessed their relative power and concluded that Russia was relatively weak. Yeltsin then limited Russian defense objectives. He explained, "I am not presenting people with a global strategic goal. I am not setting my sights on some shining peak that must be scaled. . . . No. The chief goal of this restless president is Russia's tranquility."[28]

Initially, Yeltsin was not ready to pass on the mantle of a great power. In 1992, he commented, "Russia is rightfully a great power by virtue of its history, of its place in the world, and of its material and spiritual potential." Vice President Alexander Rutskoy concurred that Russia should "retain a fitting position in world civilization and the status of a great power worthy of respect." Foreign Minister Andrei Kozyrev argued against "losing geopolitical positions that took centuries to conquer." With this in mind, Yeltsin's government began playing an active role in the former Soviet republics. Russia negotiated agreements with Georgia and South Ossetia, as well as Moldova and Transnistria, on cessation of violence. In 1993, Yeltsin explained that Russia had a "vital interest in the cessation of all armed conflicts on the territory of the former USSR" and requested United Nations authority "to grant Russia special powers as guarantor of peace and stability in this region." Russia seemed to desire a sphere of influence in Eurasia.[29]

Russian military documents, such as the Basic Provisions for Russian Military Doctrine, ascribed more limited defense objectives. The report indicated that the military should be capable of protecting the sovereignty, territorial integrity, and other vitally important interests of the Russian Federation; conduct peacekeeping operations; and terminate armed conflicts and any unlawful armed violence on the state border or the border of another state in accordance with treaty commitments. This was a limited international role largely focused on dampening conflict with Russia's neighbors. Over the next few years, Russian leaders maintained this focus on the former Soviet republics. Yevgeny Primakov, director of Russia's Foreign Intelligence Service, stated, "If the countries of Central and Eastern Europe join [NATO], the objective result will be the emergence of a barrier between Russia and the rest of the continent."[30]

But Russia's sphere of influence was shrinking along with its relative power. Yeltsin admitted, "the imperial period in Russia's history has ended." He even went so far as to state that "Russia sees the U.S., the West, and the countries of the East not merely as partners but as allies." By 1994, Russia signed the Partnership for Peace framework, stating that "Russia and NATO have agreed to prepare a wide-ranging individual program of partnership, in keeping with Russia's size, importance, and potential." Yeltsin commented, "The era of enmity, distrust, and suspiciousness is ending in the history of Russia and Germany, and in the history of Europe."[31]

Nevertheless, the idea of Russia as a great power lingered. Kozyrev commented, "Russia is doomed to be a Great Power." The politician Grigory Yavlinsky stated that the Russian army would always be "the army of a great power." Indeed, by 1995, Russian leaders were pushing back against what they saw as Western encroachment. Yeltsin warned that expansion of NATO would force Russia to "immediately launch constructive relations with all former Soviet republics. There will be a bloc. There will be two blocs. Does that promote common European security?" As tensions with NATO grew, newly appointed foreign minister Yevgeny Primakov asserted, "Russia has been and remains a great power, and its policy toward the outside world should correspond to that status." He outlined four priorities: strengthening territorial integrity, strengthening the process of reintegration, settling regional and interethnic conflicts, and preventing "hotbeds" of tension or proliferation.[32]

Tensions in Russian objectives began to be resolved in 1997, when the Russian government released several strategic documents. The most important of these was the 1997 National Security Concept, which described Russia as beset by internal problems and no longer qualified to be one of the world's strongest states. The concept noted "the change in Russia's status within the world" and vowed not to "pursue hegemonistic or expansionist goals." It acknowledged that Russia's "economic, scientific, and demographic potential is declining, . . . lagging increasingly far behind developed

countries in terms of science and technology." Despite this decrease in Russian power, the concept acknowledged, "The threat of
large-scale aggression against Russia is virtually absent for the
foreseeable future. . . . The main threats to Russia's national security come from internal political, economic, and social spheres and
are predominantly non-military." A presidential decree stated,
"The crisis in the national economy has seriously deteriorated the
opportunities for Russia." Moscow had thus adopted more limited
objectives, seeking far less authority abroad than it had in previous
decades.[33]

Despite Russia's more limited objectives, tensions grew with
the West over NATO enlargement, Kosovo, and Chechnya. Alexei
Arbatov wrote, "The bombing of Yugoslavia revived the worst in-
stincts of the Cold War." In 1999, Yeltsin selected Vladimir Putin
to succeed him. Shortly after taking over as acting president, Putin
released Presidential Decree 24, which revised the 1997 National
Security Concept. The decree criticized "the attempt to create a
structure of international relations based on the domination of developed Western countries, led by the U.S.A." Rather than seeking
"partnership" with the West, Putin sought only "cooperation" and
committed to "firmly and resolutely" defend Russian interests. The
document went so far as to note that Russian interests "predeter-
mine, in certain conditions, Russia's military presence in some strategically important regions of the world." The Soviet Union's fall
had forced Moscow to adopt more limited defense objectives. But
as Putin's more assertive tone demonstrated, the desire to return to
Moscow's heyday and increasing concerns about Western encroachment caused Russia to adopt a more confrontational style
from roughly 2000 onward.[34]

Defense Strategy: Denial

Although Russian defense objectives changed rapidly in the early
1990s, Russian strategy evolved more slowly. Russian leaders were
initially consumed with managing the Soviet Union's dismember-
ment. They had to decide which Soviet forces would become Russian and which would become part of the newly independent
republics. The status of nuclear weapons was a central question,

since Ukraine inherited 1,564 nuclear warheads, Kazakhstan 1,420, and Belarus 54. Another issue was the return of Russian forces forward deployed in East Germany and elsewhere. Gorbachev and Helmut Kohl agreed that Soviet troops would leave Germany within four years, but housing and facilities were needed. Funds were in short supply. Soviet military spending had hovered around 10 to 15 percent of gross national product. This was no longer politically acceptable. Estimated military expenditures were predicted to fall from $443 billion in 1988 to $324 billion in 1991 to just $87 billion in 1992 and $46 billion by 1995. The final amount was less than one-tenth of Soviet military spending from a decade prior.[35]

The new Russian government set about reorganizing the military and shrinking the defense enterprise. In 1992, the Russian Parliament passed a Law on Defense requiring that no more than 1 percent of the population serve in the armed forces by 1995. Russian leaders explicitly abandoned the concept of parity, which had long been the Soviet aim. Yeltsin noted, "We are departing from the ominous parity where each country was exerting every effort to stay in line, which has led to Russia having half of its population living below the poverty line." Russian force structure declined rapidly. From 1991 to 1996, the ground forces fell from 1.4 million to 460,000; air defense troops from 475,000 to 175,000; the navy from 450,000 to 190,000; the air force from 420,000 to 145,000; and the strategic rocket forces from 280,000 to 149,000. Meanwhile, paramilitary forces were cut from 520,000 to 352,000. Notably, forces for controlling territory received the largest percentage decreases, whereas paramilitary and nuclear forces were cut least.[36]

Russian experts warned that the cuts would result in "a combat-unable, poorly equipped and poorly trained, impoverished and alienated Army which will not be able to defend the country from an external threat and will itself become an internal threat." Indeed, in 1992, 71 percent of Russian officers favored restoration of the Soviet state, and roughly 65 percent preferred a military regime. Despite military pressure, however, Yeltsin resisted calls from Colonel-General Viktor Barynkin and others who argued for military funding "that corresponds to the status of a great power." This led to the 1993 Basic Provisions for Russian Military Doctrine, which stated that the "immediate threat of direct aggression . . . has considerably declined." Facing a worsening balance of conventional forces, Russia would rely more on nuclear weapons. The provisions stated that Russia reserved the right to use nuclear weapons against an attack by any state connected by an alliance or joint action with a state that does possess nuclear weapons. Nevertheless, the decree retained Yeltsin's pledge to seek "the reduction of nuclear forces to a minimal level which would guarantee the prevention of large-scale war and the maintenance of strategic stability and—in the future—the complete elimination of nuclear weapons."[37]

Russia's more limited objectives made preventing an attack on the homeland the top priority. Two strategies were available: maintaining a large conventional force or shifting toward a greater reliance on nuclear deterrence. Yeltsin's cuts to the defense budget seemed to make a conventional deterrent impossible. By 1997, Russian military spending was limited to 3.5 percent of gross national product, down from 7.2 percent in 1991. Thus, the 1997 National Security Concept stated, "Russia does not seek to maintain parity in arms and armed forces with the leading states of the world, and is oriented toward the implementation of the principle of realistic deterrence." The concept made clear, "The most important task for the Russian Federation Armed Forces is to ensure nuclear deterrence in the interests of preventing both nuclear and conventional large-scale or regional wars. . . . Russia reserves the right to use all the forces and systems at its disposal, including nuclear weapons." Moscow now created a unified missile force, while it cut two of the six branches of the armed forces.[38]

By the late 1990s, it was clear that tactical (or nonstrategic) nuclear weapons were a central focus of Russian strategy. Minister of Defense Marshal Igor Sergeyev noted the need to avoid "direct military-technical competition with the most developed countries." He commented, "Russia will not be able to support military-strategic and military-technical parity with the leading military powers of the West on a 'symmetrical' basis, especially in the area of non-nuclear armaments." A control strategy was no longer realistic, so a denial strategy became increasingly attractive. Putin persuaded Yeltsin to sign a decree authorizing the development of tactical nuclear weapons, which probably involved low-yield weapons to deter conventional attacks. The scholar Stephen Cimbala explained, "Russia's conventional military weakness makes it more reliant on nuclear weapons as weapons of first choice or first use, instead of last resort." Colonel-General Vladimir Yakovlev clarified, "The general purpose forces have been reduced, their global rearmament is impossible in the foreseeable future, and Russia is compelled to reduce the threshold for the use of nuclear weapons and extended nuclear deterrence to conflicts of lesser scales and to openly warn about that." Russia endorsed a doctrine that "unequivocally resurrects the specter of the possible use of nuclear weapons and the resort to first strike."[39]

The decision to rely more on nuclear weapons was consecrated in the 2000 National Security Concept. The concept stated, "The main task of the Russian Federation is to deter aggressions of any scale against it and its allies, including with the use of nuclear weapons." The concept blamed NATO for "the use of force beyond the zone of its responsibility and without the sanction of the UN Security Council." The Russian strategy was summarized by experts as "curbing Western superiority in conventional arms by means of Russian tactical nuclear weapons." A Russian journalist wrote, "nuclear weapons are the basis for Russia to retain its influence in the world and they are the guarantee against pressure on us from NATO." Russian military officers argued that deescalation might require "actually using nuclear weapons for showing resolve as well as for the immediate delivery of nuclear strikes against the enemy." In many ways, these concepts were reminiscent of NATO's own "flexible response" doctrine when facing overwhelming Soviet conventional strength in the 1960s. Raymond Garthoff explained that this would "substitute an objective not of winning, but of preventing the other side from winning, not of defeating and destroying the enemy's forces, but only of defeating the accomplishment of the enemy's offensive aims."[40]

The Russian reliance on nuclear weapons amounted to a strategic shift from control to denial. As Kenneth Waltz noted, nuclear weapons "enable the weak to counter some of the measures that the strong may wish to take against them." Similarly, Stephen Van Evera commented that with nuclear weapons, "even lesser powers can now stand alone against states with far greater resources."

Thus, nuclear weapons provided a denial capability—they could not help to control territory but could prevent an adversary from doing so. As Moscow faced the reality of its relative weakness, Edward Luttwak suggests that Russian leaders acted according to a "hierarchy of imperial needs" by seeking to "deny the use of their own territory to any power hostile to the empire."[41]

Defense Investments: Expendable

In line with Russian leaders' strategy, they invested a higher proportion of resources in expendable weapons systems throughout the 1990s. As Moscow eliminated excess force structure and equipment from its inventory, nuclear weapons took more and more of the budget. But later in the decade, Russian leaders invested more in nuclear weapons, seeing them as an alternative to expensive conventional forces.

In the early 1990s, Russian defense investments remained largely a by-product of Soviet spending. With falling budgets, the focus was not on what would be purchased but on what would be cut. In 1992, the Ministry of Defense proposed reducing the army to 2.1 million by 1995. The next year, Defense Minister Pavel Grachev suggested that a 1.5 million army "would be fine for a compact state without such vast borders." Russian leaders concluded, "The existing military organization is burdensome to the state. It must be reformed." At the time, Russia maintained 10,604 tanks, 17,338 armored combat vehicles, 8,107 artillery pieces, 4,161 aircraft, and 1,035 helicopters. By 1995, however, each of these categories had been cut by 15 to 40 percent, resulting in 6,696 tanks (63 percent of the 1992 total), 11,806 armored combat vehicles (68 percent), 6,240 artillery pieces (77 percent), 3,283 aircraft (79 percent), and 872 helicopters (84 percent). Meanwhile, Russia sold five aircraft carriers, leaving just a single operational carrier. These cuts devastated Russia's most mobile and sustainable power-projection forces.[42]

Nuclear weapons were initially scheduled to receive cuts as well. In 1991, the United States announced unilateral reductions to nonstrategic nuclear systems, and Gorbachev pledged to dismantle all nuclear land mines and artillery shells, as well as half of surface-to-air missile warheads, tactical naval warheads, and nonstrategic air force bombs. Yeltsin agreed to apply these constraints to Russia. When time came for actual reductions, however, Russian leaders agreed to cut strategic nuclear weapons but avoided cutting tactical nuclear weapons. Tactical nuclear weapons were protected in part because they were seen as an alternative to maintaining sustainable conventional forces. The 1997 National Security Concept warned, "The former defense system has been disrupted, and the creation of a new one is proceeding slowly. Long unprotected sections of the Russian Federation state border have appeared." Minister of Defense Igor Rodionov stated, "We might objectively face the task of increasing tactical nuclear weapons at our border," to respond to NATO activities.[43]

The poor state of Russian forces led Yeltsin to comment, "I am not merely dissatisfied. I am outraged . . . over the condition of the armed forces." Defense Minister Igor Sergeyev acknowledged that "not a single unit was combat ready except for the nuclear forces and some paratroopers." By 1998, the Defense Ministry warned, "53 percent of aircraft and 40 percent of the anti-aircraft systems, helicopters, armored equipment and artillery were in need of repair." In addition, 70 percent of naval ships required major overhauls. A government decree stated that the navy was "losing its ability to safeguard political and economic interests of the nation, and its ability to ensure full-scale security on the sea border." Despite Yeltsin's dissatisfaction, no major increase in funding was on the horizon. In fact, Russia did not acquire a single tank, artillery piece, combat aircraft, helicopter, or nuclear submarine in 1998.[44]

Defense Minister Sergeyev and General Staff Chief Anatoly Kvashnin disagreed over how to deal with the resulting conventional imbalance. Sergeyev, a former head of the Strategic Rocket Forces, argued "that given its limited resources, Moscow should pay primary attention (including the allocation of funds)" to the rocket forces. Kvashnin preferred investments in ground forces. But the missile forces eventually prevailed. Although strategic missile forces had been halved by 1995, they stayed at this level for the rest of the 1990s. Meanwhile, the ground forces were cut by over 50 percent before 1995 and by another 50 percent after. Similarly, the air force and air defense forces were cut by roughly 60 percent each between 1990 and 1995 and then were merged and cut by another 45 percent from 1995 to 2000. Spending on sustainable forces was decreasing, while expendable systems were being prioritized.[45]

By 2000, Russian leaders were facing a sharp decrease in conventional capabilities; in response, Moscow turned even more to tactical nuclear weapons. The 2000 National Security Concept warned of "the growing technological surge of some leading powers and their growing possibilities to create new-generation weapons and military hardware." The concept proposed "the use of all available means and forces, including nuclear weapons, in case of the need to repel an armed aggression." Jacob Kipp notes that the military considered tactical nuclear weapons "a counterweight to Russia's declining conventional capabilities." This decision did not come easily, but Russian leaders saw no other option. Thus, as Russia's military decline worsened through the 1990s, it came to embrace expendable systems at the expense of sustainable systems.[46]

Assessment

From 1980 to 2000, Moscow transformed its defense objectives, strategies, and investments. In the Soviet Union's last decade, its leaders continued to embrace extensive objectives, a control strategy, and investments in sustainable systems. The primary Soviet objective remained "the retention of power by the Communist party." Yet, this aim drove many Soviet leaders to focus externally, due to what Henry Kissinger called "the paradox of Russian history, . . . a fear that, unless the empire expanded, it would implode." As the Soviet Union declined in the 1980s, Gorbachev sought to implement "a doctrine that excludes rapid offensive onto enemy territory." Then, when the Soviet Union collapsed in 1991, Russian leaders revised their defense policies. Moscow was now "operating from a position of relative weakness." Facing this reality, the 1997 National Security Concept stated, "Russia's influence on resolving cardinal questions of international life which affect our state's interests has decreased significantly." Gone were Moscow's extensive aims abroad. Instead, Russian leaders adopted limited objectives, a denial strategy, and investments in expendable systems.[47]

Most alternative theories struggle to explain Russian decisions. Most structural explanations cannot explain why Soviet leaders adopted a more defensive strategy in the late Cold War and then a denial strategy in the late 1990s. Technology was certainly changing, but the Soviets largely ignored Ogarkov's efforts to field a military capable of taking advantage of technological trends. Other explanations also yield mixed results. For example, Moscow's strategy changed dramatically in this period, even though Russian strategic culture was largely consistent. Domestic explanations might stand a better chance. After all, the ends that Gorbachev and Yeltsin pursued were heavily influenced by their assessment of Russia's domestic situation. Yet, many investment decisions go against domestic pressures, such as cutting Russian ground forces rather than tactical nuclear weapons in the 1990s.

This case therefore provides support for Hypotheses 1, 3, and 5, but with an important caveat: there was a notable time lag between changes in relative power and defense policy reforms. The collapse of Russian military power in the 1990s was unmistakable. Declared defense spending declined by 98 percent in just seven years, from $142 billion in 1992 to $4 billion in 1999. Yet William Wohlforth notes that Russian leaders were slow in "their adaptation to decline in the 1990s" and that they struggled "to face necessary trade-offs." Why was Russia so slow to respond? One possible explanation is that Russian leaders did not see an immediate and significant threat until the late 1990s. Only one aspect of Stephen Walt's balance of threat theory was satisfied: NATO's fielding of offensive capabilities. But in the early 1990s, Russia had a buffer zone between it and NATO, plus NATO was withdrawing some combat forces and nuclear weapons from Europe. The United States had even declared that Russia was a partner. Therefore, in 1993, military doctrine stressed cooperation with the West and a more limited role for the Russian armed forces. Without a serious threat, reformers could not rally the political support necessary to transform Russia's defense strategy or investments.[48]

By the late 1990s, however, Russian attitudes and perceptions were changing. NATO had expanded and was moving closer to Russia's borders, decreasing the geographic distance between Russia and NATO. Meanwhile, NATO demonstrated its potent offensive capabilities—and, in the minds of some Russians, offensive intentions as well—in Iraq, Bosnia, and Kosovo. This combination of factors reshaped Russian strategy, resulting in the more realpolitik-focused National Security Concepts of 1997 and 2000. By the late 1990s, military reform appeared urgent and necessary. This accelerated the adoption of a denial strategy and expendable systems, especially tactical nuclear weapons. Thus, Russian defense policies adhered to the predictions of perceived relative power theory, but only when Moscow perceived a serious external threat. This suggests an important scope condition for the theory, which is addressed in chapter 8.[49]

CHAPTER EIGHT

Lessons and Implications

American leaders seem to believe that America's preeminent
position will last indefinitely. . . . States are free to disregard
the imperatives of power, but they must expect to pay a price
for doing so.

—KENNETH WALTZ (2000)

THE PRECEDING CHAPTERS DESCRIBED how great powers alter their
defense policies as they rise and decline. This final chapter ad-
dresses the implications for both scholars and policy makers. It begins by describing five key lessons from the historical case studies
and five areas for further study by scholars. The chapter then turns
to the consequences for the emerging Sino-American strategic
competition. Returning to the initial puzzle, this chapter explains
China's recent defense reforms and predicts its future defense policies. The book concludes by discussing how the United States
should respond, providing additional urgency for overdue reforms
to U.S. defense objectives, strategies, and investments.

Historical Lessons

This book has demonstrated that U.S., German, British, French, Japanese, and Russian defense policies changed in largely predictable ways as national power rose and fell. These patterns generally aligned with the hypotheses of perceived relative power theory, but the case studies reveal five significant caveats. First, leaders are usually slow to grasp changes in relative power, particularly when experiencing relative decline. Second, leaders can act remarkably quickly when they perceive a serious threat. Third, power changes are easier for rising states to acknowledge but politically fraught in declining states. Fourth, expected contributions by allies are an important factor in relative power calculations. And fifth, individual leadership is central to major defense reforms. Each of these lessons is described in detail below.

Defense Policies Change Slowly

In every historical case, changes in defense policies lagged changes in relative power. This delay highlights a critical weakness of structural explanations that overlook perceptions. State behavior is rooted not in power itself but in perceptions of power. As David Edelstein and others have demonstrated, national leaders are usually slow to acknowledge change and even slower to adapt to it. Therefore, defense policies often appear disconnected from relative power.[1] Coming to terms with changes in power is even more difficult in periods of relative decline.

There are several reasons that defense policies lag relative power changes. First, shifts in relative power are often difficult to discern. Although economic conditions can change quickly, these dynamics are not always visible to national leaders or to the public. This is particularly true in periods of flux, when rapid change makes it harder for leaders to discern the direction and speed of power shifts. Second, perceptions change slowly because leaders usually incorporate new data by incrementally updating reference frames. Third, leaders must build consensus in political, military, and industrial circles to pursue new policies. These initiatives take time, particularly when domestic interest groups oppose change.

Fourth, most new systems and doctrines require years, if not decades, to develop and field. For example, Germany's decision to pursue offensive sea control required not only design and acquisition of new battleships but also construction of new facilities and equipment to make them, as well as the widening of the Kiel Canal to allow their transit to the sea. For all these reasons, changes in defense policies substantially lag changes in relative power.[2]

Perceived Threats Accelerate Reforms

Although defense policies respond slowly to relative power changes, perception of a serious threat can speed up reforms. In fact, without a clear threat, leaders often disregard relative power shifts. Stephen Walt's balance of threat theory suggests that leaders identify threats by assessing other states' aggregate power, geographic proximity, offensive capabilities, and offensive intentions. As Walt has noted, "Other things being equal, states that are close by are more dangerous than those that are far away. States with large offensive military capabilities are more dangerous than those whose armed forces are largely suitable for defending their own territory. Lastly, states with clearly aggressive intentions tend to provoke more opposition than those who seek primarily to uphold the status quo." When leaders perceive a serious external threat, they are more likely to react to relative power changes. Otherwise, the impetus for expensive and politically difficult reforms is likely to be dominated by political and cultural factors. As a result, perception of a serious threat is typically a prerequisite for major defense policy reforms.[3]

The role of threat perception is particularly evident in the cases of declining powers. France perceived Germany as a serious threat for most of the interwar period, leading to major defense reforms. The same is true of Japan during World War II, when the danger of a strengthening United States could not have been clearer. Both France and Japan therefore responded rapidly to relative power changes, although both efforts were ultimately ineffective. Conversely, at the end of the nineteenth century, British leaders were divided on whether a serious external threat existed. It was not until the German threat became obvious around 1904 that

Jackie Fisher won support for major defense policy reforms. Similarly, at the end of the twentieth century, many Russian leaders believed that they faced no serious external threat. The United States and NATO were strong, but they were geographically distant and committed to cooperation with Russia. It was not until the late 1990s that Vladimir Putin and other Russian leaders shifted Russian defense policies, in part due to their view that U.S. power had encroached on Russia's sphere of influence and now posed a serious threat. When British and Russian leaders viewed external threats as low, they largely maintained their existing defense policies. These cases suggest that perception of a serious threat is usually necessary for leaders to alter defense objectives, strategies, and investments in response to relative power shifts.

Reforms Are Easier during Rise than Decline

Relative power changes are perceived and reacted to differently by rising and declining powers. Power is often a source of national pride, so rising powers are typically quick to acknowledge their ascent and adopt major defense reforms. This is true even in the absence of a serious external threat. In the United States, for example, Theodore Roosevelt won domestic support by championing U.S. strength and advocating major defense reforms, despite the lack of a clear foreign threat. This in turn accentuated the degree to which U.S. leaders and the public viewed the United States as a strong and rising power. In this sense, the pursuit of power-projection systems in rising powers is overdetermined—political, military, organizational, and strategic factors are all aligned in supporting the development of power-projection capabilities. Conversely, leaders in declining states have little political or organizational incentive to acknowledge changes in relative power, particularly absent a serious external threat.

This politicization of power accords with the literature on perception and misperception. As prospect theory suggests, individuals are strongly predisposed to avoid losses, even small losses. Even when signs of relative decline are evident, leaders often look for reasons to believe that their position is stable or that it will stabilize in the future. In the British case, political leaders discounted economic and military trends and focused instead on the strength of British colonies and alliances. The French talked about the might of defensive warfare during the interwar period. Many Japanese leaders hoped that their national willpower and supposed racial superiority would overcome the United States' industrial advantages. And Russian leaders talked about their geostrategic position as a nuclear power astride Europe and Asia as an enduring strength. In short, leaders in each declining state argued that their national strength was undiminished, despite clear signs to the contrary. As Keren Yarhi-Milo has shown, when this decline was vivid to leaders—when they lost battles or campaigns, for example—they altered their views and pursued defense policy reforms. Therefore, rapid defense policy reforms typically prove easier for rising powers than for declining powers, especially absent a clear external threat.[4]

Alliances Are Critical to Perceptions of Power

Although many structural theories focus on national power, most leaders factor alliances into their assessment of relative power. Estimation of allied strength is often a major factor for leaders considering defense reforms. Great Britain, for example, entered into alliances with Japan, France, and Russia in the early 1900s. These three nations, along with the United States, represented some of the strongest powers of the time—leaving Germany saddled with the Austrian, Italian, and Ottoman Empires. British leaders were therefore confident that they could remain relatively strong, even as German power grew. This reduced British support for drastic defense policy reforms, even if the resulting entrapment and abandonment risks simultaneously required careful strategic planning. Similarly, although Japan was economically weaker than the United States was going into World War II, many Japanese leaders thought alliances with Germany and Italy would give them an edge in a global struggle if U.S. attention was split between Europe and Asia.

If leaders include allied strength in their assessments of national power, it follows that they should adjust their objectives, strategies, and investments to conduct combined operations. Yet, in periods of high threat, national leaders often ignore the needs of allies and focus instead on domestic defense requirements. Interwar France illustrates this tendency. Rather than constructing the strategy or capabilities necessary to come to the defense of eastern European allies, leaders in Paris focused on their own narrow requirements. They also discounted expectations of allies, fearing that past promises would not turn into future actions. Therefore, although leaders often include allied strength in their relative power calculations, defense policies typically align with more parochial interests, especially in high threat environments.

Individual Leaders Drive Defense Reforms

A fifth and final lesson is that individual leaders are critical to instituting defense reforms. Overcoming the bureaucratic inertia that favors status quo policies requires sustained effort and substantial domestic political power. Therefore, defense policy reforms often demand that existing leaders embrace new ideas or be replaced by fresh leaders who favor reform. Each of the six great powers examined here had at least one leader who is often credited with championing new objectives, strategies, or investments: Theodore Roosevelt and Alfred Thayer Mahan in the United States; Kaiser Wilhelm and Alfred von Tirpitz in Germany; Jackie Fisher and a young Winston Churchill in Great Britain; André Maginot in France; Isoroku Yamamoto and Masafumi Arima in Japan; and Mikhail Gorbachev in Russia. It is impossible to explain how great-power defense policies changed in the twentieth century without referencing these leaders.

Given the importance of individual leaders, their beliefs, personalities, biases, and perceptions are hugely important. Yet, these case studies suggest that individual leaders are also shaped by strategic circumstances. For example, Theodore Roosevelt initially opposed colonialization and power projection before changing his views and championing these efforts. The same is true of other leaders, from Tirpitz to Gorbachev. In fact, leaders are often chosen for their willingness to adapt to changing strategic circumstances and push through reforms in response. Thus, there is no doubt that individual leaders are critical to instituting defense reforms, but scholars must also acknowledge that leaders' views and selection are also shaped by changes in relative power.

Questions for Further Study

This book is an initial effort to describe and validate the theory of perceived relative power. Although the historical cases analyzed herein suggest that the theory's basic premises hold—with some notable caveats—much work is left to be done on the theory's scope conditions. Five questions stand out as particularly important for specifying the conditions under which the theory holds and examining its broader implications.

First, does perceived relative power theory apply to lesser powers? Although this book focuses on great powers, the theory of perceived relative power may hold for lesser powers as well. Yet applying this theory to lesser powers raises several additional questions. Do weaker states compare their power to that of the world's greatest power? Or to their region's greatest power? Or perhaps to the state that appears the most threatening? Moreover, if lesser powers compare themselves to great powers, will they ever view themselves as strong enough to justify extensive objectives, control strategies, and sustainable investments? Answering these questions is vital to determining whether this theory can be applied more broadly and how to do so.

Second, does perceived relative power theory hold for earlier periods? This book has examined cases from the past 150 years, when denial systems such as mines and torpedoes were available. But the core logic of perceived relative power theory may also apply in earlier periods. Take, for example, the case of the Roman Empire. Edward Luttwak suggests three "changing conceptions of empire: hegemonic expansionism, . . . territorial security, . . . and finally, in diminished circumstances, sheer survival." Similarly, Iain Johnston concludes that "in the Chinese case, at least, empires, especially at peak periods of power, often exhibited offensive, coercive behavior." Johnston posits that an "empire consolidates and mobilizes resources in the earlier stages of the dynastic cycle. . . . As the dynastic cycle peaks, the empire is overextended financially and militarily. . . . As decline sets in, the state turns to less offensively coercive, more static defensive strategies." At first glance, these logics align with perceived relative power theory, but additional research is needed to confirm that this theory applies to earlier periods.[5]

Third, what are the most important drivers of perceptual change? Military outcomes persuasively communicate changes in relative power, but how else do leaders determine relative power dynamics? When is economic data sufficient to change opinions? After all, many leaders of declining powers have dismissed economic results as inaccurate or simply momentary setbacks. And different types of governments and leaders may be more willing or able to recognize and acknowledge changes in relative power. The same is true of threat perceptions. What makes some external threats more concerning than others? And how does this vary among states and leaders? Additional research is needed to explain what changes perceptions of power and threat.

Fourth, can investment patterns be quantified? Although objectives and strategies are difficult to quantify, it is easier to measure military investments. By categorizing certain investments as mobile or immobile and sustainable or expendable, it may be possible to track how much funding states direct toward different defense policies. By analyzing changes over time and across cases, scholars could evaluate whether investments follow the expected pattern. Doing so would help to identify the magnitude of change in investments due to changes in perceived relative power, which is one of the major outstanding questions from this research. Shifts in investment mixes might also help policy makers pinpoint shifts in foreign objectives and strategy.[6]

Fifth, is the balance between denial and control shifting more toward denial systems? Theorists have long argued that technological changes inherently advantage certain defense policies. But scholars have usually focused on offense and defense, rather than control and denial. The theory presented here suggests that advances in denial technologies—such as improvised explosive devices and advanced missiles—have made denial strategies easier and cheaper. This should increase spending on expendable military systems and advantage weaker actors. Scholars should be able to test this proposition. This concept could resolve some of the shortcomings of offense-defense theory. Furthermore, the increasing effectiveness of denial strategies would help to explain why the cost of projecting power is rising. This phenomenon would also have massive policy implications, particularly for the competition between China and the United States.[7]

Modern Implications

We now return to the puzzle that inspired this book: Why is China abandoning anti-access capabilities in favor of power projection? And what should the United States do in response? Answering these questions is vital if policy makers are to accurately assess and respond to the evolving Sino-American military competition. The theory of perceived relative power has implications for all states experiencing shifts in relative power, but no two are more important than China and the United States. This book therefore closes by examining Chinese and U.S. defense policies and charting their likely future path.[8]

China's Pursuit of Power Projection

The People's Republic of China is now the world's number-two economic and military power. Beijing has ascended to this position due to a remarkable economic run. Over the past three decades, China's gross domestic product jumped from under $500 billion in 1992 to over $18 trillion in 2022. The Communist Party now spends roughly forty times as much on its military as it did thirty years ago, representing an average yearly increase of 13 percent. This rapid increase in defense spending has enabled the People's Liberation Army to launch a massive military modernization program. As a result, China now has the means to challenge U.S. power and influence in East Asia and beyond. Yet, major questions remain about China's military modernization. Most importantly, why is the Communist Party shifting its military investments toward traditional means of power projection and away from the asymmetric capabilities that have called into question U.S. military dominance in Asia? Will this trend accelerate if China's rise continues? Or might it reverse if China encounters serious economic difficulties?

This book suggests that China is following the classic path of a rising power. Beijing's new focus on power projection is a natural result of a growing perception within the Communist Party that China is not only rising but increasingly in a position of strength. As Xi Jinping asserted in 2019, "The Chinese nation has achieved a tremendous transformation: It has stood up, grown rich and is becoming strong." Along these lines, the Chinese scholar Shen Dingli writes, "We are assertive to defend our rights. ... In the past, we were weak, now we are strong and don't need to accept insults." As these words suggest, China is undergoing a shift from Phase 1 to Phase 2 of perceived relative power. Just as expected, China's defense policies are transitioning from a largely anti-access approach toward power projection. Chinese leaders are adopting extensive objectives overseas. These objectives require an offensive control strategy. This strategy, in turn, requires mobile and sustainable systems.[9]

What has this shift looked like in practice? Beginning in the 1980s, China developed and fielded military systems to deny other great powers the ability to project power close to China's borders. In 1980, Deng Xiaoping called this strategy "active defense." The resulting anti-access systems included conventionally armed ballistic missiles, anti-ship cruise missiles, advanced air defenses, and diesel submarines. This approach evened the playing field between China and the United States, allowing Beijing to field comparatively cheap weapons that could neutralize Washington's more advanced and expensive platforms. For example, a Chinese conventionally armed ballistic missile costs roughly $20 million but can potentially hold at risk a U.S. aircraft carrier and its air wing, which cost at least $20 billion.[10]

In recent years, however, Beijing's posture has changed. Denny Roy predicted in the 1990s that "China's growth from a weak, developing state to a stronger, more prosperous state should result in a more assertive foreign policy." Indeed, China became more assertive and began to invest in traditional means of power projection after the great financial crisis of 2008. Elizabeth Economy writes that senior Chinese officials began to argue "that the decline of the United States and the rise of China—long predicted to occur at some time during the twenty-first century—had begun. China's military . . . started to grow its ambitions alongside its capabilities." Rush Doshi argues that a major shift in China's grand strategy began roughly fifteen years ago. Indeed, acknowledging China's new economic strength, the former commander of U.S. Pacific Command Samuel Locklear noted in 2012, "If I were China, and I was in the economic position that China is in, . . . I would consider building an aircraft carrier. And I might consider building several aircraft carriers." China did exactly this under the leadership of Admiral Wu Shengli.[11]

Today, China's leaders are building more symmetrical military forces to challenge the United States. Michael McDevitt assesses that "China wants to become a maritime power mainly because its strategic circumstances have changed dramatically over the past 20 years." Taylor Fravel concludes, "For the PRC's [People's Republic of China's] first four decades, military strategy focused on the singular challenge of countering an invasion of Chinese territory. . . . New interests overseas, and the missions they may create for the PLA [People's Liberation Army], may come to play a great role in China's military strategy going forward." This path resembles that followed by other great powers. Robert Kaplan observes, "China's naval leaders are displaying the aggressive philosophy of the turn-of-the-twentieth-century U.S. naval strategist Alfred Thayer Mahan." There are also parallels with naval developments in Wilhelmine Germany. Michael Green finds that China's recent actions are "part of a longer-term attempt by Beijing to chip away at the regional status quo." This has only accelerated since Xi Jinping took power. He has even reduced some of China's least mobile ground forces in order to fund more deployable air and naval units.[12]

Changes in relative power are not the only reason for Beijing's pursuit of power projection. As in the U.S. and German cases, multiple interwoven factors are pushing China toward new objectives, strategies, and investments. Andrew Scobell and Andrew Nathan have suggested that Chinese power projection is "largely symbolic." Similarly, Adam Liff argues that Beijing is "acquiring conspicuous prestige-driven, highly-publicized, and extremely expensive capabilities of dubious military utility for China's stated strategic priorities." Robert Ross writes that leaders in Beijing are "appeasing widespread nationalist sentiment" driven by "national-ist ambition for an aircraft carrier, . . . combined with the persistent PLA Navy's demands." And rather than being focused on the United States, Mark Cozad suggests that Chinese forces are devel-oping "sustainable, broadly-scoped capabilities that will allow them to challenge the major regional powers." All of these theories pro-vide potential explanations for China's recent behavior. Yet, as with the United States and Germany, it is notable that all these factors point in the same direction: toward China building a more robust power-projection capability and doing so just at the point Chinese leaders appear to have determined Beijing is both rising and rela-tively strong.[13]

China's recent accumulation of power leads to an obvious question: Should observers expect Chinese defense policies to shift even more toward power projection if its growth continues? This book answers in the affirmative—Chinese leaders will accelerate their embrace of power projection if they believe that China is growing more powerful. In other words, these may be just the first steps in China's development of a truly global military. Deploy-ments of Chinese ships, aircraft, and even ground forces are likely to increase if China's power grows. As the Belt and Road Initiative shows, trade will follow the flag, and the flag will follow trade. If China's interests abroad grow, Beijing will probably seek to expand its reach by fielding more sustainable power-projection forces and constructing additional military bases abroad, just as the United States, Germany, and others did during their rise. Indeed, the U.S. government asserts that Chinese leaders have "likely considered [military logistics facilities in] Cambodia, Myanmar, Thailand, Sin-gapore, Indonesia, Pakistan, Sri Lanka, United Arab Emirates, Kenya, Equatorial Guinea, Seychelles, Tanzania, Angola, and Tajik-istan, among other places."[14]

Of course, China's continued rise is by no means assured. Bei-jing faces numerous challenges, including questions about the long-term viability of its economic growth model, demographic constraints due to its one-child policy and rapidly aging popula-tion, and a more fragile political structure created by Xi Jinping's consolidation of power and elimination of the party's previous suc-cession system. Some observers, including Mike Beckley and Hal

Brands, suggest that leaders in Beijing might change their defense policies substantially if China were to stumble. Nonetheless, a question remains: Would leaders in Beijing see setbacks as an indicator of a long-term slowdown or a more temporary issue—a "body-builder with a cold," as Jude Blanchette has described it? The cases studied here suggest that national leaders are typically slow to recognize their own state's peaking power, implying that even if China's growth slows precipitously, it could take years or decades before Chinese leaders adapt their defense policies accordingly. As a result, China's embrace of power projection is probably here to stay for the foreseeable future.[15]

In short, it is no coincidence that China's rapid economic and military rise has coincided with major changes in its defense policies. Although China's anti-access systems have called into question U.S. power-projection capabilities, these capabilities will increasingly be seen as secondary priorities as Beijing embraces more extensive objectives and seeks greater control over a broader region. Beijing's new focus on power projection is directly attributable to its leaders' changing perceptions of China's relative strength vis-à-vis the United States. As Xi Jinping stated at the second Belt and Road Forum, "Today, China has reached a new historical starting point. . . . We are keenly aware that with all we have achieved, there are still many mountains to scale and many shoals to navigate." To scale those mountains, China's military leaders are aiming to "seize the strategic commanding heights of future military competition." If China's power continues to grow, leaders in Beijing will adopt more extensive objectives, offensive strategies, and sustainable systems. China's pursuit of power projection is just beginning.[16]

The United States' Occasion for Defense Reforms

U.S. strategists have long enjoyed a remarkably lucky strategic position. The United States is surrounded by "fish and friends" and has amassed more than its fair share of world power over the past seventy-five years. After World War II, the United States controlled 50 percent of the world's production. This position of strength allowed leaders in Washington to work with allies and partners around the globe to build international institutions that favored U.S. power and ideals. Washington built a global network of alliances while spreading liberal democracy and capitalism. U.S. leaders made many mistakes, but the United States' good fortune permitted it to reshape much of the world in its own image.

Today, however, many observers worry that the United States' strategic position—and the international order it created—is under unprecedented threat. Political leaders suggest that the United States is no longer "great." National security experts fret that China's growing power will eclipse that of the United States. After all, the United States now accounts for just over 20 percent of global production—its lowest percentage in the past century. The U.S. National Intelligence Council has asserted that "the United States' (and the West's) relative decline vis-à-vis the rising states is inevitable. . . . China will probably have the largest economy, surpassing that of the United States a few years before 2030." Leading academics concur, with Joseph Nye insisting that "the American century is not over" but admitting that the United States may be declining in relative terms. This increasingly anxious debate has drawn attention to the military balance in Asia, which many observers believe is deteriorating. The 2018 U.S. National Defense Strategy states bleakly, "We are emerging from a period of strategic atrophy. . . . Our competitive military advantage has been eroding."[17]

But the United States' luck has not run out. The relative decline of U.S. power is not today's only strategic shift. It has been accompanied by a second major change: technological advances that make denial cheaper and easier. As Andrew Krepinevich has noted, "The price of projecting power is going up." Today, improvised explosive devices menace ground forces, smart mines and anti-ship missiles threaten naval forces, advanced air defenses increase the risks to aircraft, and space and cyber networks are under near-constant attack. In short, technology has made control more difficult and more costly, relative to denial. One need look no further than U.S. struggles in Iraq and Afghanistan or Russian failures in Ukraine to see the damage that denial systems can inflict even on the world's most capable militaries.[18]

Until the past few years, this shift advantaged China rather than the United States. Beijing's anti-access capabilities became more potent, while Washington's global power-projection efforts proved more costly. But if China continues to follow the typical path of a perceived rising power—and this book argues that it will—it will be fighting against these technological trends. As the People's Liberation Army embraces power projection, the United States and its allies and partners will have a chance to flip the military competition on its head. By embracing defense and denial, the United States and its allies and partners can substantially raise the costs of any effort to alter the territorial status quo in East Asia.

Technological advances that favor denial benefit countries like the United States that desire to maintain the status quo. U.S. leaders already reshaped the world, so their task today is to consolidate and protect that system. Indeed, this is a natural objective for a peaking power. As the United States consolidates its objectives, U.S. strategy should focus increasingly on defense, and it should invest less in mobile forces. Eugene Gholz, Benjamin Freedman, and Enea Gjoza argue that the United States should embrace a strategy of "defensive defense." They suggest that Washington should "remember that its strategic goals are defensive, and the United States should adjust its military posture to match that reality."[19]

Changing political circumstances have created strange bedfellows. Not only are some academics supporting a more defensively oriented U.S. strategy, but this idea has also gained traction with a growing number of experts in Washington. The longtime Republican congressional staffer Chris Brose argues that U.S. leaders should adopt "defense without dominance." Bridge Colby, a former Trump administration defense official, has embraced the importance of denial. So too have researchers at the Quincy Institute—well-known for its skepticism of the conservative defense establishment—which has advocated a strategy of "flexible denial." Although the terms these experts use may vary, they all have one thing in common: a renewed focus on defense and denial.[20]

Defense and denial are often conflated, but they are not the same. A more defensive strategy would warrant less mobile systems, whereas a denial strategy would favor more expendable systems. In some cases, these strategies and systems overlap, but in many cases, they differ. Take, for example, the question of whether the United States should better fortify and defend forward bases or instead forgo these investments by relying more on small systems and distributed operations. In many ways, this is a choice between embracing defense or denial—a debate that has been raging inside the U.S. military.

Perceived relative power theory suggests that the United States is likely to embrace more defensive approaches, but denial strategies could become more appealing if U.S. leaders perceive the United States to be in a position of weakness. This is already the case for U.S. allies and partners in Asia, who are at a serious disadvantage vis-à-vis China. Therefore, one way to rationalize the ongoing debate between defense and denial would be for the United States to shift to a more defensive approach, while its allies and partners rely more heavily on denial strategies. Indeed, some experts outside the United States have already embraced this idea. To the extent that U.S. allies and partners increasingly find themselves at a disadvantage relative to China, this incentivizes them to invest more in denial capabilities. Such an approach might include "hedgehog defenses" designed to build ally and partner resilience by investing in area-denial capabilities to constrain Chinese power projection—a move that the United States should encourage and assist with. Washington might enable and support these strategies through its own capabilities and innovations, including programs like Replicator, that seek to deploy large numbers of cheap and expendable autonomous systems.

Defense officials assert that these strategies are already leading to a reversal of fortune in some war games. For many years, China prevailed in most simulations about major contingencies in Asia, such as a Taiwan invasion. But the Pentagon's more recent war games suggest that new U.S. and allied approaches are altering the military balance and often resulting in U.S. victory. This does not imply that the United States has solved the challenges posed by China's military modernization. Beijing could rely more on gray-zone coercion to alter the status quo without crossing key thresholds that might trigger outright conflict. And the Communist Party will no doubt retain the ability to carry out domestic repression at home and increasingly assertive diplomacy abroad. Allies will also worry about deterrence and reassurance if the United States shifts its defense policies—addressing these abandonment concerns is made even more difficult by growing U.S. skepticism of overseas commitments. Other tools will no doubt be necessary to address many of these challenges. But the military balance, at the very least, could be stabilized if U.S. leaders and their allies and partners are willing and able to embrace a new set of defense policies.

The question that remains, however, is whether U.S. leaders and their foreign counterparts can flip this switch. After all, this would be a momentous shift for the U.S. defense enterprise. It would be arguably the biggest change in U.S. conventional military capabilities since U.S. leaders began to view the United States as a relatively strong power in the 1890s. Since then, power projection and the maintenance of primacy have become the hallmark of U.S. military strategy. The desire for power projection has been remarkably consistent. In 1997, for example, the U.S. National Defense Panel asserted, "The cornerstone of America's continued military preeminence is our ability to project combat power rapidly and virtually unimpeded to widespread areas of the globe." Fifteen years later, despite the worsening of the United States' relative position, the 2012 U.S. Defense Strategy Guidance continued to argue, "the United States must maintain its ability to project power in areas in which our access and freedom to operate are challenged."[21]

Rather than embracing new approaches, recent U.S. initiatives have often focused on projecting power despite the increasing costs of doing so. The Air-Sea Battle Concept and its successor Joint Concept for Access and Maneuver in the Global Commons represented efforts to "double down" on power projection by disrupting Chinese anti-access capabilities. These operational concepts were designed to strike the sensors and launchers for China's long-range missiles. Proponents argued that this would "ensure that U.S. forces remain able to project power on behalf of American interests worldwide." But these approaches are increasingly in tension with the United States' objectives and the realities of the changing balance of power.[22]

Can the United States rely on primacy and power projection forever? Almost certainly not. Gone are the days in which, as Roger Cliff has commented, "if the U.S. military can arrive in force, it will almost undoubtedly win in a conventional military campaign." In fact, some experts argue that U.S. primacy is already gone. Christopher Layne warned decades ago that the United States' "preponderance cannot be maintained. . . . The changing distribution of power in the international system—specifically, the relative decline of U.S. power and the corresponding rise of new great powers—will render the strategy untenable." As a result, many scholars have called for the United States to consolidate its position. Paul MacDonald and Joseph Parent warn, "Declining powers that fail to draw in their horns tend to fall further faster." Barry Posen says the United States should shift "to a more restrained global stance." John Mearsheimer insists, "It is time for the United States to show greater restraint." Recent U.S. leaders, including Barack Obama, Donald Trump, and Joe Biden, have also called for greater restraint, particularly in the Middle East (even if they have not always executed this strategy).[23]

U.S. leaders therefore have a unique opportunity to use technology to offset the deterioration of the balance of power. There is and will continue to be substantial opposition from parts of the defense enterprise, particularly those that develop, build, train, and sustain power-projection forces. But this opposition must be overcome. U.S. leaders cannot simply ignore recent trends in relative power. As Paul Kennedy has noted, "There is a very clear connection in the long run between an individual Great Power's economic rise and fall and its growth and decline as an important military power." Just as British leaders were slow to recognize and respond to Germany's rise, U.S. leaders have been slow to recognize and respond to China's rise. But as with Great Britain, it is not too late. Secretary of Defense Jim Mattis was correct when he noted the need "to pursue urgent change at significant scale."[24]

This book suggests that the ability to adopt major defense policy reforms will depend on three factors: (1) accurate assessments of relative power dynamics; (2) perceptions of a serious external threat, most likely from the Communist Party of China; and (3) sustained efforts by U.S. leaders to overcome inherent political and bureaucratic inertia. If the United States is lucky, its leaders will be able to adopt new defense policies before it is too late. U.S. leaders have a fleeting opportunity to shift the United States' defense policies to match new realities—they must learn the lessons of history if they are to ride the tides of fortune.

Notes

Preface

Epigraph: Hirohito was referencing a proclamation on the end of World War I. Quoted in Peter Michael Wetzler, *Hirohito and War: Imperial Tradition and Military Decision Making in Prewar Japan* (Honolulu: University of Hawaii Press, 1998), 133.

1. Mark Cozad, "China's Regional Power Projection: Prospects for Future Missions in the South and East China Seas," in *Beyond the Strait: PLA Missions Other than Taiwan*, ed. Roy Kamphausen, David Lai, and Andrew Scobell (Carlisle, PA: Strategic Studies Institute, U.S. Army War College, 2008), 291. Andrew Scobell and Andrew J. Nathan, "China's Overstretched Military," *The Washington Quarterly* 35, no. 4 (October 1, 2012): 142. Also see Michael A. Glosny, Phillip C. Saunders, and Robert S. Ross, "Debating China's Naval Nationalism," *International Security* 35, no. 2 (October 1, 2010): 174–75; Robert S. Ross, "China's Naval Nationalism: Sources, Prospects, and the U.S. Response," *International Security* 34, no. 2 (2009): 46–81.

2. On China's defense policy, Michael McDevitt notes, "It wasn't until the 18th Party Congress in 2012 that maritime issues were officially identified as a national priority for the Communist Party, the state, and the country. The Chinese Communist Party leadership concluded that becoming a maritime power was essential to achieving its national goals." Michael McDevitt, "Becoming a Great 'Maritime Power': A Chinese Dream," Center for Naval Analyses, June 2016, 117–18, https://www.cna.org/archive/CNA_Files/pdf/irm-2016-u-013646.pdf; Jacqueline Newmyer, "The Revolution in Military Affairs with Chinese Characteristics," *Journal of Strategic Studies* 33, no. 4 (2010): 483–504.

3. This theory is related in many ways to concepts put forward in Paul M. Kennedy, *The Rise and Fall of the Great Powers: Economic Change and Military Conflict from 1500 to 2000* (New York: Vintage Books, 1989), xx.

4. For example, U.S. military leaders have consistently supported efforts "to ensure that U.S. forces remain able to project power on behalf of American interests worldwide." Norton A. Schwartz and Jonathan W. Greenert, "Air-Sea Battle: Promoting Stability in a Period of Uncertainty," *The American Interest*, February 20, 2012, https://www.the-american-interest.com/2012/02/20/air-sea-battle/.

Chapter One. Determinants of Defense Policies

Epigraph: Robert Gilpin, *War and Change in World Politics* (Cambridge: Cambridge University Press, 1981), 84.

1. Ends are the objectives toward which one strives. Ways are the security strategies that states adopt in pursuit of national objectives. Means are instruments, such as military investments, by which some end can be achieved. For the purposes of this book, these three elements form a state's defense policies. Note that military doctrine is often included in this hierarchy—it is not addressed in detail here but is discussed throughout this study. This is not to ignore the critical role that other elements, such as force posture, alliances, and warfighting tactics, have in determining defense policy. This study subsumes posture, alliances, and tactics into security strategies (the "ways" category), as they are inherently about how best to use fixed resources to accomplish desired ends. See Colin S. Gray, *Strategy and Defence Planning: Meeting the Challenge of Uncertainty* (Oxford: Oxford University Press, 2014), 178. Arthur F. Lykke, Jr., "Toward an Understanding of Military Strategy," in *U.S. Army War College Guide to Strategy*, ed. Joseph R. Cerami and James F. Holcomb, Jr. (Carlisle, PA: U.S. Army War College Press, 2001), 170. Steve Krasner argues that national interests are "a set of transitively ordered preferences that persist over time and are related to general societal goals." Stephen D. Krasner, *Defending the National Interest: Raw Materials Investments and U.S. Foreign Policy* (Princeton, NJ: Princeton University Press, 1978), 55.

2. As most commonly defined in the literature, such imitation or emulation "is the conscious, purposeful imitation, in full or in part, by one state of any institution, technology, or governing practice of another state." João Resende-Santos, "Anarchy and the Emulation of Military Systems: Military Organization and Technology in South America, 1870–1930," *Security Studies* 5, no. 3 (March 1, 1996): 199. See also Yu-Ming Liou, Paul Musgrave, and J. Furman Daniel, "The Imitation Game: Why Don't Rising Powers Innovate Their Militaries More?," *The Washington Quarterly* 38, no. 3 (July 3, 2015): 157–74. Kenneth N. Waltz, *Theory of International Politics* (Reading, MA: Addison-Wesley, 1979), 127. Barry R. Posen, "Nationalism, the Mass Army, and Military Power," *International Security* 18, no. 2 (1993): 82. Adam P. Liff, "Shadowing the Hegemon? Great Power

Norms, Socialization, and the Military Trajectories of Rising Powers" (PhD diss., Princeton University, 2014), 1, ProQuest (3626835). Ross, "China's Naval Nationalism."

3. John J. Mearsheimer, *The Tragedy of Great Power Politics* (New York: Norton, 2001), 165. Thomas J. Christensen and Jack Snyder, "Chain Gangs and Passed Bucks: Predicting Alliance Patterns in Multipolarity," *International Organization* 44, no. 2 (March 1990): 139. Gilpin, *War and Change in World Politics*, 29. Stephen M. Walt, *The Origins of Alliances* (Ithaca, NY: Cornell University Press, 1994), 30. Arnold Wolfers, *Discord and Collaboration: Essays on International Politics* (Baltimore: Johns Hopkins University Press, 1991), 114–15. Limited aims are necessary because, as Arnold Wolfers argues, "rational policy-makers will seek to bring policy ends and commitments to pursue them in line," creating "mutual dependence between ends and means." Wolfers, 114–15.

4. Stephen Brooks comments, "realist scholars point to three material factors other than the distribution of capabilities that affect the probability of conflict: technology, geography, and international economic pressures." Stephen G. Brooks, "Dueling Realisms," *International Organization* 51, no. 3 (July 1, 1997): 456. Jack S. Levy and William R. Thompson, "Balancing on Land and at Sea: Do States Ally against the Leading Global Power?," *International Security* 35, no. 1 (July 2010): 8. Paul M. Kennedy, *The Rise and Fall of British Naval Mastery* (London: A. Lane, 1976), 177–202. Sir Halford John Mackinder, *Democratic Ideals and Reality: A Study in the Politics of Reconstruction* (New York: Henry Holt, 1919), 150. These arguments were echoed by Nicholas Spykman, who suggested, "Who controls the rimland rules Eurasia; who rules Eurasia controls the destinies of the world." Nicholas John Spykman, *The Geography of the Peace* (New York: Harcourt, Brace, 1944), 43. Also see Nicholas John Spykman, "Frontiers, Security, and International Organization," *Geographical Review* 32, no. 3 (July 1942): 436–37. Alfred Thayer Mahan, *Mahan on Naval Warfare: Selections from the Writing of Rear Admiral Alfred T. Mahan*, ed. Allan F. Westcott (Boston: Little, Brown, 1941), 286. Mearsheimer notes, "Large bodies of water are formidable obstacles that cause significant power-projection problems for attacking armies." Geographic distance between states is another critical factor. Kenneth Boulding argues, "The further from home any nation has to operate . . . the less strength it can put in the field." Stephen Van Evera suggests that other geographic features must be considered, such as "oceans, lakes, mountains, wide rivers, dense jungles, trackless deserts, or other natural barriers that impede offensive movement or give defenders natural strong points." Mearsheimer, *The Tragedy of Great Power Politics*, 44; Kenneth Ewart Boulding, *Conflict and Defense: A General Theory* (New York: Harper, 1962), 230–32, http://catalog.hathitrust.org/Record/001109316; Stephen Van Evera, "Offense, Defense, and the Causes of War," *International Security* 22, no. 4 (April 1998): 19.

5. Thomas C. Schelling, *Arms and Influence* (New Haven, CT: Yale University Press, 1976), 234. Charles Glaser also suggests the need to include the "offense-defense balance and offense-defense distinguishability . . . as key variables." Robert Jervis, "Cooperation under the Security Dilemma," *World Politics* 30, no. 2 (January 1978): 167–214; George H. Quester, *Offense and Defense in the International System* (New Brunswick, NJ: Transaction, 2003). Charles L. Glaser, "Realists as Optimists: Cooperation as Self-Help," *International Security* 19, no. 3 (1994): 61. Gilpin, *War and Change in World Politics*, 61. Richard K. Betts, "Must War Find a Way? A Review Essay," *International Security* 24, no. 2 (October 1999): 179. Martin van Creveld, *Technology and War: From 2000 B.C. to the Present* (Toronto: Free Press, 1991), 177; James D. Fearon, "The Offense-Defense Balance and War since 1648," Stanford University, April 8, 1997, https://web.stanford.edu/group/fearon-research/cgi-bin/wordpress/wp-content/uploads/2013/10/The-Offense-Defense-Balance-and-War-since-1648.pdf, 13; Van Evera, "Offense, Defense, and the Causes of War," 16. Stephen Biddle, "Rebuilding the Foundations of Offense-Defense Theory," *The Journal of Politics* 63, no. 3 (2001): 747–48. Keir A. Lieber, *War and the Engineers: The Primacy of Politics over Technology* (Ithaca, NY: Cornell University Press, 2005), 153. Jonathan Shimshoni, "Technology, Military Advantage, and World War I: A Case for Military Entrepreneurship," *International Security* 15, no. 3 (1990): 189. Matthew Evangelista, *Innovation and the Arms Race: How the United States and the Soviet Union Develop New Military Technologies* (Ithaca, NY: Cornell University Press, 1988). Thomas G. Mahnken, *Technology and the American Way of War since 1945* (New York: Columbia University Press, 2010), 11. Van Creveld, *Technology and War*, 220.
6. See, for example, Michael Klare, *Rising Powers, Shrinking Planet: The New Geopolitics of Energy* (London: Metropolitan Books, 2008); Michael A. Barnhart, *Japan Prepares for Total War: The Search for Economic Security, 1919–1941* (Ithaca, NY: Cornell University Press, 1987), 49; Richard N. Rosecrance, *The Rise of The Trading State: Commerce and Conquest in the Modern World* (New York: Basic Books, 1986); Stephen Brooks, *Producing Security: Multinational Corporations, Globalization, and the Changing Calculus of Conflict* (Princeton, NJ: Princeton University Press, 2005); Melvyn P. Leffler, *Safeguarding Democratic Capitalism: U.S. Foreign Policy and National Security, 1920–2015* (Princeton, NJ: Princeton University Press, 2017); Jonathan N. Markowitz, *Perils of Plenty: Arctic Resource Competition and the Return of the Great Game* (Oxford: Oxford University Press, 2020), 2.
7. Allan C. Stam III, *Win, Lose, or Draw: Domestic Politics and the Crucible of War* (Ann Arbor: University of Michigan Press, 1999), 14. Peter Gourevitch, "The Second Image Reversed: The International Sources of Domestic Politics," *International Organization* 32, no. 4 (1978): 881. Harvey

M. Sapolsky, Eugene Gholz, and Caitlin Talmadge, *US Defense Politics: The Origins of Security Policy* (Abingdon, UK: Routledge, 2014), 1. Dan Reiter and Allan C. Stam, *Democracies at War* (Princeton, NJ: Princeton University Press, 2002). Richard N. Rosecrance and Arthur A. Stein, "Beyond Realism: The Study of Grand Strategy," in *The Domestic Bases of Grand Strategy*, ed. Rosecrance and Stein (Ithaca, NY: Cornell University Press, 1993), 5. Kenneth N. Waltz, "Structural Realism after the Cold War," *International Security* 25, no. 1 (July 2000): 13. Conversely, Fareed Zakaria argues, "Domestic politics has a crucial influence on foreign policy. It is a mistake, however, to place it in competition with international factors when constructing general explanations of state behavior, not least because it will lose the contest." Fareed Zakaria, "Realism and Domestic Politics: A Review Essay," *International Security* 17, no. 1 (1992): 198. Gilpin, *War and Change in World Politics*, 96–97.

8. See Charles Tilly, *Coercion, Capital, and European States, AD 990–1992*, Studies in Social Discontinuity (Cambridge, MA: Blackwell, 1992); Otto Hintze, *The Historical Essays of Otto Hintze* (New York: Oxford University Press, 1975); Hendrik Spruyt, *The Sovereign State and Its Competitors: An Analysis of Systems Change* (Princeton, NJ: Princeton University Press, 1996). Deborah Avant, "Political Institutions and Military Effectiveness: Contemporary United States and United Kingdom," in *Creating Military Power: The Sources of Military Effectiveness*, ed. Risa Brooks and Elizabeth A. Stanley (Stanford, CA: Stanford University Press, 2007), 80. On the role of regime type in determining national responses, see Daniel M. Kliman, *Fateful Transitions: How Democracies Manage Rising Powers, from the Eve of World War I to China's Ascendance* (Philadelphia: University of Pennsylvania Press, 2014), 2. Jack Snyder, *Myths of Empire: Domestic Politics and International Ambition* (Ithaca, NY: Cornell University Press, 1994), 1–2. Snyder identifies three myths that lead to overexpansion: "gains and losses are cumulative; the offensive has the advantage; and offensive threats make others more cooperative." Snyder, 3. Elizabeth Kier, *Imagining War: French and British Military Doctrine between the Wars*, Princeton Studies in International History and Politics (Princeton, NJ: Princeton University Press, 1997), 5. Stephen Peter Rosen, "Military Effectiveness: Why Society Matters," *International Security* 19, no. 4 (1995): 29; Caitlin Talmadge, *The Dictator's Army: Battlefield Effectiveness in Authoritarian Regimes* (Ithaca, NY: Cornell University Press, 2015).

9. James Q. Wilson, *Bureaucracy: What Government Agencies Do and Why They Do It* (New York: Basic Books, 2000), 14. For more on these debates, also see Stephen Peter Rosen, *Winning the Next War: Innovation and the Modern Military* (Ithaca, NY: Cornell University Press, 1991), 8–9; Michael H. Armacost, *The Politics of Weapons Innovation: The Thor-Jupiter Controversy* (New York: Columbia University Press, 1969); William A. Lucas and Raymond H. Dawson, *The Organizational Politics of Defense* (Pittsburg, PA:

International Studies Association, 1974); Michael Horowitz, *The Diffusion of Military Power: Causes and Consequences for International Politics* (Princeton, NJ: Princeton University Press, 2010), 26; Jack Snyder, "Civil-Military Relations and the Cult of the Offensive, 1914 and 1984," *International Security* 9, no. 1 (1984): 110; Jack S. Levy, "Organizational Routines and the Causes of War," *International Studies Quarterly* 30, no. 2 (June 1986): 193; Stephen M. Walt, "The Search for a Science of Strategy: A Review Essay," *International Security* 12, no. 1 (1987): 158; Kimberly Marten Zisk, *Engaging the Enemy: Organization Theory and Soviet Military Innovation, 1955–1991* (Princeton, NJ: Princeton University Press, 1993), 6; Barry R. Posen, *The Sources of Military Doctrine: France, Britain, and Germany between the World Wars* (Ithaca, NY: Cornell University Press, 1986), 47; Jack Snyder, "The Cult of the Offensive in 1914," in *The Use of Force: Military Power and International Politics*, ed. Robert J. Art and Kenneth N. Waltz (Lanham, MD: Rowman and Littlefield, 1999), 117–18; Jack L. Snyder, *The Ideology of the Offensive: Military Decision Making and the Disasters of 1914* (Ithaca, NY: Cornell University Press, 1984); Stephen Van Evera, *Causes of War: Power and the Roots of Conflict* (Ithaca, NY: Cornell University Press, 1999), 282; Kier, *Imagining War*, 15; Christensen and Snyder, "Chain Gangs and Passed Bucks," 145; Scott D. Sagan, "1914 Revisited: Allies, Offense, and Instability," *International Security* 11, no. 2 (1986): 155–56; Walt, "The Search for a Science of Strategy," 149–54; Theo Farrell and Terry Terriff, "The Sources of Military Change," in *The Sources of Military Change: Culture, Politics, Technology*, ed. Farrell and Terriff (Boulder, CO: Lynne Rienner, 2002), 4; Daniel Markey, "Prestige and the Origins of War: Returning to Realism's Roots," *Security Studies* 8, no. 4 (June 1999): 129; Michael A. Hunzeker, *Dying to Learn: Wartime Lessons from the Western Front* (Ithaca, NY: Cornell University Press, 2021); Kendrick Kuo, "Dangerous Changes: When Military Innovation Harms Combat Effectiveness," *International Security* 47, no. 2 (2022); Jonathan Askonas, "A Muse of Fire: Why the U.S. Military Forgets What It Learns in War" (PhD diss., University of Oxford, 2019).

10.	On the importance of leadership and individuals, see Elizabeth N. Saunders, *Leaders at War: How Presidents Shape Military Interventions* (Ithaca, NY: Cornell University Press, 2011); Kenneth Neal Waltz, *Man, the State, and War: A Theoretical Analysis* (New York: Columbia University Press, 1959); Robert Jervis, "The Future of World Politics: Will It Resemble the Past," *International Security* 16, no. 3 (1991): 41; Charles Kupchan, *The Vulnerability of Empire* (Ithaca, NY: Cornell University Press, 1994), 7. Kissinger quoted in Walter Isaacson, *Kissinger* (New York: Simon and Schuster, 1992), 13. For example, during a visit of King Edward to Kiel, Wilhelm II announced, "When as a little boy I was allowed to visit Plymouth and Portsmouth . . . I admired the proud English ships in those two superb harbors. Then there awoke in me the wish to build ships of my own like those some day, and when I was grown up to possess a Navy as fine as the English." Quoted in Bernhard Bülow, *Memoirs of Prince von Bülow*, trans. Fritz August Voigt (Boston: Little, Brown, 1931), 29. Some notable exceptions include Robert Jervis, *Perception and Misperception in International Politics* (Princeton, NJ: Princeton University Press, 1976), 308. Daniel L. Byman and Kenneth M. Pollack, "Let Us Now Praise Great Men: Bringing the Statesman Back In," *International Security* 25, no. 4 (April 2001): 134–42. Deborah Avant, "Political Institutions and Military Effectiveness," 81; Christensen and Snyder, "Chain Gangs and Passed Bucks," 145. Ernest R May, *"Lessons" of the Past: The Use and Misuse of History in American Foreign Policy* (New York: Oxford University Press, 1975); Richard E. Neustadt and Ernest R. May, *Thinking in Time: The Uses of History for Decision-Makers* (New York: Free Press, 1988). See also Richard Ned Lebow, *Between Peace and War: The Nature of International Crisis* (Baltimore: Johns Hopkins University Press, 1995). Yuen Foong Khong, *Analogies at War: Korea, Munich, Dien Bien Phu, and the Vietnam Decisions of 1965* (Princeton, NJ: Princeton University Press, 1992). Dan Reiter, *Crucible of Beliefs: Learning, Alliances, and World Wars* (Ithaca, NY: Cornell University Press, 1996), 2. Deborah Welch Larson, *Origins of Containment: A Psychological Explanation* (Princeton, NJ: Princeton University Press, 1985). Keren Yarhi-Milo, *Knowing the Adversary: Leaders, Intelligence, and Assessment of Intentions in International Relations* (Princeton, NJ: Princeton University Press, 2014), 3–5. Glenn Herald Snyder and Paul Diesing, *Conflict among Nations: Bargaining, Decision Making, and System Structure in International Crises* (Princeton, NJ: Princeton University Press, 1977), 332. Karl Deutsch and Richard Merritt, "Effects of Events on National and International Images," in *International Behavior: A Social-Psychological Analysis*, ed. Herbert C. Kelman (New York: Holt, Rinehart, and Winston, 1965), 182–83, referenced in Aaron L. Friedberg, *The Weary Titan: Britain and the Experience of Relative Decline* (Princeton, NJ: Princeton University Press, 2010), 16.

11. Jack Snyder first used the term "strategic culture" in 1977 when describing Soviet nuclear doctrine, defining it as "the sum total of ideas, conditioned emotional responses, and patterns of habitual behavior that members of a national strategic community have acquired through instruction or imitation and share with each other." Jack L. Snyder, *The Soviet Strategic Culture: Implications for Limited Nuclear Operations* (Santa Monica, CA: RAND, 1997), https://www.rand.org/content/dam/rand/pubs/reports/2005/R2154.pdf. See also Alexander Wendt, "Anarchy Is What States Make of It: The Social Construction of Power Politics," *International Organization* 46, no. 2 (March 1992): 395. Michael C. Desch, "Culture Clash: Assessing the Importance of Ideas in Security Studies," *International Security* 23, no. 1 (Summer 1998): 170. John A. Vasquez, *The War Puzzle*, Cambridge Studies in International Relations 27

(Cambridge: Cambridge University Press, 1993). Bradley S. Klein, "Hegemony and Strategic Culture: American Power Projection and Alliance Defence Politics," *Review of International Studies* 14, no. 2 (April 1988): 136. Markus Fischer, "Feudal Europe, 800–1300: Communal Discourse and Conflictual Practices," *International Organization* 46, no. 2 (Spring 1992): 430. Dana P. Eyre and Mark C. Suchman, "Status, Norms, and the Proliferation of Conventional Weapons: An Institutional Theory Approach," in *The Culture of National Security: Norms and Identity in World Politics*, ed. Peter J. Katzenstein (New York: Columbia University Press, 1996), 82. Alastair Iain Johnston, *Cultural Realism: Strategic Culture and Grand Strategy in Chinese History* (Princeton, NJ: Princeton University Press, 1998), 31. See also Alexander Wendt, "Constructing International Politics," *International Security* 20, no. 1 (1995): 77. Johnston, *Cultural Realism*, ix–x. Dima Adamsky, *The Culture of Military Innovation: The Impact of Cultural Factors on the Revolution in Military Affairs in Russia, the US, and Israel* (Stanford, CA: Stanford University Press, 2010), 12. Thomas U. Berger, *Cultures of Antimilitarism: National Security in Germany and Japan* (Baltimore: Johns Hopkins University Press, 1998). Fareed Zakaria, *From Wealth to Power: The Unusual Origins of America's World Role* (Princeton, NJ: Princeton University Press, 1999); Jeffrey Legro, *Cooperation under Fire: Anglo-German Restraint during World War II* (Ithaca, NY: Cornell University Press, 1995). Similarly, John Duffield argues, "culture helps to define the basic goals of the collectivity, ... shapes perceptions of the external environment, ... shapes the formulation and identification of the behaviors available, ... [and] can strongly influence the evaluation of the seemingly available options and thus the choices that are made among them." John S. Duffield, "Political Culture and State Behavior: Why Germany Confounds Neorealism," *International Organization* 53, no. 4 (September 1999): 771–72. Colin Dueck, *Reluctant Crusaders Power, Culture, and Change in American Grand Strategy* (Princeton, NJ: Princeton University Press, 2006), 15. See also Klein, "Hegemony and Strategic Culture," 135–36. Mahnken, *Technology and the American Way of War since 1945*, 3. Kennedy, *The Rise and Fall of the Great Powers*, xxiii. See also Desch, "Culture Clash," 169.

12. Duffield, "Political Culture and State Behavior," 770.

13. Posen, *The Sources of Military Doctrine*, 25. Traditional conceptions of ends, ways, and means assume that ends are determined before ways or means. Clausewitz's famous dictum that "war is the continuation of policy by other means" suggests that decisions on objectives should precede strategies or investments. However, Samuel Huntington notes that it is not always a safe assumption "that the ends of policy would be defined before strategy had to be prepared." This assumption of strategic coherence is therefore problematic and must be assessed in greater detail. See Carl von Clausewitz, *On War*, trans. Michael Eliot Howard and Peter

Paret (Princeton, NJ: Princeton University Press, 1989). Samuel P. Huntington, *The Soldier and the State: The Theory and Politics of Civil-Military Relations* (Cambridge, MA: Harvard University Press, 2002), 263.

14. As Robert Keohane suggests, "We should seek parsimony first, then add on complexity while monitoring the adverse effects this has on the predictive power of our theory: its ability to make significant inferences on the basis of limited information." Robert O. Keohane, *Neorealism and Its Critics* (New York: Columbia University Press, 1986), 187–88. As Fareed Zakaria writes, "a good account of a nation's foreign policy should include systemic, domestic, and other influences, specifying what aspects of the policy can be explained by what factors." Zakaria, "Realism and Domestic Politics," 198.

15. Peter D. Feaver et al., "Brother, Can You Spare a Paradigm? (Or Was Anybody Ever a Realist?)," *International Security* 25, no. 1 (July 2000): 174. States could also perceive their relative power to be stable—neither rising nor declining—but for the purposes of this study, stable relative power is conceptualized as a transitory period between rising and declining power.

16. One should not, however, assume that states maximizing relative power necessarily maximize military spending because, as Glaser notes, "maximizing relative power may not maximize the military capabilities that a country needs for defense and deterrence." Glaser, "Realists as Optimists," 72. As Aaron Friedberg writes, "Even if one acknowledges that structures exist and are important, there is still the question of how statesmen . . . are able to determine where they stand in terms of relative national power at any given point in history." Friedberg, *The Weary Titan*, 8. On measurements of power, see Indra de Soysa, John R. Oneal, and Yong-Hee Park, "Testing Power-Transition Theory Using Alternative Measures of National Capabilities," *Journal of Conflict Resolution* 41, no. 4 (August 1, 1997): 509–28. Paul K. MacDonald and Joseph M. Parent, "Graceful Decline? The Surprising Success of Great Power Retrenchment," *International Security* 35, no. 4 (April 2011): 22–24. Geoffrey Blainey, *The Causes of War* (New York: Free Press, 1988), 123. G. John Ikenberry, Michael Mastanduno, and William C. Wohlforth, "Unipolarity, State Behavior, and Systemic Consequences," *World Politics* 61, no. 1 (January 2009): 4. Joseph S. Nye, Jr., "The Changing Nature of World Power," *Political Science Quarterly* 105, no. 2 (Summer 1990): 177. Robert A. Dahl and Bruce Stinebrickner, *Modern Political Analysis* (Upper Saddle River, NJ: Prentice Hall, 2003), 29–33. David A. Baldwin, "Interdependence and Power: A Conceptual Analysis," *International Organization* 34, no. 4 (September 1980): 497. Zeev Maoz, "Power, Capabilities, and Paradoxical Conflict Outcomes," *World Politics* 41, no. 2 (January 1989): 240. Robert Gilpin, *U.S. Power and the Multinational Corporation: The Political Economy of Foreign Direct Investment*, The Political Economy of International Relations Series (New York:

Basic Books, 1975), 24. Richard Ned Lebow and Benjamin Valentino, "Lost in Transition: A Critical Analysis of Power Transition Theory," *International Relations* 23, no. 3 (September 1, 2009): 406–7. Nye, "The Changing Nature of World Power," 178. William Wohlforth, *The Elusive Balance: Power and Perceptions during the Cold War* (Ithaca, NY: Cornell University Press, 1993), 1–2. Others important works that note the importance of individual perceptions and biases include Feaver et al., "Brother, Can You Spare a Paradigm?," 184; Jeffrey W. Legro and Andrew Moravcsik, "Is Anybody Still a Realist?," *International Security* 24, no. 2 (October 1999): 8; Snyder, *Myths of Empire,* 128. Van Evera, *Causes of War,* 6; Stephen Van Evera, "Offense, Defense, and the Causes of War," in Art and Waltz, *The Use of Force,* 46; Yarhi-Milo, *Knowing the Adversary,* 3; Michael P. Fischerkeller, "David versus Goliath: Cultural Judgments in Asymmetric Wars," *Security Studies* 7, no. 4 (June 1998): 3. Daniel Kahneman and Amos Tversky, "Prospect Theory: An Analysis of Decision under Risk," *Econometrica* 47, no. 2 (March 1979): 288; Barbara Farnham, introduction to *Avoiding Losses/Taking Risks: Prospect Theory and International Conflict,* ed. Farnham (Ann Arbor: University of Michigan Press, 1994), 3.

17. Michael Mastanduno, David A. Lake, and G. John Ikenberry, "Toward a Realist Theory of State Action," *International Studies Quarterly* 33, no. 4 (December 1989): 468. Barry Buzan, *People, States and Fear: An Agenda for International Security Studies in the Post–Cold War Era* (Colchester, UK: ECPR Press, 2007), 241. Applying this concept to the system more generally, Glenn Snyder comments that the military balance depends on "whether the states interested in preserving the status quo were able to deny territorial gains to the expansion-minded state or states." Glenn Herald Snyder, *Deterrence and Defense: Toward a Theory of National Security* (Princeton, NJ: Princeton University Press, 1961), 41. Ivan Arreguín-Toft, "How the Weak Win Wars: A Theory of Asymmetric Conflict," *International Security* 26, no. 1 (July 2001): 96. Arreguín-Toft suggests, "Strong actors lose asymmetric conflicts when they adopt the wrong strategy vis-à-vis their weaker adversaries." Andrew Mack identifies asymmetries in resource power, arguing, "insurgents may gain political victory from a situation of military stalemate or even defeat." Arreguín-Toft, 121. Andrew Mack, "Why Big Nations Lose Small Wars: The Politics of Asymmetric Conflict," *World Politics* 27, no. 2 (January 1975): 177. See also Gil Merom, *How Democracies Lose Small Wars: State, Society, and the Failures of France in Algeria, Israel in Lebanon, and the United States in Vietnam* (Cambridge: Cambridge University Press, 2003). Zakaria, *From Wealth to Power,* 11.

18. Woosang Kim, for example, finds support for power transition theory going back as early as the Peace of Westphalia. Woosang Kim, "Power Transitions and Great Power War from Westphalia to Waterloo," *World Politics* 45, no. 1 (October 1992): 153–72. George Modelski, "The Long

Cycle of Global Politics and the Nation-State," *Comparative Studies in Society and History* 20, no. 2 (April 1978): 232–33. Gilpin, *War and Change in World Politics*, 23. See also Kupchan, *The Vulnerability of Empire*, 14. David M. Edelstein, *Over the Horizon: Time, Uncertainty, and the Rise of Great Powers* (Ithaca, NY: Cornell University Press, 2017). A. F. K. Organski, *World Politics* (New York: Knopf, 1958), 100. Dale C. Copeland, *The Origins of Major War* (Ithaca, NY: Cornell University Press, 2001), 4, 15.

19. John J. Mearsheimer, "The False Promise of International Institutions," *International Security* 19, no. 3 (1994): 12.

20. Robert Anthony Pape, *Bombing to Win: Air Power and Coercion in War* (Ithaca, NY: Cornell University Press, 1996), 16.

21. This aligns with Arreguín-Toft's description of strategy as "an actor's plan for using armed forces to achieve military or political objectives." Arreguín-Toft, "How the Weak Win Wars," 99. Also see Basil Henry Liddell Hart, *Strategy* (New York: Meridian, 1991), 321. The naval theorist Julian Corbett explains, "By general and permanent control we do not mean that the enemy can do nothing, but that he cannot interfere with our maritime trade and oversea operations so seriously as to affect the issue of the war, and that he cannot carry on his own trade and operations except at such risk and hazard as to remove them from the field of practical strategy." Julian Stafford Corbett, *Some Principles of Maritime Strategy* (London: Longmans, Green, 1918), 102–3, referenced in Stephen Cobb, *Preparing for Blockade, 1885–1914: Naval Contingency for Economic Warfare*, Corbett Centre for Maritime Policy Studies Series (Burlington, VT: Ashgate, 2013), 16. See also Pape, *Bombing to Win*, 32. See also Sam J. Tangredi, *Anti-Access Warfare: Countering A2/AD Strategies* (Annapolis, MD: Naval Institute Press, 2013), 14. "United States Strategic Bombing Survey—Summary Report (Pacific War)" (Washington, DC: Government Printing Office, 1946), 28. Archer Jones, *The Art of War in the Western World* (Urbana: University of Illinois Press, 1987), 676–78. Anti-access includes "those actions and capabilities, usually long-range, designed to prevent an opposing force from entering an operational area." Area denial includes "those actions and capabilities, usually of shorter range, designed not to keep an opposing force out, but to limit its freedom of action within the operational area." Martin E. Dempsey, *Joint Operational Access Concept (JOAC)* (Washington, DC: U.S. Department of Defense, 2012), https://permanent.fdlp.gov/gpo18049/JOACJan%25202012Signed.pdf. Tangredi, *Anti-Access Warfare*, 3. See Jervis, "Cooperation under the Security Dilemma"; Quester, *Offense and Defense in the International System*. Michael E. Brown, Owen R. Coté, Jr., Sean M. Lynn-Jones, and Steven E. Miller, eds., *Offense, Defense, and War*, An International Security Reader (Cambridge, MA: MIT Press, 2004). Sean M. Lynn-Jones, "Offense-Defense Theory and Its Critics," *Security Studies* 4, no. 4 (June 1, 1995): 667, https://doi.org/10.1080/09636419509347600. Marc Trachtenberg, "The

Meaning of Mobilization in 1914," *International Security* 15, no. 3 (1990): 120. Stephen Van Evera, "The Cult of the Offensive and the Origins of the First World War," *International Security* 9, no. 1 (1984): 58. Walt, *The Origins of Alliances*, 24. Keir A. Lieber, "Grasping the Technological Peace: The Offense-Defense Balance and International Security," *International Security* 25, no. 1 (July 1, 2000): 74.

22. This theory focuses not on the level of defense spending but on the type of systems procured. Additionally, this formulation does not include doctrine, which is more closely aligned with strategy than investments. For more on these differentiations, see Karen Ruth Adams, "Attack and Conquer? International Anarchy and the Offense-Defense-Deterrence Balance," *International Security* 28, no. 3 (January 2004): 49. Dan Reiter and Curtis Meek, "Determinants of Military Strategy, 1903–1994: A Quantitative Empirical Test," *International Studies Quarterly* 43, no. 2 (1999): 365. Posen, *The Sources of Military Doctrine*, 14. Robert Powell, "Guns, Butter, and Anarchy," *The American Political Science Review* 87, no. 1 (March 1993): 115. Joshua M. Epstein, *The Calculus of Conventional War: Dynamic Analysis without Lanchester Theory*, Studies in Defense Policy (Washington, DC: Brookings Institution, 1985). Charles A. Kupchan, "Setting Conventional Force Requirements: Roughly Right or Precisely Wrong?," *World Politics* 41, no. 4 (July 1989): 536–78. Mastanduno, Lake, and Ikenberry, "Toward a Realist Theory of State Action." James D. Morrow, "Arms versus Allies: Trade-Offs in the Search for Security," *International Organization* 47, no. 2 (March 1993): 208.

23. Charles L. Glaser, "Political Consequences of Military Strategy: Expanding and Refining the Spiral and Deterrence Models," *World Politics* 44, no. 4 (July 1992): 501. Douglas Lemke and William Reed, "Power Is Not Satisfaction: A Comment on de Soysa, Oneal, and Park," *Journal of Conflict Resolution* 42, no. 4 (August 1, 1998): 512. Randall L. Schweller, "Bandwagoning for Profit: Bringing the Revisionist State Back In," *International Security* 19, no. 1 (1994): 105. Robert Powell, "Stability and the Distribution of Power," *World Politics* 48, no. 2 (January 1996): 241. See Andrew F. Krepinevich, Jr., "The Military-Technical Revolution: A Preliminary Assessment," Office of the Secretary of Defense, last modified July 15, 1992, https://archive.org/stream/TechnicalRevolution/Technical%20Revolution_djvu.txt. Gilpin, *War and Change in World Politics*, 95. On definitions of authority, see David A. Lake, "International Authority," in *Hierarchy in International Relations* (Ithaca, NY: Cornell University Press, 2009), 17–44; Ian Hurd, "Legitimacy and Authority in International Politics," *International Organization* 53, no. 2 (1999): 379–408.

24. Schweller, "Bandwagoning for Profit," 104. Randall L. Schweller, "Neorealism's Status-Quo Bias: What Security Dilemma?," *Security Studies* 5, no. 3 (March 1996): 107. Schweller also suggests other objectives are possible, noting, "aggressor states have often sought to expand for rea-

sons other than mere survival, for example, greed, divine right, manifest destiny, and revenge." Schweller, "Neorealism's Status-Quo Bias," 115. Schweller, "Bandwagoning for Profit," 101. Note that the tendency of rising powers to revise the system is used here without normative implications. As E. H. Carr argues, "It is profoundly misleading to represent the struggle between satisfied and dissatisfied Powers as a struggle between morality on one side and power on the other. It is a clash in which, whatever the moral issue, power politics are equally predominant on both sides." Edward Hallett Carr, *The Twenty Years' Crisis, 1919–1939: An Introduction to the Study of International Relations* (New York: Harper and Row, 1964), 38. Also see Dale C. Copeland, *The Origins of Major War* (Ithaca, NY: Cornell University Press, 2001), 3. Organski, *World Politics*, 364. For a similar categorization, see Keren Yarhi-Milo, who writes that expansionism could "consist of an active plan to achieve a hegemonic international position (unlimited expansionist) or effect a change in the distribution of power that while significant, is more limited in scope (limited expansionist)." Yarhi-Milo, *Knowing the Adversary*, 14.

25. Emily O. Goldman, *Power in Uncertain Times: Strategy in the Fog of Peace* (Stanford, CA: Stanford University Press, 2011), 6–8. Gilpin, *War and Change in World Politics*, 94–95. Peter Liberman, "The Spoils of Conquest," *International Security* 18, no. 2 (1993): 127. Michael W. Doyle, *Empires* (Ithaca, NY: Cornell University Press, 1986), 44. Jervis, "Cooperation under the Security Dilemma," 169. Often conceptualizations of control are domain specific, as is Stephen D. Biddle's theory of military power, which he states applies only to "the mission of controlling territory in mid- to high-intensity continental warfare." Biddle explains that this excludes "guerilla warfare at the low end, mass destruction warfare involving nuclear, chemical, or biological weapons at the high end, . . . war at sea, . . . and strategic bombing against civilian targets." Biddle also defines "offensive military capability," which he terms "the capacity to destroy the largest possible territory for the smallest attacker casualties in the least time." Conversely, he terms defensive military capability "the ability to preserve the largest possible defensive forces over the largest possible territory with the greater attacker casualties for the longest time." Stephen D. Biddle, *Military Power: Explaining Victory and Defeat in Modern Battle* (Princeton, NJ: Princeton University Press, 2004), 6. Jones, *The Art of War in the Western World*, 676–78. Henry A. Kissinger, "The Viet Nam Negotiations," *Foreign Affairs*, January 1969, 214, https://www.foreignaffairs.com/articles/asia/1969-01-01/viet-nam-negotiations. Posen, *The Sources of Military Doctrine*, 24. Todd S. Sechser, "Goliath's Curse: Coercive Threats and Asymmetric Power," *International Organization* 64, no. 4 (October 2010): 627–60. T. V. Paul, *Asymmetric Conflicts: War Initiation by Weaker Powers*, Cambridge Studies in International Relations 33 (Cambridge: Cambridge University Press, 1994). P. L. Sullivan,

"War Aims and War Outcomes: Why Powerful States Lose Limited Wars," *Journal of Conflict Resolution* 51, no. 3 (June 1, 2007): 496–524. Robert J. Art, "To What Ends Military Power?," *International Security* 4, no. 4 (Spring 1980): 1–10. John A. Gentry, *How Wars Are Won and Lost: Vulnerability and Military Power* (Santa Barbara, CA: Praeger Security International, 2012), 18; Suzanne C. Nielsen, *An Army Transformed: The U.S. Army's Post-Vietnam Recovery and the Dynamics of Change in Military Organizations* (Carlisle, PA: U.S. Army War College, 2010); John A. Nagl, *Learning to Eat Soup with a Knife: Counterinsurgency Lessons from Malaya and Vietnam* (Chicago: University of Chicago Press, 2005); Austin Long, *The Soul of Armies: Counterinsurgency Doctrine and Military Culture in the US and UK* (Ithaca, NY: Cornell University Press, 2016); James A. Russell, *Innovation, Transformation, and War: Counterinsurgency Operations in Anbar and Ninewa Provinces, Iraq, 2005–2007* (Stanford, CA: Stanford University Press, 2010); Jeannie L. Johnson, *The Marines, Counterinsurgency, and Strategic Culture: Lessons Learned and Lost in America's Wars* (Washington, DC: Georgetown University Press, 2018).

26. Nuno P. Monteiro, *Theory of Unipolar Politics*, Cambridge Studies in International Relations 132 (New York: Cambridge University Press, 2014), 5–6. Nuno P. Monteiro, "Unrest Assured: Why Unipolarity Is Not Peaceful," *International Security* 36, no. 3 (January 2012): 12–14. Snyder, *The Ideology of the Offensive*, 19. Barry Posen, "Explaining Military Doctrine," in Art and Waltz, *The Use of Force*, 41. Posen, *The Sources of Military Doctrine*, 78–69. I am indebted to Steve Rosen for reminding me of this critical point. Posen, 69–70. Waltz, *Man, the State, and War*, 7. Jervis, *Perception and Misperception in International Politics*, 64. Jervis, "Cooperation under the Security Dilemma," 201–2. Jack S. Levy, "Declining Power and the Preventive Motivation for War," *World Politics* 40, no. 1 (October 1987): 82–107. Copeland, *The Origins of Major War*. Kier, *Imagining War*, 11. See also Barry R. Posen, *Restraint: A New Foundation for U.S. Grand Strategy* (Ithaca, NY: Cornell University Press, 2014), 69. Sagan, "1914 Revisited," 162. Douglas Lemke, "Investigating the Preventive Motive for War," *International Interactions* 29, no. 4 (October 2003): 288. Other scholars disagree; see D. S. Geller, "Power Transition and Conflict Initiation," *Conflict Management and Peace Science* 12, no. 1 (January 1, 1992): 1–16; Sam R. Bell and Jesse C. Johnson, "Shifting Power, Commitment Problems, and Preventive War," *International Studies Quarterly* 59, no. 1 (March 1, 2015): 124–32. Powell, "Stability and the Distribution of Power." Schweller, "Bandwagoning for Profit," 104. Andrew Kydd, "Sheep in Sheep's Clothing: Why Security Seekers Do Not Fight Each Other," *Security Studies* 7, no. 1 (September 1997): 114–55. Note that Archer Jones distinguishes between persisting strategies and raiding strategies—similar to control and denial strategies, respectively—as well as between offensive and defensive strategies. Jones comments, "Defend-

ers too weak to employ a persisting strategy on the defense found a raiding strategy effective because a raiding offensive was stronger than a defensive persisting strategy." Arreguín-Toft proposes four strategies, two direct and two (by implication) indirect. Each has an offensive and a defensive component. He categorizes strategic guerilla warfare, strategic bombing, blockade, and siege as indirect strategies, but they might also be termed denial strategies. Direct attack is "the use of the military to capture or eliminate an adversary's armed forces, thereby gaining control of that opponent's values." Jones, *The Art of War in the Western World*, 84–85. Arreguín-Toft, "How the Weak Win Wars," 100.

27. Goldman, *Power in Uncertain Times*, xi. Stephen Biddle, "The Past as Prologue: Assessing Theories of Future Warfare," *Security Studies* 8, no. 1 (September 1998): 4. Bernard Brodie, *Sea Power in the Machine Age* (Princeton, NJ: Princeton University Press; Oxford: Oxford University Press, 1941), 380–81. Conversely, Ron Hassner and Jason Wittenberg suggest, "weaker states have a greater incentive to construct military fortifications along borders with superior neighbors." Ron E. Hassner and Jason Wittenberg, "Barriers to Entry: Who Builds Fortified Boundaries and Why?," *International Security* 40, no. 1 (2015): 162. Denial systems, such as hidden ditches and caltrops, have existed for millennia. See, for example, Trevor N. Dupuy, *The Evolution of Weapons and Warfare* (Indianapolis: Bobbs-Merrill, 1980). Also see Michael G. Vickers, "The Structure of Military Revolutions" (PhD diss., Johns Hopkins University, 2011), ProQuest (3428567).

28. Note that this definition differs somewhat from that used by others. Railroads, for example, only moderately increase mobility since rail must typically be laid before proceeding across a hostile border. Most notably, this weakens the argument made about railroads being an offense-enhancing system in Lieber, *War and the Engineers*. As Fred Kagan finds, "It was the railroad, much more than the machine gun, that rendered combat on the Western Front so deadly and static. For the soldiers who had managed to penetrate and seize the enemy trench system found, to their dismay, that whereas their supplies and reinforcements had to walk slowly over a cratered and devastated wasteland to get to them, the enemy's supplies and reinforcements moved easily and speedily along the rail system in his rear." Frederick W. Kagan, "The Rise and Fall of Soviet Operational Act, 1917–1941," in *The Military History of the Soviet Union*, ed. Robin D. S. Higham and Frederick W. Kagan (New York: Palgrave, 2002), 81. Also see Van Evera, "Offense, Defense, and the Causes of War," 14. Jones, *The Art of War in the Western World*, 493. Sean M. Lynn-Jones, "Offense-Defense Theory and Its Critics," *Security Studies* 4, no. 4 (June 1, 1995): 667, https://doi.org/10.1080/09636419509347600. Samuel P. Huntington, "US Defense Strategy: The Strategic Innovations of the Reagan Years," in *American Defence Annual 1988*, ed. Joseph Kruzel (Lexington, MA:

Prentice Hall and IBD, 1988). Quester, *Offense and Defense in the International System*, 52. Charles L. Glaser and Chaim Kaufmann, "What Is the Offense-Defense Balance and How Can We Measure It?," *International Security* 22, no. 4 (April 1, 1998): 63. A critical part of offense-defense theory is the notion that militaries need successful doctrinal innovation and learning as well as effective training to most efficiently utilize a new weapons system. Jervis, "Cooperation under the Security Dilemma," 203. Frank A. Andrews, "Tactical Development," in *The U.S. Naval Institute on Naval Tactics*, ed. Wayne P. Hughes, U.S. Naval Institute Wheel Books (Annapolis, MD: Naval Institute Press, 2015), 47. Brodie, *Sea Power in the Machine Age*, 261. On land warfare, see Bernard Brodie and Fawn McKay Brodie, *From Crossbow to H-Bomb* (Bloomington: Indiana University Press, 1973).

29. The diagram in figure 1 represents the rise and decline of a state as a simple arc. This is not to suggest that states rise or decline smoothly or that all states experience the full cycle of rise and decline. See Mancur Lloyd Olson, *The Rise and Decline of Nations* (New Haven, CT: Yale University Press, 1982).

30. Gilpin, *War and Change in World Politics*, 187. Mastanduno, Lake, and Ikenberry, "Toward a Realist Theory of State Action," 468. See also Jeffrey W. Legro, "What China Will Want: The Future Intentions of a Rising Power," *Perspectives on Politics* 5, no. 3 (September 2007): 518.

31. Modelski, "The Long Cycle of Global Politics and the Nation-State," 224. Similarly, John A. Vasquez notes, "the stronger wants to occupy or colonize the territory of the weaker." John A. Vasquez, "Capability, Types of War, Peace," *Political Research Quarterly* 39, no. 2 (June 1, 1986): 323. Gilpin, *War and Change in World Politics*, 106. Also see W. W. Rostow, "The Stages of Economic Growth," *The Economic History Review* 12, no. 1 (1959): 5–6. See also Walt W. Rostow, *Politics and the Stages of Growth* (Cambridge: Cambridge University Press, 1971). Blainey, *The Causes of War*, 53. Erik Gartzke, "War Is in the Error Term," *International Organization* 53, no. 3 (July 1, 1999): 567–87. Also see Erik Gartzke and Dominic Rohner, "The Political Economy of Imperialism, Decolonization and Development," *British Journal of Political Science* 41, no. 3 (July 2011): 525–56.

32. Gilpin, *War and Change in World Politics*, 107. Copeland, *The Origins of Major War*, 4. John Lewis Gaddis concurs that "the point at which a great power perceives its decline to be beginning is a perilous one." John Lewis Gaddis, "The Long Peace: Elements of Stability in the Postwar International System," *International Security* 10, no. 4 (1986): 141. MacDonald and Parent, "Graceful Decline?," 9. See also G. John Ikenberry, *After Victory: Institutions, Strategic Restraint, and the Rebuilding of Order after Major Wars* (Princeton, NJ: Princeton University Press, 2001), 2. Alternatively, Levy notes that a declining power could attempt to confront a rising

challenger before that challenger becomes powerful enough to threaten its position. Levy, "Declining Power and the Preventive Motivation for War."

33. On declining states, see Tanisha M Fazal, *State Death the Politics and Geography of Conquest, Occupation, and Annexation* (Princeton, NJ: Princeton University Press, 2011). Gilpin, *War and Change in World Politics*, 185.

34. Three types of cases are possible: transitions from Phase 1 to Phase 2 (the shift from perceived weakness to perceived strength), transitions from Phase 2 to Phase 3 (the shift from perceived rise to perceived decline), and transitions from Phase 3 to Phase 4 (the shift from perceived strength to perceived weakness). These perceived power shifts are labeled *rising, declining*, and *collapsing*, respectively. Although shifts from Phase 4 to Phase 1 are also possible, perceived transitions from declining to rising often correspond to changes in governance, which permit states to aggregate capabilities with their neighbors. Thus, this type of shift is not addressed here but will be incorporated into future research projects. Yarhi-Milo, *Knowing the Adversary*. Edelstein, *Over the Horizon*.

35. Giulio Douhet, *The Command of the Air*, trans. Dino Ferrari (Maxwell, AL: Air University Press, 2019), 8; Jason Seawright and John Gerring, "Case Selection Techniques in Case Study Research: A Menu of Qualitative and Quantitative Options," *Political Research Quarterly* 61, no. 2 (February 9, 2008): 296. Note that substantial effort has been made to avoid selecting cases by their dependent variables; in fact, the case studies include several outcomes that are directly at odds with the theory presented here. On case study logic, see Andrew Bennett and Colin Elman, "Qualitative Research: Recent Developments in Case Study Methods," *Annual Review of Political Science* 9, no. 1 (June 2006): 455–76. David Collier and James Mahoney, "Insights and Pitfalls: Selection Bias in Qualitative Research," *World Politics* 49, no. 1 (October 1996): 56–91. Jack Levy, "Case Studies: Types, Designs, and Logics of Inference," *Conflict Management and Peace Science* 25, no. 1 (March 2008): 1–18. David Collier, Henry E. Brady, and Jason Seawright, "Sources of Leverage in Causal Inference: Toward an Alternative View of Methodology," in *Rethinking Social Inquiry: Diverse Tools, Shared Standards*, ed. Henry E. Brady and David Collier (Lanham, MD: Rowman and Littlefield, 2010), 184–85. James Mahoney, "After KKV: The New Methodology of Qualitative Research," *World Politics* 62, no. 1 (January 2010): 120–47. As a result, transitions from Phase 4 to Phase 1 are not specifically studied here, since these states are by definition weak throughout the entire period in question. Note that changes in relative power (power shifts) need not coincide with changes in absolute position (power transitions). As Daniel Geller writes, "dynamic power balances can be separated into two categories: transitions (a reversal of relative power position) and power shifts (power convergence or divergence)." Thus, this theory should apply to power

shifts among small states. Daniel S. Geller, "Power Differentials and War in Rival Dyads," *International Studies Quarterly* 37, no. 2 (June 1993): 175.

36. The United States, Germany, United Kingdom, France, Japan, and Russia are consistently cited as great powers through the twentieth century, with China often added late in the century. See, for example, Jacob L. Heim and Benjamin M. Miller, *Measuring Power, Power Cycles, and the Risk of Great Power War in the 21st Century* (Santa Monica, CA: RAND, 2020), https://www.rand.org/pubs/research_reports/RR2989.html.

Chapter Two. America's Rise

Epigraph: *Washington Post*, quoted in the *Congressional Record*, 55th Congress, 2nd session (1898), 573, referenced in Albert Katz Weinberg, *Manifest Destiny: A Study of Nationalist Expansionism in American History* (Baltimore: Johns Hopkins University Press, 1935), 289.

1. U.S. Intelligence Office, quoted in the *Congressional Record*, 59th Congress, 1st session (May 4, 1906), 6398, referenced in Paolo Enrico Coletta, *A Survey of U.S. Naval Affairs, 1865–1917* (Lanham, MD: University Press of America, 1987), 234.

2. Prior to the war, Navy Secretary James Dobbin suggested that U.S. naval modernization should reflect "our proper and elevated rank among the great powers of the world. . . . Our navy should, at least, be large enough to command our own seas and coast." Indeed, the U.S. Navy had over seven hundred ships, second only to the British, by the end of the war. But Washington rapidly dismantled this force. 33rd Congress, 1st session (1854), H. Ex. Doc. No. 1, Vol. III, 297–317, referenced in Harold Sprout and Margaret Tuttle Sprout, *The Rise of American Naval Power: 1776–1918* (Princeton, NJ: Princeton University Press, 1946), 141. John Bassett Moore, *A Digest of International Law*, vol. 1 (Washington, DC: Government Printing Office, 1906), 431, referenced in Weinberg, *Manifest Destiny*, 252.

3. Grover Cleveland quoted in Coletta, *A Survey of U.S. Naval Affairs, 1865–1917*, 15. Theodore Roosevelt, *Thomas H. Benton* (New York: Charles Scribner's Sons, 1906), 36, referenced in Howard K. Beale, *Theodore Roosevelt and the Rise of America to World Power*, The Albert Shaw Lectures on Diplomatic History 1953 (Baltimore: Johns Hopkins University Press, 1956), 66.

4. Figures from U.S. Bureau of the Census, "Historical Statistics of the United States: 1789–1945" (1949), 9–11. Figures from Bundesarchiv-Militararchiv, Freiburg, re-created in Kennedy, *The Rise and Fall of British Naval Mastery*, 190. Douglas A. Irwin, "Historical Aspects of U.S. Trade Policy," NBER, last modified September 2006, https://www.nber.org/reporter/summer-2006/historical-aspects-us-trade-policy#:~:text=Antebellum%20Trade%20Policy,percent%20by%20the%20Civil%20War.

5. A Vision of Britain through Time, "England and Wales, Population Tables," 1891 Census, accessed May 1, 2020, http://www.visionofbritain. org.uk/census/table_page.jsp;jsessionid=9656FC53864EA20EB28B2B81 A8D71BA3?tab_id=EW1891POP2_M2&u_id=10001043&show=&min_c=6&max_c=10. Groningen Growth and Development Centre, "The Maddison Project Database 2013," University of Groningen, last modified May 23, 2023, https://www.rug.nl/ggdc/historicaldevelopment/maddison/releases/maddison-project-database-2013?lang=en.

6. Carl Schurz, *Harper's New Monthly Magazine* 87 (1893): 738, referenced in Weinberg, *Manifest Destiny*, 252–53.

7. Theodore Roosevelt to James S. Clarkson, April 22, 1893, referenced in Beale, *Theodore Roosevelt and the Rise of America to World Power*, 47. Beale, 254. Henry Cabot Lodge to Blackwell, December 20, 1895, referenced in Beale, 51.

8. Kenneth Wimmel, *Theodore Roosevelt and the Great White Fleet: American Seapower Comes of Age* (Washington, DC: Brassey's, 1998), 48.

9. J. H. Patton, *The History of the United States of America from the Discovery of the Continent to the Close of the First Session of the Thirty-Fifth Congress* (New York: D. Appleton, 1860), 598, referenced in Mark R. Shulman, *Navalism and the Emergence of American Sea Power, 1882–1893* (Annapolis, MD: Naval Institute Press, 1995), 11.

10. Referenced in Wimmel, *Theodore Roosevelt and the Great White Fleet*, 1. Wimmel, 61. Wimmel, 9. Secretary of the Navy, *Annual Report*, 1888, iii–ix, referenced in Benjamin Franklin Cooling, *Gray Steel and Blue Water Navy: The Formative Years of America's Military-Industrial Complex, 1881–1917* (Hamden, CT: Archon Books, 1979), 80–81.

11. George Robeson in the *Congressional Record*, January 24, 1883, 1559, referenced in Shulman, *Navalism and the Emergence of American Sea Power, 1882–1893*, 105. 49th Congress, 1st Session (1886), H. Ex. Doc. No. 49, Pt. I, 9, referenced in Sprout and Sprout, *The Rise of American Naval Power*, 199–200. *Congressional Record*, April 8, 1890, 3168–69, referenced in Shulman, *Navalism and the Emergence of American Sea Power, 1882–1893*, 131–32.

12. Alfred Thayer Mahan, *The Influence of Sea Power upon History, 1660–1783* (New York: Sagamore, 1957), 34, 87. Also see Mahan, *Mahan on Naval Warfare*, 71, 98.

13. Mahan, *Mahan on Naval Warfare*, 103, 286. Alfred Thayer Mahan, *The Interest of America in Sea Power* (Cambridge: Cambridge University Press, 1897), 21, referenced in Weinberg, *Manifest Destiny*, 259. Harris Laning, *An Admiral's Yarn* (Newport, RI: Naval War College Press, 1999), 30–32, referenced in Shulman, *Navalism and the Emergence of American Sea Power, 1882–1893*, 87–88. Sea control need not be total, Mahan explained, since "control of the sea, however real, does not imply that an enemy's single ships or small squadrons cannot steal out of port, cannot cross more or less frequented tracts of ocean, make harassing descents upon unprotected

points of a long coastline, enter blockaded harbors. On the contrary, history has shown that such evasions are always possible, to some extent, to the weaker party, however great the inequality of naval strength." Mahan, *The Influence of Sea Power upon History, 1660–1783*, 14. Mahan, 31.

14. Theodore Roosevelt, speech to the Naval War College, 1897, referenced in Coletta, *A Survey of U.S. Naval Affairs, 1865–1917*, 105. Theodore Roosevelt to A. R. Cowles, January 19, 1896, referenced in Beale, *Theodore Roosevelt and the Rise of America to World Power*, 37. Theodore Roosevelt to Francis V. Greene, September 23, 1897, referenced in Beale, 37.

15. Bradley Fiske, *From Midshipman to Rear Admiral* (New York: Century, 1919), 133, referenced in Sprout and Sprout, *The Rise of American Naval Power*, 198. *Congressional Record*, 48th Congress, 1st and 2nd sessions (1884–85), 1425–26, 1453–56, 1459, and 1481, referenced in Cooling, *Gray Steel and Blue Water Navy*, 49. Secretary of the Navy, *Annual Report*, 1888, iii–ix, referenced in Cooling, 80.

16. House Naval Affairs Committee, 1880, referenced in Shulman, *Navalism and the Emergence of American Sea Power, 1882–1893*, 97. *The New York Times*, April 25, 1882, 4, referenced in Shulman, 106. 47th Congress, 1st session (1882), H. Ex. Doc. No. 1, 96, referenced in Sprout and Sprout, *The Rise of American Naval Power*, 172. Indeed, the historians Harold and Margaret Sprout observe that the *Monitor* class ships "were utterly unsuited to the one role [coastal defense] for which they had been created. . . . Their slow speed, inadequate fuel capacity, and general lack of seaworthiness, seriously handicapped every squadron to which they were attached." Sprout and Sprout, 420.

17. Secretary of the Navy, *Annual Report*, 1883. *Congressional Record*, July 24, 1886, 7474–75, referenced in Shulman, *Navalism and the Emergence of American Sea Power, 1882–1893*, 122.

18. 49th Congress, 1st session (1886), H. Report No. 993, 8, referenced in Sprout and Sprout, *The Rise of American Naval Power*, 199. W. W. Reisinger, "Torpedoes," *United States Naval Institute Proceedings* (1888), 521, referenced in Robert William Love, *History of the U.S. Navy* (Harrisburg, PA: Stackpole Books, 1992), 412. Mahan, *Mahan on Naval Warfare*, 133.

19. Wimmel, *Theodore Roosevelt and the Great White Fleet*, 63. Benjamin Harrison quoted in Cooling, *Gray Steel and Blue Water Navy*, 85. Benjamin Tracy, testimony to the House Naval Affairs Committee, January 15, 1890, 3–4, referenced in Shulman, *Navalism and the Emergence of American Sea Power, 1882–1893*, 129. John D. Alden, "Growth of the New American Navy," in *Naval Engineering and American Seapower*, ed. Randolph W. King (Baltimore: Nautical and Aviation Publishing Company of America, 1989), 43.

20. Mahan, *Mahan on Naval Warfare*, 132. Alden, "Growth of the New American Navy," 45. Alden, 44. Alden, 48.

21. Data from the *Report of the Secretary of the Navy, 1890* (Washington, DC: Government Printing Office, 1890), 17. Tracy quoted in Cooling, *Gray*

Steel and Blue Water Navy, 105. Grover Cleveland quoted in Cooling, 113. Love, *History of the U.S. Navy,* 377.

22. Alfred Thayer Mahan, *The Interest of America in Sea Power* (Cambridge: Cambridge University Press, 1897), 21, referenced in Weinberg, *Manifest Destiny,* 259. Theodore Roosevelt to Henry White, November 27, 1907, referenced in Beale, *Theodore Roosevelt and the Rise of America to World Power,* 254.

23. Theodore Roosevelt to John D. Long, August 7, 1897, referenced in Beale, *Theodore Roosevelt and the Rise of America to World Power,* 39.

24. Theodore Roosevelt, "The Issues of 1896," *Century,* November 1895, 71–72, referenced in Beale, 45–46. Theodore Roosevelt to H. White, March 20, 1896, referenced in Beale, 33. Wimmel, *Theodore Roosevelt and the Great White Fleet,* 89. Theodore Roosevelt, speech to the Ohio Naval Reserves, *New York Tribune,* July 27, 1897, referenced in Beale, *Theodore Roosevelt and the Rise of America to World Power,* 57–58. Also see Wimmel, *Theodore Roosevelt and the Great White Fleet,* 92. Theodore Roosevelt to Baron Hermann Speck von Sternburg, January 17, 1898, referenced in Beale, *Theodore Roosevelt and the Rise of America to World Power,* 56–57.

25. Charles S. Olcott, *The Life of William McKinley* (Boston: Houghton Mifflin, 1916), 379, referenced by Theodore Roosevelt, quoted in the *New York Sun,* February 13, 1898, referenced in Beale, *Theodore Roosevelt and the Rise of America to World Power,* 58–59. Weinberg, *Manifest Destiny,* 24. Beale, *Theodore Roosevelt and the Rise of America to World Power,* 58–59.

26. James Bryce, "The Policy of Annexation for America," *Forum* 24 (1897): 392, referenced in Beale, *Theodore Roosevelt and the Rise of America to World Power,* 25. Quoted in L. W. Walker, "Guam's Seizure by the United States in 1898," *Pacific Historical Review,* 1945, 1–12, referenced in Love, *History of the U.S. Navy,* 402.

27. Mahan, *Mahan on Naval Warfare,* 285. In one speech, Roosevelt commented, "Every expansion of civilization makes for peace. In other words, every expansion of a great civilized power means a victory for law, order, and righteousness. This has been the case in every instance of expansion during the present century, whether the expanding power were France or England, Russia or America." Theodore Roosevelt, "Expansion and Peace," *The Independent,* December 21, 1899, http://www.bartleby.com/58/2.html. Theodore Roosevelt, "The Strenuous Life," speech to the Hamilton Club, Chicago, April 10, 1899, referenced in Beale, *Theodore Roosevelt and the Rise of America to World Power,* 32. Theodore Roosevelt to C. Spring Rice, August 11, 1899, referenced in Beale, 79. Roosevelt, "Expansion and Peace." Theodore Roosevelt, "Grant," speech, Galena, IL, April 27, 1900), http://www.bartleby.com/58/13.html. Theodore Roosevelt to John Barrett, October 29, 1900, referenced in Beale, *Theodore Roosevelt and the Rise of America to World Power,* 38.

28. *Congressional Record,* 56th Congress, 1st session (1900), 2629, referenced in Weinberg, *Manifest Destiny,* 313. *Congressional Record,* 56th Congress,

1st session (1900), 711, referenced in Weinberg, 308. Woodrow Wilson, "The Ideals of America," *Atlantic Monthly*, 1902, 726, referenced in Weinberg, 1. Pro, Adm. 231/31, "United States, Fleet &c. 1899," Capt. C. L. Ottley, March 1900, referenced in Friedberg, *The Weary Titan*, 164.

29. Theodore Roosevelt to A. Shaw, December 26, 1902, referenced in Beale, *Theodore Roosevelt and the Rise of America to World Power*, 431. Gordon Carpenter O'Gara, *Theodore Roosevelt and the Rise of the Modern Navy* (Princeton, NJ: Princeton University Press, 1943), 8, referenced in Love, *History of the U.S. Navy*, 443. Theodore Roosevelt quoted in *New York Sun*, September 6, 1900, referenced in Beale, *Theodore Roosevelt and the Rise of America to World Power*, 69. Theodore Roosevelt quoted in *Chicago Journal*, September 8, 1900, referenced in Beale, 68.

30. Roosevelt quoted in *The New York Times*, August 27, 1907, referenced in James R. Reckner, *Teddy Roosevelt's Great White Fleet* (Annapolis, MD: Naval Institute Press, 1988), 124. Senator Beveridge to American Academy of Political and Social Science, 1907, referenced in Weinberg, *Manifest Destiny*, 277. Theodore Roosevelt to Maria Longworth Storer, October 28, 1899, referenced in Beale, *Theodore Roosevelt and the Rise of America to World Power*, 337. Theodore Roosevelt quoted in *New York Tribune*, October 27, 1900, referenced in Beale, 67.

31. Sprout and Sprout, *The Rise of American Naval Power*, 250. Theodore Roosevelt, "The American Need of a Strong Navy," speech on Lincoln Day, February 13, 1898, referenced in Samuel Fallows, ed., *Life of William McKinley, Our Martyred President* (Chicago: Regan Printing House, 1901), 381–82. Henry J. Hendrix, *Theodore Roosevelt's Naval Diplomacy: The U.S. Navy and the Birth of the American Century* (Annapolis, MD: Naval Institute Press, 2009), 22.

32. L. A. Beaumont, "Comment on Foreign Office Request for Admiralty Views Regarding Revision of Clayton-Bulwer Treaty," February 6, 1899, referenced in Friedberg, *The Weary Titan*, 164. Secretary of the Navy, *Annual Report*, 1900, referenced in Cooling, *Gray Steel and Blue Water Navy*, 135. Quoted by James D. Richardson, *A Compilation of the Messages and Papers of the Presidents, 1789–1897*, vol. 9 (Washington, DC: Bureau of National Literature and Art, 1902), 463, referenced in Coletta, *A Survey of U.S. Naval Affairs, 1865–1917*, 27.

33. Eugene C. Grace quoted during hearing before the Committee on Naval Affairs, 64th Congress, 1st session (1916), referenced in Cooling, *Gray Steel and Blue Water Navy*, 166. Craig L Symonds, *Navalists and Antinavalists: The Naval Policy Debate in the United States, 1785–1827* (Newark: University of Delaware Press, 1980), 12, referenced in Shulman, *Navalism and the Emergence of American Sea Power, 1882–1893*, 2.

34. Alfred Thayer Mahan, *Letters and Papers of Alfred Thayer Mahan*, ed. Robert Seager II and Doris McGuire (Annapolis, MD: Naval Institute Press, 1975), 86, referenced in Love, *History of the U.S. Navy*, 428. Theodore

Roosevelt, memorandum after Yonkers Conference, February 12, 1900, referenced in Beale, *Theodore Roosevelt and the Rise of America to World Power*, 103. General Board, 1901, referenced in Love, *History of the U.S. Navy*, 426.

35. Richmond Hobson, "America, Mistress of the Sea," *North American Review*, October 1902, 557, referenced in Reckner, *Teddy Roosevelt's Great White Fleet*, 4. "Brief Account of the General Board," October 26, 1903, General Records of the Navy Department, referenced in Cooling, *Gray Steel and Blue Water Navy*, 165. Coletta, *A Survey of U.S. Naval Affairs, 1865–1917*.

36. *Messages and Papers of the Presidents*, 13, 6268–69, referenced in Hendrix, *Theodore Roosevelt's Naval Diplomacy*, 136. John J. Fee, "The Rise of American Naval Power," in King, *Naval Engineering and American Seapower*, 69. Navy Yearbook, 1917, 147, referenced in Sprout and Sprout, *The Rise of American Naval Power*, 248. Wimmel, *Theodore Roosevelt and the Great White Fleet*, 188. Mahan, *Mahan on Naval Warfare*, 95. Also see Mahan, 132.

37. Roosevelt maintained an interest in some smaller craft, noting, "I have become greatly interested in submarine boats. They are in no sense substitutes for above water torpedo boats, not to speak of battleships, cruisers and the like, they may on certain occasions supplement other craft, and they should be developed." Theodore Roosevelt to Charles Joseph Bonaparte, August 28, 1905, referenced in Hendrix, *Theodore Roosevelt's Naval Diplomacy*, 152. Randolph W. King, "The Rise of American Naval Power, 1899–1913," in King, *Naval Engineering and American Seapower*, 79. Moody speech, February 16, 1904, referenced in Cooling, *Gray Steel and Blue Water Navy*, 171. Hendrix, *Theodore Roosevelt's Naval Diplomacy*, 152. "Big Battleships of High Speed," letter from U.S. Commander William S. Sims to Admiral Sir John Fisher, November 3, 1906, in *The Papers of Admiral Sir John Fisher*, ed. Peter Kemp, vol. 1 (London: Navy Records Society, 1960), 352. Theodore Roosevelt to Sims, October 13, 1906, in Hendrix, *Theodore Roosevelt's Naval Diplomacy*, 145. Captain C. W. Dyson, "The Development of Machinery in the U.S. Navy during the Past Ten Years," *Journal of the American Society of Naval Engineers* 29 (1917): 217, referenced in William M. McBride, *Technological Change and the United States Navy, 1865–1945*, Johns Hopkins Studies in the History of Technology (Baltimore: Johns Hopkins University Press, 2000), 90.

38. Gordon Carpenter O'Gara, *Theodore Roosevelt and the Rise of the Modern Navy* (Princeton, NJ: Princeton University Press, 1943), 77, referenced in Love, *History of the U.S. Navy*, 440. John Bassett Moore, *A Digest of International Law*, vol. 1 (Washington, DC: Government Printing Office, 1906), 432, referenced in Weinberg, *Manifest Destiny*, 261. "Lessons and Results of the Battleship Cruise," *Scientific American*, February 20, 1909, 146, referenced in Reckner, *Teddy Roosevelt's Great White Fleet*, 161.

39. Sprout and Sprout, *The Rise of American Naval Power,* 293.
40. Theodore Roosevelt, "Expansion and Peace," *The Independent,* December 21, 1899, http://www.bartleby.com/58/2.html.
41. Sprout and Sprout, *The Rise of American Naval Power,* 222. Alfred Thayer Mahan, *The Interest of America in Sea Power, Present and Future* (New York: Houghton, Mifflin, 1893), 35–36, referenced in Shulman, *Navalism and the Emergence of American Sea Power, 1882–1893,* 82.
42. W. P. McCann, "Report of Policy Board," January 20, 1890, in *Proceedings of the United States Naval Institute* 16/2/53 (April 1890). Theodore Roosevelt to Captain Caspar F. Goodrich, June 16, 1897, referenced in Beale, *Theodore Roosevelt and the Rise of America to World Power,* 265. Love, *History of the U.S. Navy,* xiv.

Chapter Three. Germany's Rise

Epigraph: Bülow, *Memoirs of Prince von Bülow,* 415.
1. W. O. Henderson, *The Rise of German Industrial Power, 1834–1914* (London: Temple Smith, 1975), 239. Also see Paul Michael Kennedy, *The Rise of the Anglo-German Antagonism: 1860–1914* (London: Allen and Unwin, 1982), 291–92. Holger H. Herwig, *"Luxury Fleet": The Imperial German Navy, 1888–1918* (London: Allen and Unwin, 1980), 2. Henderson, *The Rise of German Industrial Power, 1834–1914,* 198–99. Jonathan Steinberg, *Yesterday's Deterrent: Tirpitz and the Birth of the German Battle* (Aldershot, UK: Gregg Revivals, 1993), 29.
2. See table 17 in Herwig, *Luxury Fleet.* Giles MacDonogh, *The Last Kaiser: William the Impetuous* (London: Weidenfeld and Nicolson, 2000), 311.
3. Gary E. Weir, *Building the Kaiser's Navy: The Imperial Navy Office and German Industry in the von Tirpitz Era, 1890–1919* (Annapolis, MD: Naval Institute Press, 1992), 26. Alfred von Tirpitz, *My Memoirs, by Grand Admiral von Tirpitz,* vol. 1 (New York: Dodd, Mead, 1919), 72. Dirk Bönker, *Militarism in a Global Age: Naval Ambitions in Germany and the United States before World War I,* The United States in the World (Ithaca, NY: Cornell University Press, 2012), 24.
4. Hereafter, Wilhelm II is referred to simply as "Wilhelm." J. C. G. Röhl, *Germany without Bismarck* (London: London Batsford, 1967), 43. Also referenced in MacDonogh, *The Last Kaiser,* 139. Also see William II, "First Declaration of Policy," Berlin, June 25, 1888, reproduced in Christian Gauss, *The German Emperor as Shown in His Public Utterances* (New York: Scribner's, 1915), 38.
5. Referenced in Kennedy, *The Rise of the Anglo-German Antagonism,* 14. Quoted in Herwig, *Luxury Fleet,* 95. Herwig, 96. See tables 21 and 22 in Herwig.
6. John VanDerKiste, *Kaiser Wilhelm II: Germany's Last Emperor* (Stroud, UK: Sutton, 1999), 111. Wilhelm quoted in 1888, referenced in MacDonogh, *The Last Kaiser,* 110.

7. VanDerKiste, *Kaiser Wilhelm II*, 59. William II, "The English Fleet and the German Army," speech, Sandown Bay, Great Britain, August 5, 1889, reproduced in Gauss, *The German Emperor as Shown in His Public Utterances*, 48.

8. Richard Millman, *British Foreign Policy and the Coming of the Franco-Prussian War* (Oxford, UK: Clarendon, 1965), 33, referenced in Kennedy, *The Rise of the Anglo-German Antagonism*, 25. MacDonogh, *The Last Kaiser*, 106–7.

9. William II, *The Kaiser's Memoirs, 1888–1918* (New York: Narper and Brothers, 1922), 4.

10. William II, "The Emperor's First Army Bill," speech, Berlin, July 4, 1893, reproduced in Gauss, *The German Emperor as Shown in His Public Utterances*, 79. Emil Ludwig, *Kaiser Wilhelm II* (London: G. P. Putnam's Sons, 1926), 60. William II, *The Kaiser's Memoirs, 1888–1918*, 11. William II, 11.

11. Rolf Hobson, *Imperialism at Sea: Naval Strategic Thought, the Ideology of Sea Power, and the Tirpitz Plan, 1875–1914*, Studies in Central European Histories (Boston: Brill, 2002), 129. William II, "The Emperor's First Army Bill," 77. Ludwig, *Kaiser Wilhelm II*. Röhl, *Germany without Bismarck*, 167.

12. Patrick J. Kelly, *Tirpitz and the Imperial German Navy* (Bloomington: Indiana University Press, 2011), 22. Hobson, *Imperialism at Sea*, 115. Ernst Lieber papers translated in Kelly, *Tirpitz and the Imperial German Navy*, 142. Kelly, 19.

13. Stosch to Gustav Freytag, December 3, 1871, referenced in Hobson, *Imperialism at Sea*, 114. Stosch memorandum, 1873, quoted in Kelly, *Tirpitz and the Imperial German Navy*, 145.

14. Hobson, *Imperialism at Sea*, 99.

15. Michael Epkenhans, *Tirpitz: Architect of the German High Seas Fleet*, Military Profiles (Washington, DC: Potomac Books, 2008), 20. Ludwig, *Kaiser Wilhelm II*, 131. Hans Hallman, *Der Weg* (Stuttgart: Kohlhammer, 1933), 35, referenced and translated in Ivo Nikolai Lambi, *The Navy and German Power Politics, 1862–1914* (Boston: Allen and Unwin, 1984), 9. Lambi, 7. Alfred von Tirpitz, *Erinnerungen* (Leipzig: K. F. Koehler, 1919), 24, referenced in Lambi, 6.

16. See Robert K. Massie, *Dreadnought* (New York: Random House, 2012), 162–63. Wilhelm quoted in Kennedy, *The Rise of the Anglo-German Antagonism*, 237.

17. Gholz memorandum of October 16, 1889, referenced in Lambi, *The Navy and German Power Politics, 1862–1914*, 42–43. Schlieffen quoted in Snyder, *The Ideology of the Offensive*, 139. Stenzel quoted in Hobson, *Imperialism at Sea*, 143. Curt Freiherr von Maltzahn quoted in Kelly, *Tirpitz and the Imperial German Navy*, 91.

18. Tirpitz quoted in Kelly, *Tirpitz and the Imperial German Navy*, 49. Tirpitz, *My Memoirs*, 1:234. Tirpitz, 1:23; Steinberg, *Yesterday's Deterrent*, 66. Tirpitz,

My Memoirs, 1:23; Steinberg, *Yesterday's Deterrent*, 66. Lambi, *The Navy and German Power Politics, 1862–1914*, 70. Tirpitz, *My Memoirs*, 1:119–20.

19. Caprivi quoted in Hobson, *Imperialism at Sea*, 125. Hobson, 147. Tirpitz, *My Memoirs*, 1:67. Quoted in Hobson, *Imperialism at Sea*, 131.

20. Lambi, *The Navy and German Power Politics, 1862–1914*, 2. Stosch quoted in Lambi, 4. Lambi, 5.

21. Lambi, 8. William II, *The Kaiser's Memoirs, 1888–1918*, 223.

22. Michael Epkenhans, "Wilhelm II and 'His' Navy, 1888–1918," in *The Kaiser: New Research on Wilhelm II's Role in Imperial Germany*, ed. Annika Mombauer and Wilhelm Deist (Cambridge: Cambridge University Press, 2003), 22. Lambi, *The Navy and German Power Politics, 1862–1914*, 60. Admiral Knorr to William II, November 28, 1895, reproduced in *The Naval Route to the Abyss: The Anglo-German Naval Race 1895–1914*, ed. Matthew S. Seligmann, Publications of the Navy Records Society 161 (Farnham, UK: Ashgate, 2015), 15.

23. Tirpitz to Stosch, February 13, 1896, reproduced in Seligmann, *The Naval Route to the Abyss*, 40. William II, *The Kaiser's Memoirs, 1888–1918*, 78. See Lambi, *The Navy and German Power Politics, 1862–1914*, 9.

24. Lambi, *The Navy and German Power Politics, 1862–1914*, 31. Tirpitz, *My Memoirs*, 1:129. Also see Peter Padfield, *The Great Naval Race: The Anglo-German Naval Rivalry, 1900–1914* (New York: D. McKay, 1974), 113. Tirpitz, *My Memoirs*, 1:54.

25. Gauss, *The German Emperor as Shown in His Public Utterances*, 152–53. Weir, *Building the Kaiser's Navy*, 20. Quoted in Kennedy, *The Rise of the Anglo-German Antagonism*, 225.

26. Herwig, *Luxury Fleet*, 18. William II, "The Beginning of World Politics," speech, Berlin, June 16, 1896, reproduced in Gauss, *The German Emperor as Shown in His Public Utterances*, 102. Also see Epkenhans, *Tirpitz*, 16. Bülow quoted in Steinberg, *Yesterday's Deterrent*, 59–60. Also see Epkenhans, *Tirpitz*, 30. See Röhl, *Germany without Bismarck*, 162. Bülow to Eulenburg, December 26, 1897, referenced in Röhl, 252. Volker R. Berghahn, *Germany and the Approach of War in 1914* (London: Macmillan, 1973), 53. See Bönker, *Militarism in a Global Age*, 9.

27. William II, "To the Recruits for the Navy," speech, Wilhelmshaven, February 21, 1896, reproduced in Gauss, *The German Emperor as Shown in His Public Utterances*, 103. "The Chinese Situation and the Mailed Fist," letter from William II to Prince Henry, December 15, 1897, reproduced in Gauss, 120. Holstein to Paul von Hatzfeldt, April 14, 1897, referenced in Steinberg, *Yesterday's Deterrent*, 20. August Bebel, speech, March 24, 1898, quoted in Steinberg, 194–95.

28. Huntington, *The Soldier and the State*, 102, referenced in Weir, *Building the Kaiser's Navy*, 22. Steinberg, *Yesterday's Deterrent*, 117. Also see Lambi, *The Navy and German Power Politics, 1862–1914*, 115. Kelly, *Tirpitz and the Imperial German Navy*, 114.

29. Tirpitz to William II, September 28, 1899, referenced in Lambi, *The Navy and German Power Politics, 1862–1914*, 139. Also see Epkenhans, *Tirpitz*, 31. Bülow, *Reden*, vol. 1, 98, referenced in Berghahn, *Germany and the Approach of War in 1914*, 35. Kelly, *Tirpitz and the Imperial German Navy*, 179. Gauss, *The German Emperor as Shown in His Public Utterances*, 151. Gauss, 153.

30. *Die Flotte*, no. 1, January 1900, 15, referenced in Kelly, *Tirpitz and the Imperial German Navy*, 166. See Kennedy, *The Rise of the Anglo-German Antagonism*, 311. Kelly, *Tirpitz and the Imperial German Navy*, 166. Herwig, *Luxury Fleet*, 3. Bülow, *Memoirs of Prince von Bülow*, 480. Bülow, 113.

31. Epkenhans, "Wilhelm II and 'His' Navy, 1888–1918," 22. Bülow, *Memoirs of Prince von Bülow*, 423. William II, "A Place in the Sun," speech, Hamburg, June 18, 1901, reproduced in Gauss, *The German Emperor as Shown in His Public Utterances*, 181. Röhl, *Germany without Bismarck*, 130. "The Chinese Situation and the Mailed Fist," letter from William II to Prince Henry, December 15, 1897, reproduced in Gauss, *The German Emperor as Shown in His Public Utterances*, 188. Herwig, *Luxury Fleet*, 99. William II, speech, Wilhelmshaven, July 3, 1900, referenced in Epkenhans, "Wilhelm II and 'His' Navy, 1888–1918," 16. See also Ludwig, *Kaiser Wilhelm II*, 239. William II, "The Ocean Knocks at Our Door," speech, Kiel, July 3, 1900, reproduced in Gauss, *The German Emperor as Shown in His Public Utterances*, 162.

32. Quoted in Herwig, *Luxury Fleet*, 43. Röhl, *Germany without Bismarck*, 163. Col. Trench to Lascelles, August 21, 1908, referenced in Padfield, *The Great Naval Race*, 192. John Fisher, *The Papers of Admiral Sir John Fisher*, ed. Peter Kemp, vol. 2 (London: Navy Records Society, 1964), 347. Also see Kennedy, *The Rise of the Anglo-German Antagonism*, 310. Wilhelm, interview by Col. Stuart-Wortley, *Daily Telegraph*, October 28, 1908.

33. Imperial Navy Office, "Memorandum concerning the Development of Our Battleship and Large Cruiser Types," August 30, 1906, reproduced in Seligmann, *The Naval Route to the Abyss*, 215. MacDonogh, *The Last Kaiser*, 308. Sir Archibald Hurd and Henry Anson Castle, *German Sea-Power: Its Rise, Progress, and Economic Basis* (London: John Murray, 1913), x.

34. David J. Hill, memorandum of February 4, 1910, Rochester University Library, Hill Papers, referenced in John C. G. Röhl, *Kaiser Wilhelm II, 1859–1941: A Concise Life* (Cambridge: Cambridge University Press, 2014), 125. Referenced in MacDonogh, *The Last Kaiser*, 345. William II, *The Kaiser's Memoirs, 1888–1918*, 156. William II, 156. Grey quoted in Jonathan Steinberg, "Diplomatie als Wille und Vorstellung: Die Berliner Mission Lord Haldane sim Februar 1912," 263–82, in *Marine und Marinepolitik im kaiserlichen Deutschland, 1871–1914*, ed. Herbert Schottelius and Wilhelm Deist (Düsseldorf: Droste Verlag, 1972), 269, and translated in Kelly, *Tirpitz and the Imperial German Navy*, 335.

35. See MacDonogh, *The Last Kaiser*, 335. Berghahn, *Germany and the Approach of War in 1914*, 169. Admiral Holtzendorff, Commander in Chief of the High Seas Fleet, October 26, 1911, reproduced in Seligmann, *The Naval Route to the Abyss*, 324. Tirpitz to Bethmann Hollweg, October 5, 1911, in Arthur Jacob Marder, *From the Dreadnought to Scapa Flow: The Royal Navy in the Fisher Era, 1904–1919* (London: Oxford University Press, 1961), 274. Berghahn, *Germany and the Approach of War in 1914*, 169. William II quoted in Berghahn, *Germany and the Approach of War in 1914*, 144.

36. Tirpitz, *My Memoirs*, 1:76. Kelly, *Tirpitz and the Imperial German Navy*, 82. Lambi, *The Navy and German Power Politics, 1862–1914*, 76. Lambi, 76.

37. Kelly, *Tirpitz and the Imperial German Navy*, 93. Kelly, 92. Steinberg, *Yesterday's Deterrent*, 210–11. Also referenced in Lambi, *The Navy and German Power Politics, 1862–1914*, 127. Tirpitz, *My Memoirs*, 1:77.

38. Senden to Tirpitz, December 17, 1895, quoted in Kelly, *Tirpitz and the Imperial German Navy*, 109. Tirpitz to Stosch, December 21, 1895, quoted in Hobson, *Imperialism at Sea*, 222. Steinberg, *Yesterday's Deterrent*, 193–95. Weir, *Building the Kaiser's Navy*, 24. Archibald Hurd, *The German Fleet* (New York: Hodder and Stoughton, 1915), Appendix.

39. Steinberg, *Yesterday's Deterrent*, 78. MacDonogh, *The Last Kaiser*, 219. Knorr memorandum, May 2, 1897, referenced in Hobson, *Imperialism at Sea*, 231. "Notes on a Visit to Kiel and Wilhelmshaven," August 1902, quoted in Kennedy, *The Rise of the Anglo-German Antagonism*, 27.

40. William L. Langer, *The Diplomacy of Imperialism, 1890–1902* (New York: Knopf, 1951), 428. Also referenced in Lambi, *The Navy and German Power Politics, 1862–1914*, 33. Referenced in Kennedy, *The Rise of the Anglo-German Antagonism*, 224. MacDonogh, *The Last Kaiser*, 274–75. Bülow, *Memoirs of Prince von Bülow*, 513.

41. William II, *The Kaiser's Memoirs, 1888–1918*, 228. Bülow, *Memoirs of Prince von Bülow*, 305. William II, *The Kaiser's Memoirs, 1888–1918*, 228.

42. Tirpitz, speech, May 17, 1907, quoted in Kelly, *Tirpitz and the Imperial German Navy*, 282. Tirpitz to the Chancellor, November 18, 1905, reproduced in Seligmann, *The Naval Route to the Abyss*, 179. Waldersee, *Memoirs*, quoted in Kelly, *Tirpitz and the Imperial German Navy*, 233. Tirpitz to William II, 1905, quoted in Hobson, *Imperialism at Sea*, 256.

43. Tirpitz to the Chancellor, November 18, 1905, reproduced in Seligmann, *The Naval Route to the Abyss*, 182. "Sir N. O'Conor to the Marquess of Salisbury," February 7, 1898, in *British Documents on the Origins of the War, 1898–1914*, vol. 1, ed. G. P. Gooch and Harold William Vazeille Temperley (London: HMSO, 1926), 10. Lambi, *The Navy and German Power Politics, 1862–1914*, 361. Chief of the Admiralty Staff, "Memorandum concerning Warfare against England," March 1906, reproduced in Seligmann, *The Naval Route to the Abyss*, 188. Müller's report to the Emperor, October 18, 1910, in Marder, *From the Dreadnought to Scapa Flow*, 223. Berghahn, *Germany and the Approach of War in 1914*, 108.

44. Heeringen quoted in Kelly, *Tirpitz and the Imperial German Navy*, 199. Tirpitz to William II, May 17, 1914, reproduced in Seligmann, *The Naval Route to the Abyss*, 411. Dienstschrift IX, 3 quoted in Kelly, *Tirpitz and the Imperial German Navy*, 92–93. Bönker, *Militarism in a Global Age*, 121. Admiral von Knorr, May 10, 1897, quoted in Steinberg, *Yesterday's Deterrent*, 121. Immediately before war broke out in 1914, German naval plans were as follows: "1) To damage the Engl[ish] through the guard [and] blockade forces in the German Bight by a mine and U-boat offensive extending to the British coast. 2) After the power relationship has been evened through such waging of war and the English forces have been weakened through mines, destroyers and submarines, it is to be attempted under favorable circumstances to engage our fleet in battle through the preparation and involvement of all its strength." Lambi, *The Navy and German Power Politics, 1862–1914*, 422.

45. Lambi, *The Navy and German Power Politics, 1862–1914*, 35. Herwig, *Luxury Fleet*, 75.

46. Steinberg, *Yesterday's Deterrent*, 127. Tirpitz quoted in Steinberg, 126. Tirpitz memo "General Criteria for the Establishment of Our Fleet According to Ship Classes and Ship Designs," July 1897, referenced in Seligmann, *The Naval Route to the Abyss*, 42. Selborne to Marder, quoted in Arthur Jacob Marder, *British Naval Policy, 1880–1905: The Anatomy of British Sea Power* (London: Putnam, 1940), 464. Steinberg, *Yesterday's Deterrent*, 209–21.

47. Herwig, *Luxury Fleet*, 42. Steinberg, *Yesterday's Deterrent*, 146. Tirpitz, *My Memoirs*, 1:149.

48. Hobson, *Imperialism at Sea*, 240. Herwig, *Luxury Fleet*, 42. Of these ships, five battleships, four cruisers, four to six gunboats, and a torpedo-boat flotilla were to be stationed in Asia. Another five to six cruisers and one to two gunboats were devoted to the Americas. See Tirpitz to William II, September 28, 1899, reproduced in Seligmann, *The Naval Route to the Abyss*, 56. See table 1-16 in Herwig, *Luxury Fleet*. Herwig.

49. J. E. Sutton, "The Imperial Navy: 1910–1914" (PhD diss., Indiana University, 1953), 301, referenced in Padfield, *The Great Naval Race*, 179. William II, *The Kaiser's Memoirs, 1888–1918*, 156–57. William II, 156–57. Chief of the Admiralty Staff, "Memorandum concerning Warfare against England," March 1906, reproduced in Seligmann, *The Naval Route to the Abyss*, 195. Kelly, *Tirpitz and the Imperial German Navy*, 320.

50. See Weir, *Building the Kaiser's Navy*, 97. Sutton, "The Imperial Navy: 1910–1914," 308, referenced in Padfield, *The Great Naval Race*, 179. Padfield, 179. Bülow to Tirpitz, December 25, 1908, reproduced in Seligmann, *The Naval Route to the Abyss*, 291. See Bülow, *Memoirs of Prince von Bülow*. Also see Lambi, *The Navy and German Power Politics, 1862–1914*, 159.

51. Quoted in Weir, *Building the Kaiser's Navy*, 52. Tirpitz, March 17, 1909, referenced in Kelly, *Tirpitz and the Imperial German Navy*, 355. Weir,

Building the Kaiser's Navy, 198. Tirpitz, *My Memoirs*, 1:179–80. William II, *The Kaiser's Memoirs, 1888–1918*, 236–37.

52. Memorandum from Selborne, February 26, 1904, quoted in Kennedy, *The Rise of the Anglo-German Antagonism*, 270. Sir F. Lascelles to Sir Edward Gray, enclosure in Captain Dumas to Sir F. Lascelles, 1908, in *British Documents on the Origins of the War, 1898–1914*, vol. 6, ed. G. P. Gooch and Harold William Vazeille Temperley (London: HMSO, 1932), 128. The quote was revised in Tirpitz's autobiography but remains unaltered in German archives. See Kennedy, *The Rise of the Anglo-German Antagonism*, 422.

53. Quoted in Herwig, *Luxury Fleet*, 95–96.

54. Quoted in MacDonogh, *The Last Kaiser*, 349. William II, "The Old Order Changeth," speech, Aix, June 19, 1902, reproduced in Gauss, *The German Emperor as Shown in His Public Utterances*, 205. Ludwig, *Kaiser Wilhelm II*, 247. William II, *The Kaiser's Memoirs, 1888–1918*, 298.

55. Quoted in Kennedy, *The Rise of the Anglo-German Antagonism*, 330. Kennedy, 418. Ludwig, *Kaiser Wilhelm II*, 357.

56. Tirpitz, *My Memoirs*, 1:108.

Chapter Four. Britain's Apex

Epigraph: Alexander Mackintosh, *Joseph Chamberlain: An Honest Biography* (London: Hodder and Stoughton, 1914), 217.

1. Figures from Bundesarchiv-Militararchiv, Freiburg, re-created in Kennedy, *The Rise and Fall of British Naval Mastery*, 190. Kennedy, 190. Kennedy, 209.

2. League of Nations, *Industrialization and Foreign Trade*, Series of Publications II, Economic and Financial (New York: League of Nations, 1945), 56. League of Nations, 56.

3. Kennedy, *The Rise and Fall of British Naval Mastery*, 178. Great Britain, Royal Commission on the Depression of Trade and Industry, *Final Report* (London: HMSO, 1886), xxiv.

4. Kennedy, *The Rise and Fall of British Naval Mastery*, 178. J. K. Dunlop, *The Development of the British Army, 1899–1914, from the Eve of the South African War to the Eve of the Great War, with Special Reference to the Territorial Force* (London: Methuen, 1938), 12.

5. *Daily News*, October 1893, referenced in Marder, *British Naval Policy, 1880–1905*, 174. Clowes, "The Millstone round the Neck of England," *The Nineteenth Century*, March 1895, referenced in Marder, 211. Marder, 211.

6. Lord Rosebery, Colonial Institute speech, 1893, quoted in Langer, *The Diplomacy of Imperialism, 1890–1902*, 77–78. Vindex, *Cecil Rhodes; His Political Life and Speeches* (London: Chapman and Hall, 1900), 642, referenced in Langer, 79. Langer, 77–78. From Roberts memo, August 1888,

in Friedberg, *The Weary Titan,* 227. Frederick Richards, quoted in Marder, *British Naval Policy, 1880–1905,* 299.

7. Kennedy, *The Rise and Fall of British Naval Mastery,* 323. Humphrey Hugh Smith, *A Yellow Admiral Remembers* (London: Edward Arnold, 1932), 54. Bernard Mallet, *British Budgets 1887–88 to 1912–13* (London: Macmillan, 1913), 505.

8. Mallet, *British Budgets 1887–88 to 1912–13,* 502–3. Selborne to Curzon, January 4, 1903, quoted in George W. Monger, *The End of Isolation: British Foreign Policy, 1900–1907* (Westport, CT: Greenwood, 1976), 110. "The Navy Estimates and the Chancellor of the Exchequer's Memo on the Growth of Expenditure," November 15, 1901, referenced in Marder, *From the Dreadnought to Scapa Flow,* 107. Mallet, *British Budgets 1887–88 to 1912–13,* 502–3.

9. Cabinet Memorandum, April 28, 1904, quoted in Friedberg, *The Weary Titan,* 89–90. Greg Kennedy, *Imperial Defence: The Old World Order 1856–1956,* Cass Military Studies (London: Routledge, 2008), 209.

10. Marder, *British Naval Policy, 1880–1905,* 70.

11. It is worth noting that at the beginning of the twentieth century, the British Army was not one force but a combination of multiple services. The Regular Army was the primary body, and it was intended for use either at home or abroad. The Auxiliary Force was secondary and included the Volunteer Force, the Yeomanry, and the Militia. In 1898–99, Britain retained 212,393 soldiers in the Regular Army, 231,624 in the Volunteers, 11,891 in the Yeomanry, and 103,647 in the Militia. The Regular Army was well trained, but the Volunteers, Yeomanry, and Militia were not viewed as effective fighting forces. Each element had a different purpose. One respected former military officer explained, "The Regular Army—with or without the Reserves—would fight small wars. . . . The Regular Army, with the Reserves, might fight a continental war. . . . The whole Army, the Regular Army with the Auxiliary Forces, might be called upon to resist an invasion of England." The Auxiliary Forces were seen as distinct elements from the Regular Army. The Militia, for example, was viewed by supporters as "a totally different Army raised under totally different circumstances for a totally different purpose—namely for home defence." Dunlop, *The Development of the British Army, 1899–1914,* 31–59. Earl of Wemyss to the House of Lords, February 18, 1898, referenced in Dunlop, 42. Grey quoted in Marder, *From the Dreadnought to Scapa Flow,* 385. Jörn Leonhard, "Nations in Arms and Imperial Defence—Continental Models, the British Empire and Its Military before 1914," *Journal of Modern European History* 5, no. 2 (2007): 290. General Lord Wolseley, speech, Perth, December 8, 1896, quoted in Marder, *British Naval Policy, 1880–1905,* 65.

12. An alternate argument is that for many years, the British Navy saw its role more as a protector of global trade. As Vice Admiral Humphrey H.

Smith later reflected, "I don't think we thought very much about war with a big W. We looked on the Navy more as a World Police Force than as a warlike institution. We considered that our job was to safeguard law and order throughout the world." Mallet, *British Budgets 1887–88 to 1912–13*, 504. Percy Arthur Baxter Silburn, *The Colonies and Imperial Defence* (London: Longmans, Green, 1909), 250. Fisher quoted in Marder, *British Naval Policy, 1880–1905*, 65.

13. R. B. Wernham, *Before the Armada: The Emergence of the English Nation* (New York: Harcourt, Brace and World, 1966), 343. Referenced in Kennedy, *The Rise and Fall of British Naval Mastery*, 25. Quoted in Marder, *British Naval Policy, 1880–1905*, 75. Marder, *British Naval Policy, 1880–1905*, 577. Marder, 111. Andrew Lambert, "Royal Navy and the Defence of Empire, 1856–1918," 118, in Kennedy, *Imperial Defence*. Andrew Lambert, "Royal Navy and the Defence of Empire, 1856–1918," 118, in Kennedy. Lord Rendel, *The Personal Papers of Lord Rendel* (London: E. Benn, 1931), 241, in Marder, *British Naval Policy, 1880–1905*, 68.

14. April 1899 memorandum, in Marder, *British Naval Policy, 1880–1905*, 338. Selborne, "Navy Estimates, 1901–1902," January 17, 1901, 5–6, in Nicholas A. Lambert, *Sir John Fisher's Naval Revolution*, Studies in Maritime History (Columbia: University of South Carolina Press, 1999), 28. Marder, *British Naval Policy, 1880–1905*, 338.

15. Although French strategy appeared defensive, other disagreed. One naval leader suggested, "It must, however, be remembered that up to a comparatively recent date the French naval preparations were defensive rather than offensive—that is, they seemed to *fear* attack on themselves rather than making it on us." Quoted in Marder, *British Naval Policy, 1880–1905*, 3518. Marder, 370–71. Also see Lambert, *Sir John Fisher's Naval Revolution*, 64. "Value of Submarines in War," enclosed in Arnold-Forster to Selborne, August 1901, referenced in Lambert, 50. Marder, *British Naval Policy, 1880–1905*, 165.

16. Cited in Marder, *British Naval Policy, 1880–1905*, 351. The director of Naval Intelligence defined command of the sea as requiring that it "be possible to transport across the waters commanded a large Military Expedition without risk of serious loss." Cited in Marder, 65. Kennedy, *The Rise and Fall of British Naval Mastery*, 243. Reginald Custance, "Memorandum on Sea Power and the Principles Involved in it," July 1902, in Lambert, *Sir John Fisher's Naval Revolution*, 54. Fisher, *The Papers of Admiral Sir John Fisher*, 1:101.

17. In 1898, the British Regular Army included roughly 19,000 cavalry, 40,000 artillery, 8,000 engineers, 150,000 infantry, and several thousand others. This compared to over 600,000 in the German Army alone. For this reason, the influential Stanhope Memorandum made clear in 1891, "it will be distinctly understood that the probability of the employment of an Army Corps in the field in any European war is sufficiently im-

probable to make it the primary duty of the military authorities to orga-
nize our forces efficiently for the defence of this country." General
Annual Returns of the British Army for the year 1898, referenced in
Dunlop, *The Development of the British Army, 1899–1914*, 26. Data trans-
lated by Adam Blauhut in "Strength of the German Army (1890–1914),"
German History in Documents and Images, from *Social History Workbook:
Materials on Kaiserreich Statistics 1870–1914*, ed. Gerd Hohorst, Jürgen
Kocka, and Gerhard A. Ritter (Munich: Beck, 1975), 171–72. Stanhope
Memorandum, June 1, 1891, Appendix A in Dunlop, *The Development of
the British Army, 1899–1914*, 127.

18. Charles Dilke, "House of Commons Debate on Army (Supplementary)
    Estimates," UK Parliament, January 31, 1902, https://hansard.parlia-
    ment.uk/Commons/1902-01-31/debates/2e62d43d-f13c-429b-9192-
    8c7279869b83/Army(Supplementary)Estimates1901%E2%80%9302?hi
    ghlight=james%200%27mara. See Lambert, *Sir John Fisher's Naval Revo-
    lution*, 306; Jon Tetsuro Sumida, *In Defence of Naval Supremacy: Finance,
    Technology, and British Naval Policy, 1889–1914* (Boston: Unwin Hyman,
    1989); Mallet, *British Budgets 1887–88 to 1912–13*, 504.

19. "It is utterly impossible, in a country with 10,000,000 tons of floating
    commerce, to protect that floating commerce thoroughly by any number
    of fast cruisers which the taxpayers of this country would be willing to
    provide," bemoaned an admiral in 1888. Admiral Hood, Accounts and
    Papers, XIII, 1888, minutes of evidence, 34, in Marder, *British Naval Pol-
    icy, 1880–1905*, 96. Thomas Allnutt Brassey, *The Naval Annual, 1896*
    (Portsmouth, UK: Adamant Media, 2000), 68. See Lambert, *Sir John
    Fisher's Naval Revolution*, 306; Sumida, *In Defence of Naval Supremacy*;
    Mallet, *British Budgets 1887–88 to 1912–13*, 504.

20. Quoted in Marder, *British Naval Policy, 1880–1905*, 108. Selborne, "Naval
    Estimates, 1901–1902," January 17, 1901, 8, Colonial Defense Commit-
    tee papers, in Lambert, *Sir John Fisher's Naval Revolution*, 78. Marder,
    British Naval Policy, 1880–1905, 363. Admiralty, "Memorandum on Possi-
    bility of Invasion during Temporary Loss of Command of the Sea in
    Home Waters," March 31, 1903, in Lambert, *Sir John Fisher's Naval Revo-
    lution*, 60. Battenberg quoted in Marder, *British Naval Policy, 1880–1905*,
    370.

21. Reginald Bacon, "Report on Running of Submarine Boats," May 31,
    1903, in Lambert, *Sir John Fisher's Naval Revolution*, 54. Goschen, min-
    utes, January 17, 1897, in Katherine C. Epstein, *Torpedo: Inventing the
    Military-Industrial Complex in the United States and Great Britain* (Cam-
    bridge, MA: Harvard University Press, 2014), 47. Parliamentary Debates,
    4th Series, 86, 33, July 17, 1900, in Lambert, *Sir John Fisher's Naval Revo-
    lution*, 47. Sir George S. Clarke and James R. Thursfield, *The Navy and
    the Nation; or, Naval Warfare and Imperial Defence* (London: John Murray,
    1897), 301–2.

22. Marder, *British Naval Policy, 1880–1905*, 167.

23. Ottley to Vaughan Nash, May 26, 1909, in Marder, *From the Dreadnought to Scapa Flow*, 184. Fisher, *The Papers of Admiral Sir John Fisher*, 2:83. Kori Schake, *Safe Passage: The Transition from British to American Hegemony* (Cambridge, MA: Harvard University Press, 2017), 211.

24. John Fisher to King Edward, October 1906, in *Fear God and Dread Nought: The Correspondence of Admiral of the Fleet Lord Fisher of Kilverstone*, ed. Arthur Jacob Marder (Cambridge, MA: Harvard University Press, 1952), 102–3. Memorandum from Eyre Crowe, October 20, 1910, in Marder, *From the Dreadnought to Scapa Flow*, 105 Bülow, *Memoirs of Prince von Bülow*, 332.

25. Dunlop, *The Development of the British Army, 1899–1914*, 156–58. Arnold-Forster to Balfour, October 27, 1903, in J. McDermott, "The British Army's Turn to Europe," in *The War Plans of the Great Powers, 1880–1914*, ed. Paul M. Kennedy (London: Allen and Unwin, 1979), 100. War Office, "Provision of Land Forces for the Defence of the United Kingdom" and "Admiralty Remarks on the Military Paper," February 14, 1903, referenced in Lambert, *Sir John Fisher's Naval Revolution*, 56. Esher Journals, December 15, 1903, referenced in Dunlop, *The Development of the British Army, 1899–1914*, 169–71.

26. Fisher to the Earl of Rosebery, May 10, 1901, in Marder, *Fear God and Dread Nought*, 190. Fisher to Committee of Seven, May 14, 1904, in Fisher, *The Papers of Admiral Sir John Fisher*, 1:36. Lambert, *Sir John Fisher's Naval Revolution*, 4.

27. In November 1904, a special committee recommended that Britain should maintain a significant superiority of battleships and armored cruisers of the "most likely combinations" against it: "in order of probability, 1. Germany and Russia; 2. France and Russia; the United States being regarded throughout as friendly." Battenberg committee report, referenced in Marder, *British Naval Policy, 1880–1905*, 510. Fisher to Tweedmouth, September 26, 1906, in Marder, *Fear God and Dread Nought*, 91. Fisher memo, War Arrangements, in Fisher, *The Papers of Admiral Sir John Fisher*, 1:465. *Schlesische Volkszeitung*, July 15, 1906, in Marder, *From the Dreadnought to Scapa Flow*, 128. Edward Grey quoted in Marder, *Fear God and Dread Nought*, 141.

28. Admiral Wilson, "Remarks on War Plans," in Fisher, *The Papers of Admiral Sir John Fisher*, 2:454. Fisher, 2:454. Winston S. Churchill and Martin Gilbert, *The World Crisis, 1911–1918* (New York: Free Press, 2005). S. S. Hall to Fisher, April 26, 1914, in Marder, *From the Dreadnought to Scapa Flow*, 364.

29. The Peace Conference 1898–1900, *Admiralty Papers*, P.R.O ADM 116/98. Churchill and Gilbert, *The World Crisis, 1911–1918*. Also see Lambert, *Sir John Fisher's Naval Revolution*, 163. Wilson, June 27, 1905, in Marder, *British Naval Policy, 1880–1905*, 504. Marder, 504.

30. *The Standard*, May 29, 1912, referenced in Kennedy, *The Rise and Fall of British Naval Mastery*, 205.

31. A 1902 Admiralty memorandum to the Royal Commission on Food Supplies argued, "a dispersion of strength for [attack or defense of commerce] is the strategy of the weak and cannot materially influence the ultimate result of the war." Marder, *British Naval Policy, 1880–1905*, 97.

32. Johannes Lepsius, Albrecht Mandelssohn Bartholdy, and Friedrich Thimme, *Die Grosse Politik, 1871–1914* (Berlin: Deutsche Verlagsgesellschaft für Politik und Geschichte, 1925), 194–95, referenced in Marder, *British Naval Policy, 1880–1905*, 479. Admiralty statement to the Royal Commission on Food Supply in War Time, 1904, in Marder, 84. Quoted in Marder, *From the Dreadnought to Scapa Flow*, 113.

33. Ottley in response to June 24, 1905, note from Fisher, in Marder, *British Naval Policy, 1880–1905*, 502–3. Note that these plans were created in part to defend Fisher against attacks from his critic Charles Beresford and may not reflect Fisher's true desires for a warfighting construct. Fisher, *The Papers of Admiral Sir John Fisher*, 2:326. Fisher, 2:351.

34. Arnold-Forster, Proposed Army Organization Scheme, Command Paper 1910, August 1, 1904, in Dunlop, *The Development of the British Army, 1899–1914*, 179–80. Fisher, *The Papers of Admiral Sir John Fisher*, 2:360. Asquith to Campbell-Bannerman, December 30, 1906, in Lambert, *Sir John Fisher's Naval Revolution*, 138.

35. Churchill and Gilbert, *The World Crisis, 1911–1918*, 23. Churchill and Gilbert, 23. M. Macdonald, *The Times*, March 3, 1908. Asquith to McKenna, January 1, 1909, in Marder, *From the Dreadnought to Scapa Flow*, 120. Churchill and Gilbert, *The World Crisis, 1911–1918*, 23.

36. As late as October 1911, Fisher wrote, "Never in our whole history have we been so powerful or so feared as at the present moment." Fisher quoted in Reginald Bacon, *The Life of Lord Fisher of Kilverstone, Admiral of the Fleet*, 2 vols. (London: Hodder and Stoughton, 1929), 2:133. Churchill, speech, November 10, 1911, quoted in Lambert, *Sir John Fisher's Naval Revolution*, 15. E. L. Woodward, *Great Britain and the German Navy* (Oxford, UK: Clarendon, 1935), 230–31. On the other hand, a retired military expert argued, "any deviation of a policy which centres the control of the Empire's first line of defence in the United Kingdom would be fatal to the Empire, though not necessarily fatal to the Colonies or to England." Silburn, *The Colonies and Imperial Defence*, 149.

37. Kennedy, *The Rise and Fall of British Naval Mastery*, 228. Fisher to Churchill, June 24, 1912, quoted in Marder, *From the Dreadnought to Scapa Flow*, 469. Fisher to Committee of Seven, May 14, 1904, in Fisher, *The Papers of Admiral Sir John Fisher*, 1:161.

38. Fisher notes on new proposals to the Committee of Seven, May 14, 1904, in Fisher, *The Papers of Admiral Sir John Fisher*, 1:22.

39. The concept behind the dreadnought favored primacy. As one leader noted, "Whatever type the French have, we must go one better." Bacon, *Life of Lord Fisher of Kilverstone*, 1:170, citing J. L. Garvin. William White quoted in Marder, *British Naval Policy, 1880–1905*, 536.

40. Fisher to Committee of Seven, May 14, 1904, in Fisher, *The Papers of Admiral Sir John Fisher*, 1:41. Kerr quoted in Marder, *British Naval Policy, 1880–1905*, 399. Fisher to Cabinet, December 1904, in Fisher, *The Papers of Admiral Sir John Fisher*, 1:221–22. Fisher, 1:221–22.

41. Fisher, speech to the Royal Academy, May 14, 1903, in Bacon, *The Life of Lord Fisher of Kilverstone*, 2:202. Bacon quoted in Marder, *British Naval Policy, 1880–1905*, 363. Admiralty, "Submarine Boats," March 1905, in Lambert, *Sir John Fisher's Naval Revolution*, 122. By the summer of 1910, maneuvers of the HMS *D1* reportedly "opened the eyes of the First Sea Lord, Admiral Sir Arthur Wilson, to the offensive possibilities of submarines which he had hitherto regarded as defensive vessels." Lord Keyes, *Memoirs*, 23, referenced in Lambert, 207. Also see Richmond to Keyes, June 29, 1942, in Lord Keyes, *Keyes Papers*, vol. 2, ed. Paul Halpern (London: William Clowes, 1981), 251, referenced in Christopher M. Bell, *The Royal Navy, Seapower and Strategy between the Wars* (Basingstoke, UK: Macmillan, 2000), 189. Balfour to Selborne, January 7, 1904, in Lambert, *Sir John Fisher's Naval Revolution* 67. First draft of Churchill and Gilbert, *The World Crisis, 1911–1918*. Referenced in Lambert, *Sir John Fisher's Naval Revolution*, 301. Earl of Selborne to Fisher, May 14, 1904, in Fisher, *The Papers of Admiral Sir John Fisher*, 1:xviii.

42. Fisher to Prince of Wales, October 16, 1907, quoted in Lambert, *Sir John Fisher's Naval Revolution*, 174. Admiralty, "Remarks on M.I.D. Paper 13A," July 14, 1903, quoted in Lambert, 57. Captain George Egerton, February 6, 1903, quoted in Lambert, 58. Fisher to Committee of Seven, May 14, 1904, quoted in Fisher, *The Papers of Admiral Sir John Fisher*, 1:68–69. Attachment sent from Fisher to Earl of Selborne, October 19, 1904, in Fisher, 1:11. Balfour to Fisher, January 3, 1904, quoted in Lambert, *Sir John Fisher's Naval Revolution*, 66.

43. Meeting minutes, November 25, 1903, in Lambert, *Sir John Fisher's Naval Revolution*, 66. Army Debates, 1906, and Army Estimates, 1906–1907, referenced in Dunlop, *The Development of the British Army, 1899–1914*, 247–50. Dunlop, 247–50. Haldane, "Autobiography," referenced in Dunlop, 241–42. Balfour, speech, York, January 13, 1910, in Marder, *From the Dreadnought to Scapa Flow*, 358.

44. Beresford quoted in Lambert, *Sir John Fisher's Naval Revolution*, 165. Custance to Selborne, September 31, 1904, in Lambert, 60. Fisher, *The Papers of Admiral Sir John Fisher*, 2:90. Churchill memorandum "Trade Protection on and after the Outbreak of War," August 23, 1913, in Marder, *From the Dreadnought to Scapa Flow*, 365. Marder, 196.

45. Fisher, notes to the Committee of Seven, May 14, 1904, in Fisher, *The Papers of Admiral Sir John Fisher*, 1:31. Fisher, memorandum for Lord Selborne, October 20, 1904, in Fisher, 25. Reginald Bacon quoted in Lambert, *Sir John Fisher's Naval Revolution*, 199. McKenna to Asquith, December 17, 1910, quoted in Lambert, 195. Mark Kerr, "Greek Naval Construction Policy," September 1913, referenced in Lambert, 290.

46. Lambert, *Sir John Fisher's Naval Revolution*, 10. Fisher to Corbett, June 22, 1914, quoted in Lambert, 303.

47. Esher to Balfour, July 23, 1912, in Lambert, 254.

48. Churchill's memorandum of January 10, 1914, quoted in Marder, *From the Dreadnought to Scapa Flow*, 322–23.

49. Mallet, *British Budgets 1887–88 to 1912–13*, 505. Sir Edward Grey to Sir Rennell Rodd, January 13, 1913, quoted in Marder, *From the Dreadnought to Scapa Flow*, 272.

50. Spending trends in the British army were another matter. Britain continued to invest in ground-force mobility, even decreasing the army's size to maximize its ability to deploy abroad. Yet, the army was shrinking in part to allow for the growth of the navy, which was the defensive arm of the British military. As British naval spending ramped up, First Lord Goschen announced, "These are not Estimates of provocation—they are estimates of self-defense. . . . If foreign countries look at these Estimates they must not compare them with what they spend upon their navies. They must consider comparatively what they spend on their armies, because the squadrons which we send to sea are the *corps d'armee* that we place upon our frontiers as they place *corps d'armee* upon theirs." Goschen, in Hansard, March 2, 1896, quoted in Marder, *British Naval Policy, 1880–1905*, 264. Fisher referenced in Marder, 355.

51. Upon the completion of Fisher's scheme, Britain shifted nine fleets from the Mediterranean and Chinese fleets to the Channel and the new Atlantic fleets. Custance, June 2, 1902, in Marder, *British Naval Policy, 1880–1905*, 518. As *The Naval and Military Record* concluded in 1901, "certain limitations must hamper the expansion of a naval Power. . . . [Singapore] requires a large garrison. Thus, the limitations of seapower begin to be felt when territorial expansion can no longer be safeguarded exclusively by the guns of the fleet, backed by minor garrisons." *The Naval and Military Record* (London), December 26, 1901, referenced in Kennedy, *The Rise and Fall of British Naval Mastery*, 198.

52. This is not to suggest that this more locally concentrated force was properly prepared for war. Admiral Sir Percy Scott reflected, "We had no up-to-date mine layers, nor an efficient mine; no properly fitted mine sweepers; no arrangements for guarding our ships against mines' no efficient method of using our guns at night; no anti-Zeppelin guns; no anti-submarine precautions; no safe harbour for our Fleet. . . . Our torpedoes were so badly fitted that in the early days of the war they went under the

German ships instead of hitting them." Percy Scott, *Fifty Years in the Royal Navy* (London: J. Murray, 1919), 201, referenced in Marder, *From the Dreadnought to Scapa Flow*, 435. From Edward Vose Gulick, *Europe's Classical Balance of Power*, 29, referenced in Friedberg, *The Weary Titan*, 15.

Chapter Five. France's Apex

Epigraph: Anthony P. Adamthwaite, *Grandeur and Misery: France's Bid for Power in Europe, 1914–1940* (London: Arnold, 1995), 64.

1. Judith M. Hughes, *To the Maginot Line: The Politics of French Military Preparation in the 1920's*, Harvard Historical Monographs 64 (Cambridge, MA: Harvard University Press, 2006), 12. Anthony P. Adamthwaite, *France and the Coming of the Second World War, 1936–1939* (London: Cass, 1977), 5. Alistair Horne, *To Lose a Battle: France 1940* (London: Penguin, 2007), 58. Churchill and Gilbert, *The World Crisis, 1911–1918*.

2. Anthony Kemp, *The Maginot Line: Myth and Reality* (New York: Stein and Day, 1982), 11. Denise Artaud, "Reparations and War Debts: The Restoration of French Financial Power, 1919–1929," in *French Foreign and Defence Policy, 1918–1940: The Decline and Fall of a Great Power*, ed. Robert W. D. Boyce (London: Routledge, 1998), 95. Desch, "Culture Clash," 162. Desch, 162. Adamthwaite, *Grandeur and Misery*, 142. Adamthwaite, *France and the Coming of the Second World War, 1936–1939*, 4. Horne, *To Lose a Battle*, 640; Adamthwaite, *Grandeur and Misery*, 224.

3. Adamthwaite, *Grandeur and Misery*, 6. Adamthwaite, *France and the Coming of the Second World War, 1936–1939*, 17.

4. Adamthwaite, *Grandeur and Misery*, 40.

5. See The Avalon Project, "The Versailles Treaty June 28, 1919: Part V," Lillian Goldman Law Library, Yale Law School, accessed May 1, 2020, http://avalon.law.yale.edu/imt/partv.asp.

6. Adamthwaite, *Grandeur and Misery*, 135.

7. Adamthwaite, 59. Adamthwaite, *France and the Coming of the Second World War, 1936–1939*, 8. Also see Hughes, *To the Maginot Line*, 21. Hughes, 83.

8. Horne, *To Lose a Battle*, 63. Adamthwaite, *Grandeur and Misery*, 89.

9. Thomas Jones, *Whitehall Diary*, edited by Keith Middlemas, vol. 1 (London: Oxford University Press, 1969), 116–17, referenced in Adamthwaite, *France and the Coming of the Second World War, 1936–1939*, 3. Artaud, "Reparations and War Debts," 97.

10. Hughes, *To the Maginot Line*, 163, 205.

11. Horne, *To Lose a Battle*, 32. Hughes, *To the Maginot Line*, 58. Adamthwaite, *Grandeur and Misery*, 40.

12. J. E. Kaufmann and H. W. Kaufmann, *Fortress France: The Maginot Line and French Defenses in World War II* (Mechanicsburg, PA: Stackpole Books, 2007), 3. Kemp, *The Maginot Line*, 57. Hughes, *To the Maginot Line*, 201.

13. Guillaumat quoted in Kier, *Imagining War,* 42. Martin S. Alexander, "In Defense of the Maginot Line," in Boyce, *French Foreign and Defence Policy, 1918–1940,* 170. Fayolle quoted in Kier, *Imagining War,* 44.

14. Kier, *Imagining War,* 45. Posen, *The Sources of Military Doctrine,* 117. Kier, *Imagining War,* 41.

15. Horne, *To Lose a Battle,* 71. Williamson Murray, "Armored Warfare: The British, French, and German Experiences," in *Military Innovation in the Interwar Period,* ed. Williamson Murray and Allan R. Millett (Cambridge: Cambridge University Press, 1996), 32. Kier, *Imagining War,* 45.

16. Hughes, *To the Maginot Line,* 71. Buat quoted in Kier, *Imagining War,* 43. Foch quoted in Kier, 42.

17. Horne, *To Lose a Battle,* 89. Hughes, *To the Maginot Line,* 139. Posen, *The Sources of Military Doctrine,* 131.

18. Gamelin quoted in Kier, *Imagining War,* 43. Horne, *To Lose a Battle,* 75. J. E. Kaufmann and H. W. Kaufmann, *The Maginot Line: None Shall Pass* (Westport, CT: Praeger, 1997), 6–7.

19. Hughes, *To the Maginot Line,* 215.

20. Vivian Rowe, *The Great Wall of France: The Triumph of the Maginot Line* (New York: Putnam, 1961), 17. Rowe, 17.

21. Hughes, *To the Maginot Line,* 178. Horne, *To Lose a Battle,* 117.

22. Kemp, *The Maginot Line,* 20. Martin S. Alexander, *The Republic in Danger: General Maurice Gamelin and the Politics of French Defence, 1933–1940* (Cambridge: Cambridge University Press, 2002), 189. Rowe, *The Great Wall of France,* 46. Posen, *The Sources of Military Doctrine,* 102. British Committee of Imperial Defense, 1938, quoted in Posen, 114. Posen, 114.

23. Rowe, *The Great Wall of France,* 48. Rowe, 50. Quoted in Eugen Weber, *The Hollow Years: France in the 1930s* (New York: Norton, 1994), 244–45. Adamthwaite, *Grandeur and Misery,* 187. Also see Hughes, *To the Maginot Line,* 231.

24. Adamthwaite, *France and the Coming of the Second World War, 1936–1939,* 29. Adamthwaite, *Grandeur and Misery,* 137. Joseph A. Maiolo, *Cry Havoc: How the Arms Race Drove the World to War, 1931–1941* (New York: Basic Books, 2010), 81. Maiolo, *Cry Havoc,* 90. Rowe, *The Great Wall of France,* 57–58.

25. Adamthwaite, *France and the Coming of the Second World War, 1936–1939,* 30. Peter Jackson, "Intelligence and the End of Appeasement," in Boyce, *French Foreign and Defence Policy, 1918–1940,* 250–51. Martin S. Alexander, "In Defense of the Maginot Line: Security Policy, Domestic Politics and the Economic Depression in France," in Boyce, 178. Adamthwaite, *France and the Coming of the Second World War, 1936–1939,* 39. *FRUS,* 1937, I, 89, referenced in Adamthwaite, 61. Adamthwaite, 88.

26. Alan Bullock, *Hitler: A Study in Tyranny* (London: Odhams, 1952), 135. Adamthwaite, *France and the Coming of the Second World War, 1936–1939,* 39. Quoted in Weber, *The Hollow Years,* 146.

27. Gamelin described the military's main tasks as "1. the defense of France and her empire; 2. offensive action against Italy on the Alps and in Africa; 3. if possible and at a convenient time offensive action against Germany in order to divert part of the German forces for the benefit of our Central European allies." Adamthwaite, *France and the Coming of the Second World War, 1936–1939*, 62. Rowe, *The Great Wall of France*, 93. Maiolo, *Cry Havoc*, 178. Horne, *To Lose a Battle*, 76. Adamthwaite, *Grandeur and Misery*, 203. Also see Adamthwaite, *France and the Coming of the Second World War, 1936–1939*, 54. Hughes, *To the Maginot Line*, 234–35.

28. P. M. H. Bell, *France and Britain, 1900–1940: Entente and Estrangement* (New York: Routledge, 2013), 230. Jackson, "Intelligence and the End of Appeasement," 250. Adamthwaite, *Grandeur and Misery*, 214. Also see Adamthwaite, *France and the Coming of the Second World War, 1936–1939*, 226. Adamthwaite, 258. Henry Morgenthau, *From the Morgenthau Diaries*, ed. J. M. Blum (Boston: Houghton Mifflin, 1959), 525, referenced in Adamthwaite, *Grandeur and Misery*, 140.

29. French troops on the continent assumed a "protective posture for the defense of the national territory." Hughes, *To the Maginot Line*, 193. Adamthwaite, *France and the Coming of the Second World War, 1936–1939*, 221. Horne, *To Lose a Battle*, 233, 137. Winston Churchill, *The Second World War*, vol. 2, *Their Finest Hour* (Boston: Houghton Mifflin, 1985), 36–39. Bell, *France and Britain, 1900–1940*, 233.

30. Rowe, *The Great Wall of France*, 21. Posen, *The Sources of Military Doctrine*, 106–7. Posen, 106–7.

31. Rowe, *The Great Wall of France*, 59–60. Alexander, "In Defense of the Maginot Line," 167. Kaufmann and Kaufmann, *Fortress France*, 3. Posen, *The Sources of Military Doctrine*, 102.

32. Kier, *Imagining War*, 16. Kier, 12. Kier, 53. Kier, 54.

33. Hughes, *To the Maginot Line*, 205.

34. Kier, *Imagining War*, 75. Philip Charles Farwell Bankwitz, *Maxime Weygand and Civil-Military Relations in Modern France* (Cambridge, MA: Harvard University Press, 1967), 122. Posen, *The Sources of Military Doctrine*, 118–19. Hughes, *To the Maginot Line*, 205.

35. Kemp, *The Maginot Line*, 24. Rowe, *The Great Wall of France*, 49. Alexander, "In Defense of the Maginot Line," 168–69.

36. Rowe, *The Great Wall of France*, 52. Hughes, *To the Maginot Line*, 213. Posen, *The Sources of Military Doctrine*, 111. Hughes, *To the Maginot Line*, 223. Hughes, 218–19.

37. Horne, *To Lose a Battle*, 242. Nicholas Atkin, *The French at War, 1934–1944* (Harlow, UK: Longman, 2001), 34. Rowe, *The Great Wall of France*, 61. See also Kemp, *The Maginot Line*, 19.

38. Horne, *To Lose a Battle*, 80. Hughes, *To the Maginot Line*, 248. Also see Kaufmann and Kaufmann, *Fortress France*, 4. Adamthwaite, *France and the Coming of the Second World War, 1936–1939*, 171. Adamthwaite, *Grandeur*

and Misery, 203. Also see Adamthwaite, *France and the Coming of the Second World War, 1936–1939*, 37, 54. Winston S. Churchill, *The Gathering Storm* (New York: Houghton Mifflin, 1948), 170–71.

39. Robert J. Young, *In Command of France: French Foreign Policy and Military Planning, 1933–1940* (Cambridge, MA: Harvard University Press, 1978), 179. Horne, *To Lose a Battle*, 115. Alexander, *The Republic in Danger*, 37. Bankwitz, *Maxime Weygand and Civil-Military Relations in Modern France*, 159. Bankwitz, 166.

40. Horne, *To Lose a Battle*, 177–78, 143. Bankwitz, *Maxime Weygand and Civil-Military Relations in Modern France*, 131. Bankwitz, 123. Horne, *To Lose a Battle*, 94. Also see Kemp, *The Maginot Line*, 82. Horne, *To Lose a Battle*, 28–29.

41. Kaufmann and Kaufmann, *Fortress France*, 15. Kaufmann and Kaufmann, 91. *The Maginot Line—the Facts Revealed (by a French Officer)* (London: Duckworth, 1939), 10.

42. A publication by a French officer later described the line as including six elements: "1. Cover, so as to hide it completely. 2. Observation points. 3. Obstacles to hold up the enemy on the whichever side they attack. 4. Protection against enemy artillery from whatever direction it may come. 5. Firing facilities against all attacks—e.g., artillery, tanks, aeroplanes, infantry. 6. Communications permitting of the revictualling of the troops and the evacuation of the wounded." *The Maginot Line—the Facts Revealed (by a French Officer)*, 27. Rowe, *The Great Wall of France*, 45–46. Horne, *To Lose a Battle*, 73–74. Alexander, "In Defense of the Maginot Line," 185. Fabry quoted in Kier, *Imagining War*, 67.

43. Gamelin quoted in Kier, *Imagining War*, 43. Horne, *To Lose a Battle*, 115. Maiolo, *Cry Havoc*, 86–87. Alexander, *The Republic in Danger*, 149. Also see Kier, *Imagining War*, 47.

44. Horne, *To Lose a Battle*, 117. Eugenia C. Kiesling, "Resting Uncomfortably on Its Laurels," in *The Challenge of Change: Military Institutions and New Realities, 1918–1941*, ed. Harold R. Winton and David R. Mets, Studies in War, Society, and the Military (Lincoln: University of Nebraska Press, 2000), 18. Kiesling, 19. Horne, *To Lose a Battle*, 116.

45. *The Maginot Line—the Facts Revealed (by a French Officer)*, 55. Adamthwaite, *France and the Coming of the Second World War, 1936–1939*, 162. Also see Maiolo, *Cry Havoc*, 181. Adamthwaite, *Grandeur and Misery*, 223. From René Girault and Robert Frank, *Turbulente Europe et nouveaux mondes (1914–1941): Histoire des relations internationales contemporaines*, vol. 2 (Paris: Payot, 2004), 242. Horne, *To Lose a Battle*, 127.

46. Hughes, *To the Maginot Line*, 250–51. Kemp, *The Maginot Line*, 59. Alexander, "In Defense of the Maginot Line," 183. *The Maginot Line—the Facts Revealed (by a French Officer)*, 70.

47. Horne, *To Lose a Battle*, 94. Horne, 179. Quoted in Weber, *The Hollow Years*, 253. Horne, *To Lose a Battle*, 118.

48. Kemp, *The Maginot Line*, 54. Kemp, 54. Kemp, 54. Had this area been re-inforced by mines, the German attack might have been slowed. However, the Maginot Line "completely lacked anti-personnel mines, relying mainly on anti-tank barriers, other obstacles and supporting fires to stop the infantry." French funds went to fortifications instead of mines be-cause France desired to retain control of its territory, rather than simply deny that control to the Germans. This tendency continued even though "anti-personnel mines would have rendered the Maginot Line extremely difficult to penetrate and would probably have allowed a reduction of in-terval troops." Kaufmann and Kaufmann, *The Maginot Line*, 59. See Er-nest R. May, *Strange Victory: Hitler's Conquest of France* (New York: Hill and Wang, 2001). Kaufmann and Kaufmann, *Fortress France*, 133. Theo-dore Draper, *Six Weeks War: France May 10–June 25, 1940* (New York: Vi-king, 1944), 10, quoted in Kaufmann and Kaufmann, *The Maginot Line*, 112.

49. Marc Bloch, *Strange Defeat: A Statement of Evidence Written in 1940* (New York: Norton, 1999), 52. Kemp, *The Maginot Line*, 78. Stanley Hoffmann, "The Trauma of 1940," in *The French Defeat of 1940: Reassessments*, ed. Joel Blatt (Providence, RI: Berghahn Books, 1998), 369. Hughes, *To the Maginot Line*, 205.

50. Adamthwaite, *France and the Coming of the Second World War, 1936–1939*, 24.

51. Kier, *Imagining War*, 7. Eugenia C. Kiesling, *Arming against Hitler: France and the Limits of Military Planning* (Lawrence: University Press of Kansas, 1996), 117. Douglas Porch, "Review: Military 'Culture' and the Fall of France in 1940: A Review Essay," *International Security* 24, no. 4 (Spring 2000): 173. Porch also argues, "Because Kier confuses strategy and doc-trine, she mistakenly exaggerates the impact of military doctrine on the fall of France in 1940. . . . Strategy and policy determine a military orga-nization's offensive or defensive posture, not its doctrine. Doctrine is the way an army organizes to fight, that is, the procedures and methods it ap-plies in combat. Doctrines are important especially for armies whose nu-merous articulated components must be coordinated to operate in unison. Strategy, on the other hand, is how a nation organizes its strength toward achieving a political goal in war." Porch, 165–68. Desch, "Culture Clash," 162. Kier, *Imagining War*, 53–54.

52. Kier, *Imagining War*, 53–54.

53. See also Posen, *The Sources of Military Doctrine*, 109. Rowe, *The Great Wall of France*, 89–90. Adamthwaite, *France and the Coming of the Second World War, 1936–1939*, 355. Alexander Werth, *France and Munich: Before and After the Surrender* (New York: Harper and Brothers, 1939), 141, ref-erenced in Adamthwaite, 107–8. H. C. Hillmann, "Comparative Strength of the Great Power," in *The World in March 1939—Survey of International Affairs, 1939–1946*, ed. Arnold Toynbee and Frank T. Ashton-Gwatkin

(London: Royal Institute of International Affairs and Oxford University Press, 1952), 446, referenced in Posen, *The Sources of Military Doctrine*, 235. *FRUS*, 1937, I, 78, referenced in Adamthwaite, *France and the Coming of the Second World War, 1936–1939*, 61.

54. Eliot A. Cohen and John Gooch, *Military Misfortunes: The Anatomy of Failure in War* (New York: Free Press, 1990), 206.

Chapter Six. Japan's Decline

Epigraph: Tangredi, *Anti-Access Warfare*, 144. Masanori Itō and Roger Pineau, *The End of the Imperial Japanese Navy* (Westport, CT: Greenwood, 1984), 36.

1. Louise Young, *Japan's Total Empire: Manchuria and the Culture of Wartime Imperialism* (Berkeley: University of California Press, 1999), 428–29. Stephen E. Pelz, *Race to Pearl Harbor: The Failure of the Second London Naval Conference and the Onset of World War II*, Harvard Studies in American–East Asian Relations 5 (Cambridge, MA: Harvard University Press, 1974). This estimate suggested that Japan had just one-twentieth the U.S. steel-production capacity. Snyder, *Myths of Empire*, 112. H. P. Willmott, *Empires in the Balance: Japanese and Allied Pacific Strategies to April 1942* (Annapolis, MD: Naval Institute Press, 1982), 57–58.

2. See, for example, O. Tanin and E. Yohan, *When Japan Goes to War* (London: Lawrence and Wishart, 1936). James B. Wood, *Japanese Military Strategy in the Pacific War: Was Defeat Inevitable?* (Lanham, MD: Rowman and Littlefield, 2007), 53. Wood, 46. Hatsuho Naitō, *Thunder Gods: The Kamikaze Pilots Tell Their Story* (Tokyo: Kodansha, 1989), 229. Mark Stille, *The Imperial Japanese Navy in the Pacific War* (New York: Osprey, 2014), 367. See also Willmott, *Empires in the Balance*, 98.

3. David C. Evans and Mark R. Peattie, *Kaigun: Strategy, Tactics, and Technology in the Imperial Japanese Navy, 1887–1941* (Annapolis, MD: Naval Institute Press, 1997), 1. Barnhart, *Japan Prepares for Total War*, 17. Snyder, *Myths of Empire*, 126. Snyder, 126. James Buckley Crowley, *Japan's Quest for Autonomy: National Security and Foreign Policy, 1930–1938* (Princeton, NJ: Princeton University Press, 2015), 196.

4. Evans and Peattie, *Kaigun*, 19.

5. Barnhart, *Japan Prepares for Total War*, 23. David J. Lu, *From the Marco Polo Bridge to Pearl Harbor: Japan's Entry into World War II* (Washington, DC: Public Affairs Press, 1961), 30. Barnhart, *Japan Prepares for Total War*, 38. Barnhart, 88–89. Willmott, *Empires in the Balance*, 55.

6. Roosevelt to William Leahy, August 22, 1937, referenced in Barnhart, *Japan Prepares for Total War*, 123. Barnhart, 106–7. Barnhart, 132. Roland H. Worth, *No Choice but War: The United States Embargo against Japan and the Eruption of War in the Pacific* (Jefferson, NC: McFarland, 1995), 108. Worth, 116.

7. Worth, *No Choice but War*, 177. U.S. Department of State, "Political Estimate," August 20, 1941, in Worth, 20. Worth, 39. Hull to Roosevelt, February 12, 1941, referenced in Barnhart, *Japan Prepares for Total War*, 219. On Hull's arguments for a stronger stance on Japanese expansionism, see Cordell Hull and Andrew Henry Thomas Berding, *The Memoirs of Cordell Hull* (New York: Macmillan, 1948). Worth, *No Choice but War*, 63. Worth, 48.

8. Worth, *No Choice but War*, 144. Worth, 137. Herbert Feis, *The Road to Pearl Harbor: The Coming of the War between the United States and Japan* (Princeton, NJ: Princeton University Press, 1950). "Diary of Admiral Kichisaburo Nomura, June–December 1941," in *The Pacific War Papers: Japanese Documents of World War II*, ed. Donald M. Goldstein and Katherine V. Dillon (Washington, DC: Potomac Books, 2004), 187. Worth, *No Choice but War*, 203. In September 1941, Admiral Nomura noted that U.S. polling "favoring the checking of Japan's development at the risk of a war has suddenly increased from 51% in July to 70% today." "Diary of Admiral Kichisaburo Nomura, June–December 1941," 178.

9. Barnhart, *Japan Prepares for Total War*, 261. John Toland, *The Rising Sun: The Decline and Fall of the Japanese Empire, 1936–1945* (New York: Random House, 1970), 128. Toland, 95. Rikihei Inoguchi, Tadashi Nakajima, and Roger Pineau, *The Divine Wind: Japan's Kamikaze Force in World War II* (Westport, CT: Greenwood, 1978), xiv. Inoguchi, Nakajima, and Pineau, xiii. Toland, *The Rising Sun*, 112.

10. Nomura also advised, "I do not think it opportune to wage a great protracted war when the country is in an exhausted condition after the Manchurian Incident and the succeeding four years of the China Affair." "Diary of Admiral Kichisaburo Nomura, June–December 1941," 205. "Extracts from the Diary of Marquis Koichi Kido," in Goldstein and Dillon, *The Pacific War Papers*, 123–24. Toland, *The Rising Sun*, 112. John W. Dower, *War without Mercy: Race and Power in the Pacific War* (New York: Pantheon Books, 1986), x. "Diary of Admiral Kichisaburo Nomura, June–December 1941," 193. Crowley, *Japan's Quest for Autonomy*, 187. Nobutake Kondo, "Some Opinions Concerning the War," 1947, in Goldstein and Dillon, *The Pacific War Papers*, 307. Richard O'Neill, *Suicide Squads, W.W. II: Axis and Allied Special Attack Weapons of World War II, Their Development and Their Missions* (New York: St. Martin's, 1981), 144. Jisaburo Ozawa, "Development of the Japanese Navy's Operational Concept against America," in Goldstein and Dillon, *The Pacific War Papers*, 73–74.

11. John Ellis, *Brute Force: Allied Strategy and Tactics in the Second World War* (New York: Viking, 1990), 443–46. Andrieu D'Albas, *Death of a Navy: Japanese Naval Action in World War II* (New York: Devin-Adair, 1957), 17. Akira Iriye, *The Origins of the Second World War in Asia and the Pacific* (New York: Routledge, 1987), 160. "Extracts from the Diary of Marquis

Koichi Kido," 130. "Extracts from the Diary of Marquis Koichi Kido," 119. "Extracts from the Diary of Marquis Koichi Kido," 132. Toland, *The Rising Sun*, 86. Toland, 86. Meirion Harries and Susie Harries, *Soldiers of the Sun: The Rise and Fall of the Imperial Japanese Army* (New York: Random House, 1991), 394–95. Harries and Harries. Harries and Harries, 23. "Extracts from the Diary of Marquis Koichi Kido," 135.

12. Toland, *The Rising Sun*, 95. Toland, 132. Stimson diary entry of November 26, 1941, referenced in Barnhart, *Japan Prepares for Total War*, 236. Barnhart, 35–37. "Diary of Admiral Kichisaburo Nomura, June–December 1941," 216.

13. Masataka Chihaya, "General Characteristics of Yamato Class Battleships," in Goldstein and Dillon, *The Pacific War Papers*, 92.

14. Itō and Pineau, *The End of the Imperial Japanese Navy*, 54. Paul S. Dull, *A Battle History of the Imperial Japanese Navy (1941–1945)* (Annapolis, MD: United States Naval Institute Press, 1978), 133. Willmott, *Empires in the Balance*, 71. Evan Thomas, *Sea of Thunder: Four Commanders and the Last Great Naval Campaign, 1941–1945* (New York: Simon and Schuster, 2006), 84.

15. Willmott, *Empires in the Balance*, 89. Evans and Peattie, *Kaigun*, 137. Ozawa, "Development of the Japanese Navy's Operational Concept against America," 71–72. Sadao Asada, *From Mahan to Pearl Harbor: The Imperial Japanese Navy and the United States* (Annapolis, MD: Naval Institute Press, 2013).

16. Toland, *The Rising Sun*, 130. "Japanese Monograph No. 102: Submarine Operations December 1941–April 1942," Office of the Chief Military History Department of the Army, 1953, in Goldstein and Dillon, *The Pacific War Papers*, 233. Albert Axell and Hideaki Kase, *Kamikaze: Japan's Suicide Gods* (New York: Longman, 2002), 30. Itō and Pineau, *The End of the Imperial Japanese Navy*, 51. On the other hand, Willmott writes, "Perhaps the most striking feature of Japanese doctrine was that it eschewed interest in the concept of command of the sea. . . . The Japanese sought not command of the sea but 'sea control.'" H. P. Willmott, *The Barrier and the Javelin: Japanese and Allied Pacific Strategies to April 1942* (Annapolis, MD: Naval Institute Press, 1982), 16. Wood, *Japanese Military Strategy in the Pacific War*, 13–14. Willmott, *The Barrier and the Javelin*, 79.

17. Mark R. Peattie, *Sunburst: The Rise of the Japanese Naval Air Power, 1909–1941* (Annapolis, MD: Naval Institute Press, 2001), 195. Harries and Harries, *Soldiers of the Sun*, 394. Worth, *No Choice but War*, 161. Dull, *A Battle History of the Imperial Japanese Navy (1941–1945)*, 453. Atsushi Oi, "The Japanese Navy in 1941," 1951, in Goldstein and Dillon, *The Pacific War Papers*, 11–12. Masataka Chihaya, "Organization of the Naval General Staff Headquarters in Tokyo," in Goldstein and Dillon, *The Pacific War Papers*, 39. Dull, *A Battle History of the Imperial Japanese Navy (1941–1945)*, 452.

18. Wetzler, *Hirohito and War,* 175. Japan had followed France's lead in adopting elements of the Jeune École, since the torpedo boat was seen as "an ideal weapon for Japan's defense: it was inexpensive and easy to deploy among the Japanese islands." But such expendable vessels were out of fashion by the early 1900s. Evans and Peattie, *Kaigun,* 15.

19. Stille, *The Imperial Japanese Navy in the Pacific War,* 13. Naitō, *Thunder Gods,* 229.

20. Itō and Pineau, *The End of the Imperial Japanese Navy,* 34. Carl Boyd and Akihiko Yoshida, *The Japanese Submarine Force and World War II,* Bluejacket Books (Annapolis, MD: Naval Institute Press, 2002), 4. Not all mobility was highly advanced; Japanese troops gained an advantage by riding bicycles in Malaya. Stille, *The Imperial Japanese Navy in the Pacific War,* 17. Stille, 58.

21. Peattie, *Sunburst,* 40. Peattie. Peattie, 124. Peattie, 58. Peattie. Peattie, 83.

22. Peattie, 40. Willmott, *The Barrier and the Javelin,* 415. Willmott, 60. Willmott, 159. Oi, "The Japanese Navy in 1941," 20.

23. Oi, "The Japanese Navy in 1941," 17. Stille, *The Imperial Japanese Navy in the Pacific War,* 326. Evans and Peattie, *Kaigun,* 218.

24. Evans and Peattie, *Kaigun,* 218. Evans and Peattie, 218.

25. Axell and Kase, *Kamikaze,* 199.

26. Although a reporter who was on the *Enterprise* would publish a story noting that success at Midway was due to the breaking of Japanese naval codes, the Japanese proceeded unaware. Axell and Kase, 68. Axell and Kase, 71. D'Albas, *Death of a Navy,* 114. Willmott, *The Barrier and the Javelin,* 72. Itō and Pineau, *The End of the Imperial Japanese Navy,* 57. Thomas, *Sea of Thunder,* 66.

27. Naitō, *Thunder Gods,* 93. Dull, *A Battle History of the Imperial Japanese Navy (1941–1945),* 181. Toland, *The Rising Sun,* 352. Toland, 419, 422. "United States Strategic Bombing Survey—Summary Report (Pacific War)," 5.

28. Willmott, *The Barrier and the Javelin,* 513. Wood, *Japanese Military Strategy in the Pacific War,* 94. Itō and Pineau, *The End of the Imperial Japanese Navy,* 84. D'Albas, *Death of a Navy,* 239. Willmott, *Empires in the Balance,* 89. Nobutake Kondo, "Some Opinions Concerning the War," 317.

29. Dull, *A Battle History of the Imperial Japanese Navy (1941–1945),* 267. Itō and Pineau, *The End of the Imperial Japanese Navy,* 18. D'Albas, *Death of a Navy,* 255. D'Albas, 152.

30. Toland, *The Rising Sun,* 446–47. Dull, *A Battle History of the Imperial Japanese Navy (1941–1945),* 260. Herbert P. Bix, *Hirohito and the Making of Modern Japan* (New York: Perennial, 2002), 422.

31. D'Albas, *Death of a Navy,* 267. Masataka Chihaya, "Importance of the Japanese Naval Bases Overseas," 1947, in Goldstein and Dillon, *The Pacific War Papers,* 65. Inoguchi, Nakajima, and Pineau, *The Divine Wind,* 24. Toland, *The Rising Sun,* 506. Toland, 701.

32. Thomas, *Sea of Thunder*, 63. Dull, *A Battle History of the Imperial Japanese Navy (1941–1945)*, 460.

33. Evans and Peattie, *Kaigun*, 445. D'Albas, *Death of a Navy*, 294. Toland, *The Rising Sun*, 427. Naitō, *Thunder Gods*, 85. Tangredi, *Anti-Access Warfare*, 141.

34. Oi, "The Japanese Navy in 1941," 14. Stille, *The Imperial Japanese Navy in the Pacific War*, 326. From 1942 to 1945, the United States produced roughly five times the tonnage of battleships, carriers, destroyers, and cruisers as Japan. In submarines, however, the U.S. lead was only two times that of Japan. Evans and Peattie, *Kaigun*, 366. Naitō, *Thunder Gods*, 22. Naitō, 43. Naitō, 192.

35. Andrew Adams, *Born to Die: The Cherry Blossom Squadrons* (Los Angeles: Ohara, 1973), 19. Inoguchi, Nakajima, and Pineau, *The Divine Wind*, 7. Inoguchi, Nakajima, and Pineau, 27. Inoguchi, Nakajima, and Pineau, 20. Dull, *A Battle History of the Imperial Japanese Navy (1941–1945)*, 454. Naitō, *Thunder Gods*, 21. O'Neill, *Suicide Squads, W.W. II*, 107.

36. Thomas, *Sea of Thunder*, 149.

37. Willmott, *The Barrier and the Javelin*, 29. Willmott, 29. Adams, *Born to Die*, 10.

38. Adams, *Born to Die*, 16. Inoguchi, Nakajima, and Pineau, *The Divine Wind*, 39–40. Naitō, *Thunder Gods*, 29.

39. Naitō, *Thunder Gods*, 177. Naitō, 24. Inoguchi, Nakajima, and Pineau, *The Divine Wind*, 138. O'Neill, *Suicide Squads, W.W. II*, 268. Naitō, *Thunder Gods*, 25. Naitō, 25.

40. O'Neill, *Suicide Squads, W.W. II*, 83. D'Albas, *Death of a Navy*, 268–69. D'Albas, 84. D'Albas, 100. D'Albas, 22–24. D'Albas, 226–27. D'Albas, 279.

41. Naitō, *Thunder Gods*, 182. O'Neill, *Suicide Squads, W.W. II*, 157. O'Neill, 118. O'Neill, 169. Inoguchi, Nakajima, and Pineau, *The Divine Wind*, 160. Inoguchi, Nakajima, and Pineau, 151. Inoguchi, Nakajima, and Pineau, 28.

42. Naitō, *Thunder Gods*, 187. Axell and Kase, *Kamikaze*, 42. Axell and Kase, 206. Axell and Kase, 180–81. Adams, *Born to Die*, 52. Adams, 109. Thomas, *Sea of Thunder*, 48.

43. Oi, "The Japanese Navy in 1941," 12.

44. Worth, *No Choice but War*, 183.

45. Evans and Peattie, *Kaigun*, xxii. Naitō, *Thunder Gods*, 120. Jim Bresnahan, introduction to *Refighting the Pacific War: An Alternative History of World War II*, ed. Bresnahan (Annapolis, MD: Naval Institute Press, 2011), 14. Evans and Peattie, *Kaigun*, 492. Willmott, *The Barrier and the Javelin*, 521–22.

46. Willmott, *Empires in the Balance*, 74. "Extracts from the Diary of Marquis Koichi Kido," 121. For more on this topic, see James William Morley and Nihon Kokusai Seiji Gakkai, eds., *The Fateful Choice: Japan's Advance*

into Southeast Asia, 1939–1941: Selected Translations from Taiheiyō sensō e no michi, kaisen gaikō shi (New York: Columbia University Press, 1980). Richard Overy, *Why the Allies Won* (New York: Norton, 1997), 1.

47. Dull, *A Battle History of the Imperial Japanese Navy (1941–1945)*, 452. Miles Kahler, "External Ambition and Economic Performance," *World Politics* 40, no. 4 (July 1988): 430. Evans and Peattie, *Kaigun*, 402. "Diary of Admiral Kichisaburo Nomura, June–December 1941," 146. Wetzler, *Hirohito and War*, 206. Overy, *Why the Allies Won*, 15.

48. Willmott, *Empires in the Balance*, 62. Barnhart, *Japan Prepares for Total War*, 267. Willmott, *Empires in the Balance*, 71. Axell and Kase, *Kamikaze*, 26.

49. Toland, *The Rising Sun*, 838–39.

Chapter Seven. Russia's Decline

Epigraph: Mikhail Sergeevich Gorbachev, *Perestroika: New Thinking for Our Country and the World* (New York: Perennial Library, 1988), 4–5.

1. Edward Luttwak, *The Grand Strategy of the Soviet Union* (New York: St. Martin's, 1983), 137. Luttwak, 30. We now know that these estimates overstated Soviet spending, but they still reflected the consensus opinion of the U.S. intelligence community at the time. Luttwak, 21. Vyacheslav Molotov quoted in V. M. Zubok, *A Failed Empire: The Soviet Union in the Cold War from Stalin to Gorbachev* (Chapel Hill: University of North Carolina Press, 2007), 227.

2. Stephen White, *Gorbachev and After*, Cambridge Soviet Paperbacks 3 (Cambridge: Cambridge University Press, 1992), 106. U.S. Central Intelligence Agency (CIA), "A Comparison of Soviet and U.S. Gross National Products, 1960–1983," 1984, 3, http://www.foia.cia.gov/sites/default/files/document_conversions/89801/DOC_0000498181.pdf. Leonid Abalkin and Nikolai Shmelev quoted in CIA, 109. A. S. Cherniaev, *My Six Years with Gorbachev*, trans. Robert English and Elizabeth Tucker (University Park: Pennsylvania State University Press, 2000), 50–51.

3. The most common motivations for Gorbachev's increasingly expansive reform agenda are often described as due to learning, increasing power, and external pressure. Archie Brown, *The Gorbachev Factor* (Oxford: Oxford University Press, 1996), 13.

4. Harriet Fast Scott and William Fontaine Scott, *Soviet Military Doctrine: Continuity, Formulation, and Dissemination* (Boulder, CO: Westview, 1988), 69. Leonid Brezhnev, "Speech to the Fifth Congress of the Polish United Workers' Party," November 13, 1968, accessed at https://loveman.sdsu.edu/docs/1968BrezhnevDoctrine.pdf. Moreover, one estimate of the defense burden suggests that the Soviet defense sector required 6–9 percent of its rolled steel and 23–25 percent of its rolled aluminum, and it employed over 8 percent of its total labor force. Vitaly V. Shlykov, "The

Economics of Defense in Russia and the Legacy of Structural Militariza-
tion," in *The Russian Military: Power and Policy*, ed. Steven E. Miller and
Dmitri Trenin, American Academy Studies in Global Security (Cam-
bridge, MA: MIT Press, 2004), 159. Jacques Sapir, *The Soviet Military
System* (Cambridge, UK: Polity, 1991), 27. Sapir, 277. Chernyaev diary,
January 1977, referenced in Sapir, 255. Sapir, 267.

5. Anatoly Dobrynin, *In Confidence: Moscow's Ambassador to Six Cold War
Presidents* (Seattle: University of Washington Press, 2001), 540. Also see
Zubok, *A Failed Empire*, 274. Richard Halloran, "Pentagon Draws Up
First Strategy for Fighting a Long Nuclear War," *The New York Times*,
May 30, 1982, quoted in Michael MccGwire, *Military Objectives in Soviet
Foreign Policy* (Washington, DC: Brookings Institution, 1987), 290.
Quoted in Zubok, *A Failed Empire*, 276. MccGwire, *Military Objectives in
Soviet Foreign Policy*, 293–95. Robert M. Gates, *From the Shadows: The Ul-
timate Insider's Story of Five Presidents and How They Won the Cold War*
(New York: Simon and Schuster, 2007), 265–66. A similar argument is
made in Jack F. Matlock, *Autopsy on an Empire: The American Ambassador's
Account of the Collapse of the Soviet Union* (New York: Random House,
1995). Also see Zubok, *A Failed Empire*, 273. Additionally, in the summer
of 1984, a CIA document reportedly concluded, "The Soviets have concluded that the danger of war is greater than it was before the INF decision, that Soviet vulnerability is great and will grow. ... These
perceptions, perhaps driven by a building defense budget, new initiatives
in continental defense, improvements in force readiness, and a poten-
tially massive space program, may be propelling the U.S.S.R. to take national readiness measures at a deliberate pace." Jay Mallin, Sr., "Split
Voiced by CIA, Pentagon on Buildup," *Washington Times*, July 27, 1984,
referenced in MccGwire, *Military Objectives in Soviet Foreign Policy*, 303.

6. Chernyaev diary, December 30, 1979, referenced in Zubok, *A Failed Empire*, 264. Quoted in White, *Gorbachev and After*, 8.

7. See Bruce Parrott, "Soviet National Security under Gorbachev," *Problems
of Communism* 37, no. 6 (1988), 7. Cherniaev, *My Six Years with Gorbachev*,
42. Also see Chernyaev diary, referenced in Zubok, *A Failed Empire*, 284.
Mikhail Sergeevich Gorbachev, *Memoirs* (New York: Doubleday, 1996),
189. *Izvestiia*, September 9, 1986, referenced in Malvin M. Helgesen,
"Civil-Military Relations under Gorbachev," in *The Dynamics of Soviet
Defense Policy*, ed. Bruce Parrott (Washington, DC: Wilson Center Press,
1990), 53. Ed A. Hewett, "The Soviet Economy and Soviet National Security," in Parrott, 121. Gorbachev, October 1986, quoted in Zubok, *A
Failed Empire*, 292.

8. Warsaw Pact spending was 95 percent of NATO's, according to one figure. Sapir, *The Soviet Military System*, 26. Hewett, "The Soviet Economy
and Soviet National Security," 129. Noel E. Firth and James H. Noren,
Soviet Defense Spending: A History of CIA Estimates, 1950–1990, Texas

A&M University Military History Series 58 (College Station: Texas A&M University Press, 1998), 125. Dale R Herspring, *The Soviet High Command, 1967–1989: Personalities and Politics* (Princeton, NJ: Princeton University Press, 1990). Chernyaev's notes on the December 1, 1986, meeting are quoted in Zubok, *A Failed Empire*, 295.

9. Gorbachev, *Memoirs*, 147. Gorbachev, 147. Gorbachev, 215. Alexei Arbatov, "Parity and Reasonable Sufficiency," *International Affairs*, October 1988, 76. See Christoph Bluth, *The Collapse of Soviet Military Power* (Brookfield, VT: Dartmouth, 1995), 84. David Holloway, "State, Society, and the Military under Gorbachev," *International Security* 14, no. 3 (1989): 6.

10. Gorbachev, *Perestroika*, xiii. White, *Gorbachev and After*, 114. Gorbachev, *Memoirs*, 237. Gorbachev, 199. Georgi Arbatov, *The System: An Insider's Life in Soviet Politics* (New York: Three Rivers, 1993), 321–22. Also see Zubok, *A Failed Empire*, 282. Robert H. Donaldson and Joseph L. Nogee, *The Foreign Policy of Russia: Changing Systems, Enduring Interests* (Armonk, NY: M. E. Sharpe, 1998), 97.

11. *Pravda*, August 12, 1989, referenced in Donaldson and Nogee, *The Foreign Policy of Russia*, 87. *Pravda*, January 9, 1989, referenced in Helgesen, "Civil-Military Relations under Gorbachev," 62. Ed A. Hewett, "The Soviet Economy and Soviet National Security," 62. Hewett, 129. George H. W. Bush and Brent Scowcroft, *A World Transformed* (New York: Vintage, 1999), 135. Robert W. Strayer, *Why Did the Soviet Union Collapse? Understanding Historical Change* (Armonk, NY: M. E. Sharpe, 1998), 135. White, *Gorbachev and After*, 123. See *Pravda*, May 22, 1991, referenced in White, 139.

12. William F. Buckley, Jr., "The Sinatra Doctrine," *National Review Online*, accessed December 29, 2015, http://www.nationalreview.com/article/210798/sinatra-doctrine-william-f-buckley-jr. "The Soviet-Finish Declaration: New Thinking in Action," *Izvestiia*, October 27, 1989, 1, referenced in Christopher Jones, "The Post-Soviet Military and the Future of Europe," in *Soviet Military Power in a Changing World*, ed. Susan L. Clark (Boulder, CO: Westview, 1991), 29. Cherniaev, *My Six Years with Gorbachev*, 225. Cherniaev, 147. Cherniaev, 293. Gorbachev, *Memoirs*, 388.

13. V. Karpov quoted in October 1979, referenced in Raymond L. Garthoff, "Continuity and Change in Soviet Military Doctrine," in Parrott, *The Dynamics of Soviet Defense Policy*, 165. P. I. Trifonenkov quoted in Garthoff, 147. Garthoff, 154. Thomas W. Wolfe, *Soviet Strategy at the Crossroads* (Cambridge, MA: Harvard University Press, 1964), 7–8. Luttwak cautions that, throughout Russian history, "there was an unusually great disparity between the very great defensive strength of the country and its far smaller capacity to wage war offensively against serious opposition. Two compelling reasons immediately present themselves to explain the contrast: the fragility of autocratic rule, and military backwardness." Luttwak,

The Grand Strategy of the Soviet Union, 14. MccGwire, *Military Objectives in Soviet Foreign Policy*, 299. Petrov comments made in December 1984, quoted in Rose E. Gottemoeller, "Intramilitary Conflict in the Soviet Armed Forces," in Parrott, *The Dynamics of Soviet Defense Policy*, 91.

14. Cherniaev, *My Six Years with Gorbachev*, 118. D. T. Yazov, "On the Military Balance of Forces and Nuclear-Missile Parity," *Pravda*, February 8, 1988, translated in Andrei A. Kokoshin, *Soviet Strategic Thought, 1917–91*, CSIA Studies in International Security (Cambridge, MA: MIT Press, 1998), 133. Michael MccGwire, "A Soviet View of World War," referenced in Parrott, *The Dynamics of Soviet Defense Policy*, 187.

15. *The Program of the Communist Party of the Soviet Union* (Moscow: Novosti, 1986), 544, quoted in Scott and Scott, *Soviet Military Doctrine*, 102. Zubok, *A Failed Empire*, 292. *Pravda*, July 27, 1987, referenced in Garthoff, "Continuity and Change in Soviet Military Doctrine," 174. *Pravda*, July 27, 1987, referenced in Edward Warner III and David Ochmanek, "Conventional Arms Control: Soviet Approaches and Objectives," in Parrott, 339. Mikhail Gorbachev, *Realities and Guarantees for a Secure World* (Moscow: Novosti, 1987), referenced in Bluth, *The Collapse of Soviet Military Power*, 85.

16. William E. Odom, *The Collapse of the Soviet Military* (New Haven, CT: Yale University Press, 2000), 15. Cherniaev, *My Six Years with Gorbachev*, 84. Garthoff, "Continuity and Change in Soviet Military Doctrine," 174. Robert Hall, *Soviet Military Art in a Time of Change* (London: Brassey's, 1991), 59–61, referenced in Bluth, *The Collapse of Soviet Military Power*, 79. Firth and Noren, *Soviet Defense Spending*, 107. Pavel Baev, *The Russian Army in a Time of Troubles* (Thousand Oaks, CA: Sage, 1996), 20. A. S. Milovidov, *Military-Theoretical Heritage of V. I. Lenin and Problems of Contemporary War* (Moscow: Voyenizdat, 1987), 251, quoted in Baev, 20. *Political Report of the CPSU Central Committee to the 27th Party Congress* (Moscow: Novosti, 1986), 85, referenced in Scott and Scott, *Soviet Military Doctrine*, 101.

17. Bluth, *The Collapse of Soviet Military Power*, 76. Summary of comments by Soviet Defense Minister General Iazov, November 26, 1987, quoted in Bluth, 76. Cherniaev, *My Six Years with Gorbachev*, 192. Cherniaev, 192. Mikhail Gorbachev, "Speech to the United Nations General Assembly," December 7, 1988, accessed at https://digitalarchive.wilsoncenter.org/document/address-mikhail-gorbachev-un-general-assembly-session-excerpts.

18. Gorbachev, "Speech to the United Nations General Assembly." Bluth, *The Collapse of Soviet Military Power*, 98. Gorbachev, *Memoirs*, 514.

19. Gorbachev, *Memoirs*, 455. Gorbachev, 456. Carolina Vendil Pallin, *Russian Military Reform: A Failed Exercise in Defence Decision Making*, Routledge Contemporary Russia and Eastern Europe Series 14 (London: Routledge, 2009), 65. Gorbachev, *Memoirs*, 439. F. Ladygin, "In the

Condition of Partnership," *Pravda*, December 7, 1990, 5, referenced in Susan L. Clark, "Soviet Nuclear Forces and the New European Security Environment," in Clark, *Soviet Military Power in a Changing World*, 107. Alexei Arbatov, "Military Doctrines," in *Disarmament and Security 1987 Yearbook*, ed. Yevgeny Primakov (Moscow: Novosti Press Agency, 1988), 200, referenced in Clark, 94. They did, however, note, "It is even possible that significant changes have already taken place, but have not yet been announced." Scott and Scott, *Soviet Military Doctrine*, 125. See also Gorbachev, *Perestroika*, 205.

20. Cherniaev, *My Six Years with Gorbachev*, 193. Gorbachev, *Perestroika*, 127. Gorbachev, 205.

21. Gorbachev, *Perestroika*, 83. A. A. Grechko, *The Armed Forces of the Soviet State* (Moscow: Voyenizdat, 1975), 197, referenced in Harriet Fast Scott and William Fontaine Scott, *The Armed Forces of the USSR* (Boulder, CO: Westview, 1979), 155. Babadzhanian quoted in Gottemoeller, "Intramilitary Conflict in the Soviet Armed Forces," 89. Adamsky, *The Culture of Military Innovation*, 57.

22. V. V. Serebryannikov, *Basis of Marxist-Leninist Teachings on War and Army* (Moscow: Voyenizdat, 1982), 173, quoted in Scott and Scott, *Soviet Military Doctrine*, 149. Sapir, *The Soviet Military System*, 19. Ogarkov quote referenced in Phillip A. Petersen and Notra Trulock III, "Soviet Views and Policies toward Theater War in Europe," in Parrott, *The Dynamics of Soviet Defense Policy*, 241–42. *Pravda*, October 21, 1981, referenced in Bluth, *The Collapse of Soviet Military Power*, 69. Bluth, 63. L. I. Brezhnev, *By Lenin's Course* (Moscow: Politizdat, 1982), 538, quoted in Scott and Scott, *Soviet Military Doctrine*, 124.

23. Nikolai Ogarkov, *Izvestiia*, May 9, 1983, and May 9, 1984, quoted in Gottemoeller, "Intramilitary Conflict in the Soviet Armed Forces," 88. Helgesen, "Civil-Military Relations under Gorbachev," 49. Akhromeyev quoted in February 1985, referenced in Petersen and Trulock, "Soviet Views and Policies toward Theater War in Europe," 243. *Pravda*, September 11, 1983, quoted in Gottemoeller, "Intramilitary Conflict in the Soviet Armed Forces," 89. D. A. Volkogonov, "Imperatives of the Nuclear Age," *Krasnaya Zvezda*, May 22, 1987, 3, quoted in Scott and Scott, *Soviet Military Doctrine*, 113.

24. See Yevgeny Primakov, ed., *Disarmament and Security 1987 Yearbook* (Moscow: Novosti Press Agency, 1988), referenced in Bluth, *The Collapse of Soviet Military Power*, 93. Bluth, 93. Scott and Scott, *Soviet Military Doctrine*, 285–86. Scott and Scott, 64.

25. Alexander Prokhanov, "The Tragedy of Centralism," *Literaturnaya Rossia*, January 5, 1990, translated in *Current Digest of the Post-Soviet Press* 42, no. 4 (1990): 1–2, referenced in Christopher Jones, "The Post-Soviet Military and the Future of Europe," in Clark, *Soviet Military Power in a Changing World*, 31–32. Jones, 47. The Warsaw Pact noted four objec-

tives: "increase strategic attack forces three-fold, increase ground forces two-fold, increase air forces two-fold, increase naval forces by a factor of three." Bluth, *The Collapse of Soviet Military Power*, 76. Figures compiled for International Institute for Strategic Studies, "The Military Balance," 1987, 231–32, referenced in Sapir, *The Soviet Military System*, 12. Conversely, in 1988, Chief of the General Staff Akhromeyev noted that NATO had superiority in aircraft, aviation, helicopters, and anti-tank complexes, while the Warsaw Pact held numerical superiority in tactical rocket launchers (a 7.6-fold advantage), tanks, rocket launchers, artillery, and armored combat vehicles. See Bluth, *The Collapse of Soviet Military Power*, 77. Bluth, 77. S. L. Sokolov, "On Guard over the Peace and Security of the Motherland," *Pravda*, February 23, 1987, 2, quoted in Scott and Scott, *Soviet Military Doctrine*, 102.

26. Numbers quoted in interview with Col. General Nikolai Chervov, *Moscow World Service*, January 11, 1990. Jones, "The Post-Soviet Military and the Future of Europe," 54.

27. Bluth, *The Collapse of Soviet Military Power*, 261. Boris Nikolayevich Yeltsin, *The Struggle for Russia*, trans. Catherine A. Fitzpatrick (New York: Belka, 1994), 35. See also Yeltsin, 35. Robbin F. Laird, "Conclusion: Rethinking the Role of Soviet Military Power," in Clark, *Soviet Military Power in a Changing World*, 301–5. On the coup's roots and implications for civil-military relations, see Stephen M. Meyer, "How the Threat (and the Coup) Collapsed: The Politicization of the Soviet Military," *International Security* 16, no. 3 (1991): 5. See also John B. Dunlop, *The Rise of Russia and the Fall of the Soviet Empire* (Princeton, NJ: Princeton University Press, 1993). Gorbachev, *Memoirs*, xxvii.

28. World Bank, "GDP, PPP (current international $)," 2015, https://data.worldbank.org/indicator/NY.GDP.MKTP.PP.CD?locations=RU. Yeltsin, *The Struggle for Russia*, 293.

29. John Erickson, " 'We Have Plenty to Defend Ourselves With . . .': Russian Rhetoric, Russian Realism," in *The Russian Military into the Twenty-First Century*, ed. Stephen J. Cimbala, Cass Series on Soviet (Russian) Military Theory and Practice (London: Frank Cass, 2001), 12. Pallin, *Russian Military Reform*, 10–11. Interview with *Izvestiia*, October 8, 1993, referenced in Baev, *The Russian Army in a Time of Troubles*, 108. Suzanne Crow, "Russia Asserts Its Strategic Agenda," *RFE/RL Research Report* 2, no. 50 (1993): 1–8. See also Baev, *The Russian Army in a Time of Troubles*, 151.

30. Russian Federation, "Basic Provisions of the Military Doctrine of the Russian Federation," Decree 1833, November 2, 1993. "Russia Issues a Warning on NATO Expansion," *Current Digest of the Post-Soviet Press* 45, no. 47 (1993): 11–13, referenced in Baev, *The Russian Army in a Time of Troubles*, 240.

31. Baev, *The Russian Army in a Time of Troubles*, 107. Yeltsin quoted in Donaldson and Nogee, *The Foreign Policy of Russia*, 219. See Michael Mihalka,

"European-Russian Security and NATO's Partnership for Peace," *RFE/ RL Research Report* 3, no. 33 (1994): 44. *Izvestiia*, August 31, 1994, translated in Donaldson and Nogee, *The Foreign Policy of Russia*, 257.

32. Baev, *The Russian Army in a Time of Troubles*, 34. Grigorii Yavlinskii in "Comments on US National Strategy and Hearing in the Defense Committee of the Duma," *Moskovskii Komsomolets*, October 26, 1994, referenced in Erickson, "We Have Plenty to Defend Ourselves With," 11. Yeltsin quoted in *ITAR-TASS*, September 8, 1995, referenced in Stephen J. Blank, "The New Turn in Russian Defense Policy: Russia's Defense Doctrine and National Security Concept," in Cimbala, *The Russian Military into the Twenty-First Century*, 56. Erickson, "We Have Plenty to Defend Ourselves With," 12. See also Donaldson and Nogee, *The Foreign Policy of Russia*, 116. Quoted in Donaldson and Nogee, 116.

33. For background, see Celeste A. Wallander, "Russian National Security Policy in 2000," *PONARS Policy Memo* 102 (January 2000), https://csis-website-prod.s3.amazonaws.com/s3fs-public/legacy_files/files/media/csis/pubs/pm_0102.pdf. See also Ivan Rybkin, *Rossiiskie Vesti*, May 13, 1997, referenced in Erickson, "We Have Plenty to Defend Ourselves With," 12. Russian Federation, "National Security Concept," December 26, 1997. Russian Federation, "The World Ocean," Presidential Decree 11, January 11, 1997.

34. Alexei Arbatov, "The Transformation of Russian Military Doctrine: Lessons Learned from Kosovo and Chechnya," in *The Marshall Center Papers*, no. 2 (Garmisch-Partenkirchen, Germany: George C. Marshall Center, 2000), 9, referenced in Jacob W. Kipp, "Russia's Nonstrategic Nuclear Weapons," *Military Review*, June 2001, http://fmso.leavenworth. army.mil/documents/russias_nukes/russias_nukes.htm. Russian Federation, "National Security Concept," January 10, 2000.

35. Bluth, *The Collapse of Soviet Military Power*, 143. When the Soviet Union fell, its armed forces numbered 2.7 million, of which only 2.1 million were resident within Russian borders. Baev, *The Russian Army in a Time of Troubles*, 72. Sapir, *The Soviet Military System*, 259. Figures cited in Steven E. Miller, "Moscow's Military Power: Russia's Search for Security in an Age of Transition," in Miller and Trenin, *The Russian Military*, 11. This reflected a decrease in defense spending from 21 percent of the budget in 1994 to under 15 percent in 2002. Alexei G. Arbatov, "Military Reform: From Crisis to Stagnation," in Miller and Trenin, 100.

36. Thomas L. Friedman, "Reducing the Russian Arms Threat," *The New York Times*, June 17, 1992. See International Institute for Strategic Studies, *The Military Balance* (London: Brassey's, 1991–97); and Pallin, *Russian Military Reform*, 81.

37. Quoted in Baev, *The Russian Army in a Time of Troubles*, 174. Donaldson and Nogee, *The Foreign Policy of Russia*, 141. Pallin, *Russian Military Reform*, 11. On the other hand, John Erickson observes, "In the military

doctrine itself there was little concession to the reality of Russia's shrinking geostrategic space." Erickson, "We Have Plenty to Defend Ourselves With," 10. Russian Federation, "Basic Provisions of the Military Doctrine of the Russian Federation," Decree 1833, November 2, 1993. Russian Federation.

38. Russian Federation, "National Security Concept," December 26, 1997. Steven J. Zaloga, "Soviet/Russian Strategic Nuclear Forces, 1945–2000," in Higham and Kagan, *The Military History of the Soviet Union*, 216.

39. Zaloga, "Soviet/Russian Strategic Nuclear Forces, 1945–2000," 216. "The Main Factors Which Determine Russia's Military-Technical Policy on the Eve of the 21st Century," *Krasnaya zvezda*, December 9, 1999, referenced in Timothy L. Thomas, "Russia's Asymmetrical Approach to Information War," in Cimbala, *The Russian Military into the Twenty-First Century*, 104. "Yeltsin Signs Decree on Tactical Nuclear Weapons," *Arms Control Today*, April–May 1999, 18–19. Stephen Cimbala, "Nuclear Crisis-Management and Information Warfare," *Parameters* 29, no. 2 (1999): 118. Peter Rainow, "If War Will Come Tomorrow," in Cimbala, *The Russian Military into the Twenty-First Century*, 33. "Yakovlev on 40th Anniversary of Rocket Forces," *Moscow Vek*, 1999, referenced in Mark Schneider, *The Nuclear Forces and Doctrine of the Russian Federation* (Washington, DC: National Institute Press, United States Nuclear Strategy Forum, 2006). Erickson, "We Have Plenty to Defend Ourselves With," 23.

40. Russian Federation, "National Security Concept," January 10, 2000. "Lecture Background Notes Recommend Focus on Modernization of Russia's Armed Forces," *Samara Soldat Otechestva*, February 23, 2005, translation referenced in Schneider, *Nuclear Forces and Doctrine of the Russian Federation*. Dmitriy Yevstafyev, "Putin's Position on Arms Control, Disarmament as Derived from Public Statements, Actions in Previous Posts," *Yadernyy Kontrol*, March–April 2000, translation referenced in Schneider. A. V. Nedelin, "Nuclear Weapon Use to De-escalate Mil Operations," *Moscow Voyennaya Mys*, May 1, 1999, translation referenced in Schneider. The U.S. government assessed, "The overall reduction in Russian military capabilities, especially the conventional forces, has caused Russian military planners to emphasize Moscow's threat to use nuclear weapons to deter a large-scale conventional attack, a policy that Moscow stated in its military doctrine published in October 1999 and reiterated in January 2000 and again in April 2000." U.S. Department of Defense, *Proliferation: Threat and Response* (Washington, DC: Government Printing Office, 2001), 53. Garthoff, "Continuity and Change in Soviet Military Doctrine," 178.

41. Kenneth N. Waltz, "Peace, Stability, and Nuclear Weapons," in Art and Waltz, *The Use of Force*, 366. Stephen Van Evera, "Primed for Peace: Europe after the Cold War," *International Security* 15, no. 3 (1990): 13. Luttwak, *The Grand Strategy of the Soviet Union*, 77.

42. Dale R. Herspring, ed., *Putin's Russia: Past Imperfect, Future Uncertain* (Lanham, MD: Rowman and Littlefield, 2007). Baev, *The Russian Army in a Time of Troubles*, 73. Russian Federation, "National Security Concept," December 26, 1997. Baev, *The Russian Army in a Time of Troubles*, 82. Christopher C. Lovett, "The Soviet Cold War Navy," in Higham and Kagan, *The Military History of the Soviet Union*, 255.

43. Kipp, "Russia's Nonstrategic Nuclear Weapons." Aleksander Golts, "The Army of Russia: 11 Lost Years," *Armiya Rossii: Ordinadtsat Poteryannykh*, December 31, 2004, translation referenced in Schneider, *Nuclear Forces and Doctrine of the Russian Federation*. Russian Federation, "National Security Concept," December 26, 1997. Igor Rodionov, " 'Neobkhidimo reformirovat' ne chasti sistemy voyennoy bezopasnosti gosudarstva, a vsyu ee v tselom," *Nezavisimoye voyennoye obozreniye*, November 1996, quoted in Kipp, "Russia's Nonstrategic Nuclear Weapons."

44. *Current Digest of the Post-Soviet Press* 49, no. 21 (1997): 1, referenced in Donaldson and Nogee, *The Foreign Policy of Russia*, 8. Stephen J. Blank, "Valuing the Human Factor: The Reform of Russian Military Manpower," *The Journal of Slavic Military Studies* 12, no. 1 (March 1999): 83. "Defense Chief Describes Army's Woes," *The Monitor* 4, no. 69 (April 9, 1998). Barry Renfrow, "Russia Tries to Save Military," Associated Press, July 2, 1999. Russian Federation, "The World Ocean," Presidential Decree 11, January 11, 1997. "Russian Army Woes Outlined," *The Monitor* 4, no. 230 (December 14, 1998).

45. Herspring, *Putin's Russia*. Partially as a result, the ground forces were reinstated from their downgrading in 1997, and the SRF was instead downgraded to a command. The SRF would eventually be split into the Strategic Missile Troops and the Space Troops. Sergeyev would eventually resign in March 2001. See figures in Marcel de Haas, "Russia's Military Reforms: Victory after Twenty Years of Failure?," Clingendael Paper No. 5 (Netherlands Institute of International Relations, November 2011), 10, https://www.clingendael.org/sites/default/files/2016-02/20111129_clingendaelpaper_mdehaas.pdf.

46. Russian Federation, "National Security Concept," January 10, 2000. Kipp, "Russia's Nonstrategic Nuclear Weapons."

47. Michael MccGwire, *Military Objectives in Soviet Foreign Policy* (Washington, DC: Brookings Institution, 1987), 37–38. Henry Kissinger, *Diplomacy* (New York: Simon and Schuster, 1995), 143. Gottemoeller, "Intramilitary Conflict in the Soviet Armed Forces," 110. The sheer magnitude of the changes in the size of the Russian military forced a rapid reassessment. In 1985, the Soviet armed forces included five million people, but Russia had only two and a half million when the Soviet Union collapsed, falling to one and a half million by 1995 and one million by 1999. Russian Federation, "National Security Concept," December 26, 1997.

48. See, for example, the categories developed by Pavel K. Baev, "The Trajectory of the Russian Military: Downsizing, Degeneration, and Defeat," in Miller and Trenin, *The Russian Military*, 46. Baev, 46.Wohlforth also suggests three assumptions underscoring Russian thinking, including the view that Russia is a "great Eurasian power" and a "temporarily wounded world power seeking to restore its rightful place, and that Russia's interests demand a sphere of influence in the former Soviet territory." William C. Wohlforth, "Heartland Dreams: Russian Geopolitics and Foreign Policy," in *Perspectives on the Russian State in Transition*, ed. Wolfgang F. Danspeckgruber (Princeton, NJ: Princeton University Press, 2006), 268. Although Charles Dick notes that an early draft of the 1993 military doctrine "implied that the U.S.A. and NATO really were hostile," the final document stated that Russia "does not regard any state as its enemy." See Charles J. Dick, "The Military Doctrine of the Russian Federation," *The Journal of Slavic Military Studies* 7, no. 3 (September 1994): 495. This contrasts with Marshal Ogarkov's comment in the 1980s that "we are witnessing the creation of a military alliance between the U.S., China, and Japan that is similar to the infamous Rome-Berlin-Tokyo 'axis' of the 1930s." Ogarkov quoted in Jeremy R. Azrael, *The Soviet Civilian Leadership and the Military High Command, 1976–1986* (Santa Monica, CA: RAND, 1987), 18.

49. These trends have continued, and by 2005, the Russian Defense Ministry's official newspaper noted, "Despite various assurances, Russia's traditional geopolitical rivals are continuing to take advantage of the historical moment—the temporary weakness of a great state. Stronger states are striving to reinforce their positions around the entire perimeter of Russian borders. . . . Russia survived thanks largely to its military potential, above all nuclear." Oleg Falichev, "Russia: Editorial Remarks for Reprinted Interview with RVSN Commander Solovtsov," *Moscow Krasnaya Zvezda*, January 12, 2005, translation referenced in Schneider, *Nuclear Forces and Doctrine of the Russian Federation*.

Chapter Eight. Lessons and Implications

Epigraph: Waltz, "Structural Realism after the Cold War," 37.

1. Edelstein, *Over the Horizon*.
2. Philip E. Tetlock, "Theory-Driven Reasoning about Plausible Pasts and Probable Futures in World Politics: Are We Prisoners of Our Preconceptions?," *American Journal of Political Science* 43, no. 2 (1999): 335–66.
3. Walt, *The Origins of Alliances*. "Balancing Threat: The United States and the Middle East—An Interview with Stephen M. Walt," *Yale Journal of International Affairs*, July 2010, 10–16, https://www.yalejournal.org/publications/balancing-threat-the-united-states-and-the-middle-east.

4. See Kahneman and Tversky, "Prospect Theory." Yarhi-Milo, *Knowing the Adversary*.

5. Luttwak also notes that when the Roman republic was relatively strong and rising, "the Romans generally solved the security problems of their growing empire by furthering expansion." He notes, "at any one moment large troop concentrations could be assembled for wars of conquest." Luttwak goes on to comment that in the late republic and early principate period, Rome remained strong, and the marching camp was established; but "the strategic mobility of Roman forces was undoubtedly reduced by this tiring and time-consuming camp-building routine." He later describes how "perimeter defense inaugurated by the Flavians required an investment of colossal proportions" and how the "defense against high intensity threats was mobile and offensive, not static: combat was to take place *beyond* the border than within it. In other words, the complex of fixed defenses built along the *limes* served only as a *supporting infrastructure* for offensive operations." As Roman power began to decline, however, Luttwak describes how "the overall strategy of the empire was transformed from hegemonic expansionism to territorial defense. . . . The army also needed a sustained defensive capability over the full length of a land perimeter that was 6,000 miles long." Luttwak also notes that "decline did not occur suddenly during the late fourth century" but left "purely territorial forces incapable of mobile field operations." Finally, in the final stage, Rome became relatively weak and adopted "defense-in-depth strategies" focused on rearward defense, providing "interception only inside imperial territory," rather than forward defense, "in advance of the frontier." Edward N. Luttwak, *The Grand Strategy of the Roman Empire: From the First Century A.D. to the Third* (Baltimore: Johns Hopkins University Press, 1984), 4. Alastair Iain Johnston, "Cultural Realism and Strategy in Maoist China," in Katzenstein, *The Culture of National Security*, 261. Johnston, *Cultural Realism*, 57.

6. It may also be possible to use emerging research methods, such as computer-assisted content analysis, to assess the degree to which policy makers discuss certain types of defense policies and track changes over time. By doing so, it might be possible to correlate changes in defense policies to changes in perceptions of relative power.

7. If one accepts that status quo actors are typically defensive and revisionist actors are typically offensive, then this theory should also explain whether a military technological innovation would advantage not only strong or weak actors but also status quo or revisionist actors. See Charles L. Glaser, "The Security Dilemma Revisited," *World Politics* 50, no. 1 (October 1997): 171–201.

8. The theory presented here also applies to a broader set of powers beyond China and the United States. For example, it could be applied to India (a weak but rising power) and Russia (a weak and declining power), helping

to forecast their likely future defense policies. This theory might also be applied to smaller regional powers, helping to explain different military procurement patterns emerging across Asia and the Middle East. This theory therefore provides an opportunity for insight into a variety of military competitions.

9. Mu Xuequan, "Xi Stresses Unity, Striving for National Rejuvenation at PRC Anniversary Reception," *Xinhua*, September 30, 2019, http://xinhuanet.com/english/2019-09/30/c_138437557.htm; Olga Khazan, "China Pushes 'Progress, Constant Progress,'" *NamViet News*, November 15, 2012, https://namvietnews.wordpress.com/2012/11/15/china-pushes-progress-constant-progress/. Notably, prior to the Persian Gulf War, some Chinese leaders may have thought they could already compete symmetrically with the United States. However, Samuel Tangredi writes that the U.S. victory "justified the acquisition of sensors and weapons systems optimized for the denial of contested area rather than the control of it." After all, as U.S. Lieutenant General H. R. McMaster notes, "There are only two ways to fight the US: stupidly or asymmetrically." Tangredi, *Anti-Access Warfare*, 23.

10. Deng Xiaoping speech of September 1980, referenced in Taylor M. Fravel, *Active Defense: China's Military Strategy since 1949* (Princeton, NJ: Princeton University Press, 2019), 1.

11. Rush Doshi, *The Long Game: China's Grand Strategy to Displace American Order* (New York: Oxford University Press, 2021). Denny Roy, "Hegemon on the Horizon? China's Threat to East Asian Security," *International Security* 19, no. 1 (Summer 1994): 159. Elizabeth C. Economy, *The Third Revolution: Xi Jinping and the New Chinese State* (New York: Oxford University Press, 2018), 8. Doshi, *The Long Game*. Samuel J. Locklear III, "Defense Department News Briefing in the Pentagon Briefing Room," U.S. Indo-Pacific Command, December 6, 2012, http://www.pacom.mil/Media/Speeches-Testimony/Article/565147/defense-department-news-briefing-in-the-pentagon-briefing-room/.

12. McDevitt, "Becoming a Great 'Maritime Power,'" 117–19. Fravel, *Active Defense*, 276. Robert D. Kaplan, "The Geography of Chinese Power: How Far Can Beijing Reach on Land and at Sea?," *Foreign Affairs* 89, no. 3 (May–June 2010): 34. Markus Brunnermeier, Rush Doshi, and Harold James, "Beijing's Bismarckian Ghosts: How Great Powers Compete Economically," *The Washington Quarterly* 41, no. 3 (Fall 2018): 163, https://www.tandfonline.com/doi/full/10.1080/0163660X.2018.1520571. Michael J. Green, "Safeguarding the Seas," *Foreign Affairs*, December 2, 2013, http://www.foreignaffairs.com/articles/140307/michael-j-green/safeguarding-the-seas.

13. Scobell and Nathan, "China's Overstretched Military," 142. Adam P. Liff, "Shadowing the Hegemon? Great Power Norms, Socialization, and the Military Trajectories of Rising Powers" (PhD diss., Princeton University, 2014), 29, https://dataspace.princeton.edu/bitstream/88435/dsp014x-

51hj17w/1. Robert Ross in Glosny, Saunders, and Ross, "Debating China's Naval Nationalism," 174–75. See also Ross, "China's Naval Nationalism." Cozad, "China's Regional Power Projection," 291. It is also possible that these theories combine to explain Chinese naval modernization. For example, Michael Glosny and Phillip Saunders write that the People's Liberation Army is likely to "develop a limited power-projection capability that increases China's ability to defend regional interests in contingencies not involving the United States, to protect expanding overseas interests, to perform nontraditional missions, to conduct military diplomacy, to demonstrate international responsibility, and to increase China's prestige." Glosny, Saunders, and Ross, "Debating China's Naval Nationalism," 165.

14. U.S. Department of Defense, *Military and Security Developments Involving the People's Republic of China*, November 29, 2022, https://media.defense. gov/2022/Nov/29/2003122279/-1/-1/1/2022-military-and-security-de-velopments-involving-the-peoples-republic-of-china.pdf.

15. Hal Brands and Michael Beckley, *Danger Zone: The Coming Conflict with China* (New York: Norton, 2022).

16. Xi Jinping, "Working Together to Deliver a Brighter Future for Belt and Road Cooperation," speech, Beijing, China, April 26, 2019, Ministry of Foreign Affairs of the People's Republic of China, https://www.fmprc. gov.cn/mfa_eng/zxxx_662805/t1658424.shtml. Elsa B. Kania and John K. Costello, "The Strategic Support Force and the Future of Chinese Information Operations," *The Cyber Defense Review*, Spring 2018, 105–21, https://cyberdefensereview.army.mil/Portals/6/Documents/CDR%20 Journal%20Articles/The%20Strategic%20Support%20Force_Kania_Costello.pdf.

17. The National Intelligence Council also argues that five military competitions will define the character of the future security environment: "Access vs. Anti-Access. The US ability to project air and maritime forces is in competition with China's burgeoning capabilities to deter and deny such force projection. The outcome of this competition will impact the ability of either side to control the maritime and air approaches to East Asia and the US ability to assure allies in the region." U.S. National Intelligence Council, *Global Trends 2030: Alternative Worlds* (Washington, DC: Government Printing Office, 2013), 72. Joseph S. Nye, *Is the American Century Over?* (Cambridge, MA: Polity, 2015). U.S. Department of Defense, *U.S. National Defense Strategy Summary*, 2018, 1, https://dod.defense.gov/ Portals/1/Documents/pubs/2018-National-Defense-Strategy-Summary. pdf; Benjamin M. Jensen, *Forging the Sword: Doctrinal Change in the U.S. Army* (Stanford, CA: Stanford University Press, 2016); Janine Davidson, *Lifting the Fog of Peace: How Americans Learned to Fight Modern War* (Ann Arbor: University of Michigan Press, 2011).

18. Sydney J. Freedberg, Jr., "The Next War," *Government Executive*, August 15, 2012, http://www.govexec.com/magazine/features/2012/08/next-war/57392/.

19. Eugene Gholz, Benjamin Friedman and Enea Gjoza, "Defensive Defense: A Better Way to Protect U.S. Allies in Asia," *The Washington Quarterly* 42, no. 4 (2019): 184–85, https://doi.org/10.1080/01636 60X.2019.1693103.

20. Elbridge A. Colby, *The Strategy of Denial: American Defense in an Age of Great Power Conflict* (New Haven, CT: Yale University Press, 2021). Christian Brose, *The Kill Chain: Defending America in the Future of High-Tech Warfare* (New York: Hachette Books, 2020).

21. National Defense Panel, *Transforming Defense: National Security in the 21st Century* (Arlington, VA: National Defense Panel, December 1997). U.S. Department of Defense, "Defense Strategic Guidance," 2012.

22. Andrew F. Krepinevich, "Why Air Sea Battle?," Center for Strategic and Budgetary Assessments, 2010, 7, https://csbaonline.org/uploads/documents/2010.02.19-Why-AirSea-Battle.pdf. As Jennifer Lind and Daryl Press note, "It might make military sense to blind the adversary and disrupt its command and control—but are the strategic risks of this so high, that those strategic considerations should outweigh the military considerations?" Jennifer Lind and Daryl G. Press, "Geography, Technology, and Crisis Escalation in U.S.-China Relations," U.S.-China Working Group paper, April 7, 2014. Schwartz and Greenert, "Air-Sea Battle."

23. Roger Cliff, Mark Burles, Michael S. Chase, Derek Eaton, and Devin L. Pollpeter, *Entering the Dragon's Lair: Chinese Antiaccess Strategies and Their Implications for the United States* (Santa Monica, CA: RAND, 2007), 2. Christopher Layne, "From Preponderance to Offshore Balancing," in Art and Waltz, *The Use of Force*, 289. Joshua Shifrinson, *Rising Titans, Falling Giants: How Great Powers Exploit Power Shifts* (Ithaca, NY: Cornell University Press, 2018). Paul K. MacDonald and Joseph M. Parent, *Twilight of the Titans: Great Power Decline and Retrenchment* (Ithaca, NY: Cornell University Press, 2018), 198. Barry Posen, "Pull Back: The Case for a Less Activist Foreign Policy," *Foreign Affairs* 92, no. 1 (January–February 2013): 127. John Mearsheimer, "Imperial by Design," *National Interest* 111 (January–February 2011): 34.

24. Kennedy, *The Rise and Fall of the Great Powers*, xxii. Gilpin, *War and Change in World Politics*, 196–97, 11.

Index